WOMEN
BEHIND
THE CAMERA

WOMEN BEHIND THE CAMERA

Conversations with Camerawomen

Alexis Krasilovsky

PRAEGER

Westport, Connecticut
London

Library of Congress Cataloging-in-Publication Data

Krasilovsky, Alexis.
　　Women behind the camera : conversations with camerawomen / Alexis
Krasilovsky.
　　　　p.　　cm.
　　Includes bibliographical references and index.
　　ISBN 0–275–95744–6 (alk. paper).—ISBN 0–275–95745–4 (pbk. :
alk. paper)
　　　　1. Women cinematographers—United States—Interviews.　I.　Title.
TR849.A1K72　1997
778.5′3′0922—dc20　　　96–42684

British Library Cataloguing in Publication Data is available.

Library of Congress Catalog Card Number: 96–42684
ISBN: 0–275–95744–6
　　　　0–275–95745–4 (pbk.)

First published in 1997

Praeger Publishers, 88 Post Road West, Westport, CT 06881
An imprint of Greenwood Publishing Group, Inc.

Printed in the United States of America

(∞)™

The paper used in this book complies with the
Permanent Paper Standard issued by the National
Information Standards Organization (Z39.48–1984).

10　9　8　7　6　5　4　3　2　1

Copyright Acknowledgments

The author and publisher gratefully acknowledge permission to use excerpts from the following:

Krasilovsky, Alexis. "Estelle F. Kirsh." *Angles: Women Working in Film & Video* 2, no. 4 (1995): 14–17.

Krasilovsky, Alexis. "Interview with Jo Carson." *Behind the Lens Annual Newsmagazine* (winter 1989–90): 4–5, 10–15.

Krasilovsky, Alexis. "Interview with Kristin Glover." *Behind the Lens Annual Newsmagazine* (1992): 1, 3, 5.

Krasilovsky, Alexis. "Liz Bailey: Interview with the President of Behind the Lens." *Behind the Lens Annual Newsmagazine* (January 1988): 28–32.

Krasilovsky, Alexis. "A Sharper Image." *Angles: Women Working in Film & Video* 2, no. 4 (1995): 10–11.

Krasilovsky, Alexis. "Women Behind the Camera: Interview with Leslie Hill." *Journal of Film and Video* 48, no. 4 (winter 1996–97): 38–53.

To my mother,
who taught me to fight,
and to Estelle Kirsh,
who taught me what to fight for.

Contents

Photographs   *ix*

Acknowledgments   *xiii*

Abbreviations   *xv*

Introduction   *xvii*

I. The Pioneers: Starting Out Before 1970

1. Brianne Murphy, ASC   *3*

2. Juliana Wang   *14*

3. Estelle F. Kirsh   *18*

4. Emiko Omori   *25*

5. Judy Irola, ASC   *31*

II. The Pioneers of Second-Wave Feminism

6. Leslie Hill *41*

7. Kristin Glover *59*

8. Lisa Seidenberg *69*

9. Susan Walsh *78*

10. Liz Bailey *91*

11. Laurel Klick *98*

12. Madelyn Most *102*

III. The Second Wave: Starting Out in Independent Film

13. Cathy Zheutlin *113*

14. Dyanna Taylor *124*

15. Sandi Sissel, ASC *131*

16. Geraldine Kudaka *139*

17. Amy Halpern *148*

18. Nancy Schreiber, ASC *158*

19. Jo Carson *164*

IV. Emerging Camerawomen

20. Sabrina Simmons *173*

21. Karen Williams Kane *183*

22. Sandy Butler *189*

23. Alicia Sehring *196*

Selected Bibliography *205*

Index *209*

Photographs

1. Brianne Murphy, ASC. Photograph courtesy of Brianne
    Murphy.   3

2. Juliana Wang. Photograph courtesy of Juliana Wang.   14

3. Estelle F. Kirsh. Photograph courtesy of Kathleen O'Reilly.   18

4. Emiko Omori (center), with the cast of *Hot Summer Winds*.
    Photograph courtesy of Mitzi Trumbo.   25

5. Judy Irola, ASC. Photograph courtesy of Judy Irola.   31

6. Leslie Hill, shooting Christmas Eve on *Looking for Mr.
    Goodbar* (1976). Photograph courtesy of Kathy Fields.   41

7. *Blue Thunder* camera crew (1981): John Alonzo, Director of
    Photography in white cap, front row; Leslie Hill, Camera
    Assistant (and the only woman), standing next to Alonzo.
    Photograph courtesy of Leslie Hill.   51

8. Kristin Glover DP'ing and directing her film short, *Ah Paris?*,
    November 1987. Photograph courtesy of Kristin Glover.   59

9.   Lisa Seidenberg on location in Kom Pung Speu, Cambodia,
      out on patrol with Cambodian militia, shooting for *World
      Monitor* (1989). Photograph courtesy of Lisa Seidenberg.   69

10.   *American Gigolo* (1978–1979), Richard Gere, Paul Schrader,
      and John Bailey, DP, with Camera Assistants Susan Walsh (l)
      and Leslie Hill (r). Photograph courtesy of Leslie Hill.   78

11.   Liz Bailey operating on PBS Special *Watch Me Move: An
      Anthology of Dance in Black America*, for PBS. Photograph
      courtesy of Mitzi Trumbo.   91

12.   Liz Bailey and son, David D'Antoni, on the set of *Sidewalk
      Motel*. Photograph courtesy of Liz Bailey.   97

13.   Laurel Klick. Photograph courtesy of Laurel Klick.   98

14.   Madelyn Most (bottom row, second from left) at the
      Ultracam Symposium at Leonetti's, Hollywood. (December 3,
      1984). Other Behind the Lens members include: left to right
      (top row): Alexis Krasilovsky, Melinda Sue Gordon, Alicia
      Craft Sehring, Suzy Groves, Judy Reidel, Valerie Davidson,
      Laurie Towers. (bottom row) Pat Harrison, Jane Brenner, Jo
      Carson, and Liz Bailey. Photograph by Jean Mason.
      Photograph courtesy of Behind the Lens.   102

15.   Cathy Zheutlin, Director/Camera: *The Great Peace March*, on
      location in New York City (1987). Photograph courtesy of
      Stel Sandris.   113

16.   Dyanna Taylor (with Panastar). Photograph courtesy of
      Ulrich Bonnekamp.   124

17.   Sandi Sissel, ASC. On location in India for *Salaam Bombay*
      (1988). Photograph courtesy of Sooni Taraporeuala.   131

18.   Geraldine Kudaka. Photograph courtesy of Behind the Lens.   139

19.   Amy Halpern, in her film *Falling Lessons*. Photograph courtesy
      of Amy Halpern.   148

20.   Nancy Schreiber, ASC. Photograph courtesy of Amalie
      Rothschild.   158

21.   Jo Carson. Photograph courtesy of Alexis Krasilovsky.   164

22.   Sabrina Simmons, cinematographer, on location in Memphis,
      Tennessee, for *What Memphis Needs* (1990). Photograph
      courtesy of Alexis Krasilovsky.   173

23.   Karen Williams Kane, AC, and Jack Brown, AC, with
      Mitchell R-35. Photograph courtesy of Dennis Yeandle.   183

24.   Sandy Butler at the N.O.W. Equality Walk. Photograph
courtesy of Alexis Krasilovsky.   189

25.   (r to l:) Alicia Craft Sehring, First Assistant Camerawoman,
and Alex Phillips, ASC, Director of Photography, on location
in Mexico for *Born in East L.A.* Photograph courtesy of Alicia
Craft Sehring.   196

Acknowledgments

I am grateful to the following individuals for their contributions to my manuscript: Dr. Lenore Weitzman, my teacher at Yale, who taught me the value of interviewing women in terms of their careers; Kris Malkiewicz, whose resistance to my attempts to change *cameraman* to *cameraperson*— while typing the manuscript for his book, *Film Lighting*, when I was a student at California Institute of the Arts—first made me notice how few books or periodicals relating to the field of cinematography included camerawomen; Dr. Gelya Frank, whose practice of compassionate anthropological techniques was an inspiration; Herbert Krill, who taught me perseverance; the many members of Behind the Lens: An Association of Professional Camerawomen, especially Liz Bailey, Leslie Hill, Kelly Elder McGowen, and Estelle Kirsh, for their advice; Reseda Mickey, friend, secretary, and editor; Richard Bellikoff, for his computer assistance; Dr. Charles Musser of Yale University, for his editorial suggestions and support; Dr. Harriet Margolis of Victoria University of Wellington, whose copyediting and encouragement were essential to the completion of the project; and, finally, Nelson Finney, who cared for our son while I interviewed camerawomen.

Without grants from the California N.O.W. Foundation or the Affirmative Action Program and Creativity and Research Committee at California State University, Northridge, or the help of Studio Transcription Services and Bobbi Owens, the preparation of this manuscript would have been impossible. Special thanks go to Mary Yost, my agent, and Nina Pearlstein, my editor at Praeger. I am also grateful for the support of Dr. Judith Marlane, Chair of the Radio-Television-Film Department; Gail Said Johnson and other staff members of the Computer Center; and Virginia Elwood, Librarian, Oviatt Library, California State University, Northridge. Also much appreciated has been the assistance of Pamela Rosenberg of Women in Film, Los Angeles; Denise Mulvey of Toronto Women in Film; and Marianne Davis of the American Society of Cinematographers.

Abbreviations

AC   Assistant Cameraperson

ACTT   Alliance of Cinematographic and Television Technicians (England)

AFI   American Film Institute

AMPTP   Alliance of Motion Picture and Television Producers (the producers' organization that represents the major studios and major independents, located in Southern California)

ASC   American Society of Cinematographers

BBC   British Broadcasting Corporation

BNC   Blimped Newsreel Camera: a blimped, 35mm Mitchell camera. The BNCR (a reflex model) was the most widely used camera for television series in the 1970s.

BTL   Behind the Lens: An Association of Professional Camerawomen

DP   Director of Photography

EEOC   Equal Employment Opportunity Commission

ENG   Electronic News Gathering, e.g. video

HMIs   H (symbol for mercury) M (medium arc) I (iodides): daylight color temperature lighting instruments

IA   International Photographers' Guild, Local 600—International Alliance of Theatrical and Stage Employees. (Note: IATSE Local 659, the Hollywood union that shoots most U.S. union features and television programs, merged on May 16, 1996, with New York's Local 644 and Chicago's Local 666. Their new name is Local 600.)

IBEW   International Brotherhood of Electrical Workers, Local 45—Broadcast Television Recording Engineers

MOW   Movie of the Week

NABET   National Association of Broadcast Employees and Technicians—AFL-CIO-CLC (including, for example, the former Association of Film Craftsmen, Local No. 531—Hollywood. NABET Locals 531 and 15, including Hollywood, New York, San Francisco, and other local chapters, merged with IA in the early 1990s.)

PA   Production Assistant

POV   Point of View

SMPTE   Society of Motion Picture Technicians and Engineers

SOC   Society of Operating Cameramen

WIF   Women in Film

Introduction

Most film books refer to came*ramen*.[1] Yet the number of highly trained and experienced camerawomen over the last fifteen years has grown significantly. For example, the number of camerawomen in the International Photographers' Guild, IA Local 659 (the Hollywood portion of the union that shoots most American union features and television programs, now referred to as Local 600) more than quadrupled between 1981 and 1996 to 425, or 11.24 percent of total membership.[2]

Women Behind the Camera is about the aspirations and obstacles, satisfactions and conflicts, failures and successes, experienced by a representative range of American camerawomen. Among the twenty-three camerawomen interviewed between 1988 and 1996 for this study are six directors of photography (including all four female members of the prestigious American Society of Cinematographers); three camera operators; two special effects camerawomen; three documentary camerawomen (although at least ten of the others have also shot documentaries); two camerawomen working primarily in video; one experimental filmmaker who also works as a gaffer on features; and six camera assistants (including three who are currently working primarily as producer/directors). A majority of the camerawomen are currently in a union and working.

The filmographies of a vast majority of the camerawomen included in this study testify to the wealth and breadth of their experience, from *Working Girls* (Judy Irola, Director of Photography), *Honey, I Shrunk the Kids* (Jo Carson, Matte Photography Camera Operator), to *Star Trek VI: The Undiscovered Country* (Kristin Glover, "A" Camera Operator). Credits as camera operators and assistants include numerous documentaries, television shows, commercials, music videos, and features such as *Close Encounters of the Third Kind*, *Continental Divide*, and *Silverado*.

I have tried to underscore the significance of the overall achievements of women in cinematography in my interviews with Liz Bailey, Sandy Butler, Jo Carson, Kristin Glover, Amy Halpern, Leslie Hill, Judy Irola, Karen Williams Kane, Estelle Kirsh, Laurel Klick, Geraldine Kudaka, Madelyn Most, Brianne Murphy, Emiko Omori, Nancy Schreiber, Alicia Sehring, Lisa Seidenberg, Sabrina Simmons, Sandi Sissel, Dyanna Taylor, Susan Walsh, Juliana Wang, and Cathy Zheutlin.

Many of these camerawomen have won awards. Brianne Murphy was the cinematographer on *The Magic Tide*, which won eleven international awards. *Carved in Silence*, shot by Emiko Omori, won a Golden Cine Award. Cannes Film Festival Camera d'Ors were awarded to Judy Irola, Director of Photography on *Northern Lights*, and Sandi Sissel, Director of Photography on *Salaam Bombay*. Blue Ribbons at the American Film Festival were awarded to *Miles to Go* and *Annapurna: A Woman's Place*, both shot by Dyanna Taylor, as well as to *Possum Living*, directed and shot by Nancy Schreiber. Nancy Schreiber also shot the Academy Award–nominated film *Seeing Red*.

Of the many Emmy Award–winning shows shot by women included in the study, *Mother Teresa* was shot by Sandi Sissel, *Frontline*'s "Men Who Molest" was shot by Dyanna Taylor, and a story on lesbian mothers for *New York Illustrated* was shot by Juliana Wang. *Winds of War*, on which Laurel Klick did Optical Camera and Line-Up, won an Emmy for Outstanding Individual Achievement in Special Visual Effects.

Other camerawomen working primarily in the United States have included Karen Edmundson Bean, Sandra Chandler, Carolyn Chen, Joan Churchill, Catherine Coulson, Michelle Crenshaw, Roxanne di Santo, Joey Forsyte, Patricia Hill, Ellen Kuras, Heather MacKenzie, Jo Mayers, Kelly Elder McGowen, Teresa Medina, Kathleen O'Reilly, Marie Pedersen, Tama Takahashi Pollard, Lisa Rinzler, Tara Summers, Patty Vanover, Amy Vincent, Alicia Weber, Joan Weidman, Claudia Weill, Lorna Wiley, and Elizabeth Ziegler. Some of these camerawomen are highly active; others are no longer working or have entered other fields, such as directing.

My book, which does not purport to be definitive, excludes many successful camerawomen of note, including still camerawomen, such as Melinda Sue Gordon and Kim Gottlieb-Walker; experimental filmmakers, such as Babette Mangolte; artists who have pioneered women's experimental cinematographic vision, such as Carolee Schneemann; women who have primarily filmed pornography, such as Roberta Findlay;[3] and camerawomen who have worked primarily on in-house industrials.

While this study focuses on American camerawomen, notable achievements have also been made by camerawomen in other countries, including: Sally Bongers (Australia); Director of Photography Cathryn Robertson (Canada), and Judith Lindo, Lori P. Longstaff, and Kerry Smart, Canadian camera assistants; Nurith Aviv (France), who has worked with director Agnes Varda; Sabeena Gadihoke (India); Akiko Ashisawa (Japan); director Márta Mészáros (Hungary), who also shot some of her earlier films; Mairi Gunn (New Zealand); and Mia Turos (Sweden). Of the several Soviet camerawomen working today, Tatiana Loginova is a "stage camerawoman" employed at Belorusfilm, whose credits include *A Wreath of Sonnets* and *The Use of the Genius*; while Marina Goldovskaya, who shot and directed numerous documentaries—including *The Shattered Mirror*, winner of numerous international awards—now lives in the United States.

While Toronto Women in Film and Television has published an outstanding guide for camerawomen in Canada—*Take Two: A Woman's Guide to Technical Jobs in the Film and Television Industry*,[4] few studies exist to date of American women in the film and television industries other than as writers, producers, and directors. Jesse Maple's moving personal account of what it meant to be the sole Black union camerawoman in 1974 included advice for other women trying to survive as camerawomen.[5] Ally Acker's *Reel Women: Pioneers of the Cinema, 1896 to the Present* largely excludes camerawomen.[6] A 1991 study conducted by Women in Film and the National Commission on Working Women of Wider Opportunities for Women, "What's Wrong with This Picture: The Status of Women on Screen and behind the Camera in Entertainment TV," reports that "women continue to fare poorly on television—both on screen and behind the camera—despite significant gains over time and some notable but scattered breakthroughs."[7] The study reports that women producers are 15 percent of all producers on entertainment series, women writers are 25 percent of all writers, and women directors are 9 percent of all directors,[8] but excludes camerawomen, whose numbers trail far behind. In comparison, *A Statistical Profile of Women in the Canadian Film and Television Industry* reported that, in 1990, "only 2 percent of directors of photography are female, as are only

1 percent of gaffers, 3 percent of grips and 4 percent of people working in special effects."[9] A 1993 report in *Premiere*, "The Numbers Never Lie: Tracking the Progress of Women in the Industry," cites an estimated 15 percent female membership in IA Local 659, along with other statistics for women working "above the line" as actors, directors, and screenwriters, and in other technical positions "below the line."[10] But *The Hollywood Reporter*'s 1993 Special Issue, "Women in Entertainment," fails to include any camerawomen among over ninety-five profiles of successful women.[11]

THE EARLIEST "MOVING PICTURE" CAMERAWOMEN

To the dismay of film historians everywhere, much of early film history neither has been documented nor preserved. It is therefore impossible to provide a definitive history of the earliest women pioneers in cinematography. Whatever research can be conducted in this area, however, is important towards the creation of camerawomen's community with the past, for, like the "women's art and thought and action" sought after by Adrienne Rich, women's cinematographic vision "will continue to be seen as deviant, its true meaning distorted or buried, as long as women's work can be dismissed as 'exceptional,' an interesting footnote to the major texts."[12]

Women considering entering the field of cinematography today would be much heartened by Alice Guy Blaché's pronouncement in 1914 that:

There is nothing connected with the staging of a motion picture that a woman cannot do as easily as a man, and there is no reason why she cannot master every technicality of the art. The technique of the drama has been mastered by so many women that it is considered as much her field as a man's and its adaptation to picture work in no way removes it from her sphere. The technique of motion-picture photography, like the technique of the drama, is fitted to a woman's activities.[13]

For many years deprived by film historians of her status as a well-known film director, Alice Guy Blaché was credited in *The Moving Picture World* of 1912 with having operated the camera as early as 1895 or 1896.[14] Guy learned the art of cinematography by spending "months of study in the laboratory of the Gaumont Company in Paris at a time when motion-picture photography was in the experimental stage," and later continued her experiments in America in her laboratory in the Solax Studios, which she owned.[15] "We discovered many little tricks," Guy later wrote, "such as:

Films turned in reverse . . . ; *Films slowed down or accelerated* by a turn of the handle . . . ; *Stops*, permitting one to displace an object which in projection would seem to be animated by a supernatural life . . . ; *Double exposures*; *Fade-outs . . .* " (Guy's emphasis)[16] "The other film producers who sprang up concurrently used our discoveries as soon as we made them," concluded Guy, and Columbia University was interested in forming a cinematography college with her during her lifetime.[17]

The earliest professional American "moving picture camerawoman" was Katherine Russell Bleecker, who began her work in 1913. She owned her own motion picture equipment, and, according to the *Sunday New York Times Magazine* (November 21, 1915), was hired to document prison conditions in Sing Sing and other prisons, thus contributing to prison reform.[18] "When dealing with violence and masochism," said Haskell Wexler, seventy years after Bleecker began her cinematography, "if there is a woman on the crew, I feel embarrassed at being part of a system that needs to make those kind of films. A woman's presence makes one's social conscience more acute."[19] One wonders if film history might have evolved differently if there had been ongoing participation of women in the area of cinematography, instead of sporadic activity by women such as Guy, Bleecker, and Erica Anderson, who shot the 1957 Academy Award–winning documentary *Albert Schweitzer*.[20]

INTERVIEWING CAMERAWOMEN: A SUMMARY

The interviews that appear in this book have been organized in historical categories, based on the year each woman began her career in cinematography. Among them are many "firsts." For example, of those women starting out before 1970, Brianne Murphy was the first woman to gain membership to the prestigious American Society of Cinematographers; Juliana Wang was the first woman to join IA Local 644 as a director of photography; Estelle Kirsh was the first woman camera assistant in IA promoted to camera operator by a director of photography (in this case, Brianne Murphy); Emiko Omori was the first president of NABET Local 532, and Judy Irola was one of the first camerawomen to work at KQED, in San Francisco.

The pioneers of Second Wave feminism include Leslie Hill, the first woman to be admitted to the IATSE-AMPTP Camera Training Program. Kristin Glover was the first female camera assistant to work on a Paramount three-camera television show. Lisa Seidenberg was one of the first camerawomen at WNET-13 in New York. Susan Walsh was one of the first women elected to the Executive Board of IA Local 659 and the first president of Behind the Lens: An Association of Professional Camerawomen. Liz Bailey, working at WBRZ, in Baton Rouge, was the first camerawoman in Louisiana. And Madelyn Most was one of the first female camera assistants to work at the BBC, in London.

Of those Second Wave feminists who started out in independent film, special effects camerawoman Jo Carson was the first to put stepper motors and a motion-control computer onto a pitching lens with a snorkel type of arrangement. Dyanna Taylor was part of the first all-woman crew to film a mountaineering expedition, to Annapurna I in Nepal. And Sandi Sissel was the first woman to work on a $12 million feature as director of photography.

Sabrina Simmons was one of the first and only African American women whose careers began through IA's Camera Assistant Training Program. Among other emerging camerawomen, Karen Williams Kane is the first to specialize in high-speed cinematography. Sandy Butler is the first woman to serve on the executive board of Local 16 in San Francisco. Yet, as Emiko Omori said, "Most pioneers are reluctant pioneers."

This study does not attempt to explore fully the broader sociological context for those women pioneering in the film industry as camerawomen. However, their struggle parallels those of women in other male-dominated fields, such as longshorewomen, women plumbers, and women coal miners. Their advances parallel those made by men and women in the civil rights movement. Indeed, several women interviewed address the similarity of their struggle to the struggles of minorities.

This study stresses the relationship of camerawomen to the film industry, and, in keeping with the lives of the individual women interviewed, focuses only on alternative workings of power and aesthetics in the cases of women whose work also entailed independent cinematography, all-women film collectives, or individual filmic visions. Most of the women interviewed work in a highly proscribed situation—the Hollywood crew:

The camera crew by its nature presents a special situation for a camerawoman. This crew is hierarchical, with specifically defined responsibilities for each member, limiting parameters, mutually exclusive roles. The camera crew consists of: the director of photography, or cinematographer, who is responsible for the overall "look" of the film and the lighting; the camera operator who actually operates the camera; the first assistant, in charge of equipment, who pulls focus and "zooms" during shots; and the second assistant, who loads film, slates, marks feet, and generally assists the first assistant. A camera crew is an entity which is supposed to work together as a unit; but it is definitely not a team of equals. There is a distinct stratification, status, rank, whatever you choose to call it, and professional jealousy often not far below the surface. "Moving up" to a higher classification is difficult, not encouraged, governed by almost byzantine rules . . . Male crew members have had their ideas about "women's place" reinforced by their experiences, by the long-standing tradition of all-male crews. Most are not used to dealing with women on the set, let alone recognizing them as equals, peers, colleagues.[21]

On the other hand, camerawomen have acknowledged many individual men for their support, including instructors, such as James Pasternak; camera rental house owners Denny Clairmont and Otto Nemenz; gaffer Martin Andrews; directors Jonathan Demme and George Lucas; producer Mark Obenhaus; cameraman Allen Willis; and directors of photography William Fraker, Woody Omens, Steven Poster, Robert Primes, Richard Walden, and Haskell Wexler.

Many camerawomen have experienced the joy of reaching out to a greater, more challenging world than the one their mothers envisioned for them. They have experienced the satisfactions of developing and using mental and physical strength—lifting heavy camera equipment on the set—and technological savvy. But many have worked in the film industry for years as the token women on otherwise all-male crews. For some, being interviewed for this study represents a significant breakthrough from their isolation.

Their stories—sometimes humorous, but often painful—range from the union camerawomen with years of experience in dealing with hostile working environments to the young camera operator who worked through her eighth month of pregnancy on a supportive set. In conducting the interviews, I soon found that the process was not a one-way street,[22] despite having traded my own cinematography career for a more distancing role in academia. Not only was the editing of the interviews "a collaborative act,"[23] but it brought overwhelming validation to years of pioneering efforts both for those interviewees with a feminist consciousness and for the interviewer. As Maria Mies has stated, "Women cannot appropriate their own history unless they *begin to collectivize their own experiences* (Mies's emphasis)."[24]

Despite discriminatory hiring practices, isolation, and sexual harassment, many camerawomen have successfully transcended, or, increasingly, have never perceived themselves as victims, but rather see themselves as dynamic, strong, committed professionals.

Haskell Wexler has stated: "Women in the business, all the minority groups have to struggle. The ones that were able to make it really had to excel, they really had to shine. They had to be so much better than guys doing the same job in order to have it."[25]

In "struggling," some camerawomen have faced both discrimination and sexual harassment.[26] "Sexual harassment in the film business," said Estelle Kirsh, "runs from inane verbal harassment, to physical assault, to sabotage of equipment."

Attorney Gloria Allred, who has represented camerawomen in Los Angeles, has stated:

Camerawomen are often in only token numbers. . . . They fear asserting their rights to be free of sex discrimination because they fear being retaliated against by not getting a promotion, or by being demoted, or by being terminated, or by not getting another job, because they have stood up for themselves. . . . It's only because of the women who were brave enough to file lawsuits that women ever won the opportunity to be behind the camera in the first place.[27]

Some of the hurdles that the camerawomen pioneers overcame are now doors that have opened for younger women serious about camerawork. What was once viewed as a subject rife with stories of victimization is quickly changing, in part, to episodes of female camaraderie. In addition to informal networks of friends, Behind the Lens: An Association of Professional Camerawomen (1984–1996) served as a dynamic support group of camerawomen joining together to provide a forum of communication and exchange of information among women and men throughout the industry. Some camerawomen have been reluctant to associate themselves with women's groups, fearful of negative connotations, or because they are "not joiners." However, a majority of the camerawomen interviewed for this book were members of Behind the Lens, which networked with other industry organizations, including the Chicago Film and Video Network; Cinewomen (Los Angeles); Films de Femmes (France); Independent Feature Project; Interguild Women's Caucus; Media Network (New York); National Organization of Women; Women in Film, "whose annual Film Festival and Crystal Awards [were] shot by co-members of Behind the Lens"; and Women Make Movies (New York);[28] as well as the Society of Operating Cameramen and the Swedish Institute of Cinematography.

The strength of numbers is what is needed to create significant jobs for camerawomen, and with these jobs, a filmic vision of their own.[29] As Geraldine Kudaka wrote in a 1986 Behind the Lens Newsletter editorial:

As women in a traditionally male dominated field, the issues at stake are more than simply jobs and paychecks. The issues extend beyond the question of benefits. It is my belief that all women must look to the future, to the world we are creating, to the world we bring children into, and in this light, we women of the industry must see the question of Union Versus Non-Union as an issue which will not only affect us now, but will affect our jobs ten years down the road.[30]

Ten years later, IA Locals 659, 644, and 666 merged into one International Photographers' Guild—Local 600, with a union leadership actively supportive of women and minorities. As of June 1996, the Women's Steering Committee of Local 600 joined forces with the Women's Steering Committees of the Screen Actors Guild, the American Federation of Television and Radio Artists, the Writers Guild of America, and the Directors Guild of America. On August 31, 1996, Behind the Lens dissolved. Whether most of the issues pertinent to camerawomen have dissolved remains to be seen.

Ironically, some of the same issues concerned Alice Guy Blaché more than eighty years ago:

There is no doubt in my mind that a woman's success in many lines of endeavor is still made very difficult by a strong prejudice against one of her sex doing work that has been done only by men for hundreds of years. Of course this prejudice is fast disappearing, and there are many vocations in which it has not been present for a long time. In the arts of acting, music, painting, and literature, woman has long held her place among the most successful workers, and when it is considered how vitally all of these arts enter into the production of motion pictures, one wonders why the names of scores of women are not found among the successful creators of photodrama offerings.[31]

Perhaps in response, bridging the community of lost years of women's history, Adrienne Rich states: "There is a natural fear that if we do not enter the common world of men, as asexual beings or as 'exceptional' women, do not enter it on its terms and obey its rules, we will be sucked back into the realm of servitude, whatever our temporary class status or privileges"[32]

If, as Adrienne Rich concludes, the most important task is "to make visible the full meaning of women's experience,"[33] surely camerawomen are the most suited to this challenge. With what dream vision, what technical innovations, what "machisma" will we accomplish the task of "reinvent[ing] cinema as a narrative and visual form"?[34] In becoming "the subjects of the look,"[35] will we indeed replace "possession and the erotic" with "the sphere of ecstatic contemplation and mystical experience"?[36] As filmmaker Shirley Clarke stated in the late 1960s, those formative years of the women's movement, "To begin with, none of us is only masculine or only feminine. This we have finally learned."[37]

The filmic language of women may only yet be forming, and presently centered in the feminist avant-garde. But in the collaborative medium that is Hollywood filmmaking, the extension of women's power on the set to the power of our imagery may be intrinsically related.

NOTES

1. E.g., Kris Malkiewicz, *Film Lighting: Talks with Hollywood's Cinematographers and Gaffers* (New York: Prentice Hall, 1986); Leonard Maltin, *Behind the Camera: The Cinematographer's Art* (New York: New American Library, 1971); and Dennis Schaefer and Larry Salvato, *Masters of Light: Conversations with Contemporary Cinematographers* (Berkeley: University of California Press, 1988).

In 1987, the Women's Caucus of the University Film and Video Association voted unanimously to recommend that UFVA adopt the following policy: "UFVA urges all film/video professionals and academics to use non-sexist nomenclature in interviews, panel discussions, scholarly or professional articles, lectures and textbooks."

2. David Robb, "Women's Picture Brighter at Hollywood Camera Local 659," *Daily Variety* (15 November 1991):8; David Heuring, "Visionary Women: Pre-Eminent Women Cinematographers Lisa Rinzler, Ellen Kuras, Jo Mayers, Nancy Schreiber, Roxanne di Santo, Judy Irola and Sandi Sissel Discuss the Challenges and Rewards of Their Craft," *Film & Video* 13, no. 2 February 1996: 44.

3. Molly Haskell, "Are Women Directors Different?" in Karyn Kay and Gerald Peary, *Women and the Cinema: A Critical Anthology* (New York: E.P. Dutton, 1977), 434; Kathleen Carroll, "A Film First By and About Women," *Sunday Daily News*, Entertainment Section (29 April 1973):7.

4. Karen Laurence, Nan Weiner, and Elaine Cooper, *Take Two: A Woman's Guide to Technical Jobs in the Film and Television Industry*, Toronto Women in Film (Toronto: University of Toronto Press, 1993).

5. Jesse Maple, *How to Become a Union Camerawoman: Film-Videotape* (New York: LJ Film Productions, 1977).

6. Ally Acker, *Reel Women: Pioneers of the Cinema, 1896 to the Present* (New York: Continuum Publishing Co., 1991).

7. Sally Steenland, *What's Wrong with This Picture?: The Status of Women on Screen and behind the Camera in Entertainment TV* (Washington, D.C.: National Commission on Working Women of Wider Opportunities for Women; Los Angeles: Women in Film, November 1990), 2.

8. Ibid., 3.

9. *A Statistical Profile of Women in the Canadian Film and Television Industry*, project report prepared by Peat, Marwick, Stevenson, and Kellogg for Toronto Women in Film and Television (Toronto: Toronto Women in Film and Television, 1990), quoted in *Take Two*, by Karen Laurence, 5.

10. Caroline Kirk Cordero, "The Numbers Never Lie: Tracking the Progress of Women in the Industry," *Premiere*, Special Issue (1993):33–36.

11. "Women in Entertainment," *The Hollywood Reporter*, Special Issue (December 7, 1993).

12. Adrienne Rich, "Conditions for Work: The Common World of Women," foreword to *Working It Out: Twenty-Three Women Writers, Artists, Scientists and Scholars Talk about Their Lives and Work*, eds. Sara Ruddick and Pamela Daniels (New York: Pantheon Books, 1977), xxiii.

13. Alice Guy, "Woman's Place in Photoplay Production," in *Women and the Cinema: A Critical Anthology*, ed. Karyn Kay and Gerald Peary (New York: E.P. Dutton, 1977), 339–340 (reprinted from *Moving Picture World* [11 July 1914]); Alice Guy, Appendix H to *The Memoirs of Alice Guy Blaché*, trans. Roberta and Simone Blaché, ed. Anthony Slide (Metuchen, N.J.: The Scarecrow Press, 1986), 26–27.

14.

From Levine, and from others, I learned that Madame Alice Blaché became associated with the Gaumont Company very early in the game, when Mr. Gaumont was absorbed with the scientific department of production or merely engaged in photographing moving objects. She *inaugurated* the presentation of little plays on the screen by that company some sixteen or seventeen years ago, operating the camera, writing or adapting the photodramas, setting the scenes and handling the actors. I had an opportunity to see how efficient she was in her diversity of roles before the day was over and was amazed at her skill, especially in directing the action of a complicated scene.

Louis Reeves Harrison, "Studio Saunterings," *The Moving Picture World* 12 no. 11 (15 June 1912):1007–1011, reprinted in Alice Guy, Appendix D to *Memoirs*, 110.

15. Alice Guy, "Woman's Place in Photoplay Production," in *Women and the Cinema*, ed Karyn Kay and Gerald Peary, 340.

16. Alice Guy, *Memoirs*, 26–27.

17. Ibid., 69.

18. Suzy Groves, "Katherine Russell Bleecker: The First Professional Moving Picture Camerawoman," *Behind the Lens Newsletter* 3, no. 4 (June 1985):1–2.

19. Haskell Wexler, quoted in "Women on Film Crews: Views from the Top," by Susan M. Walsh, *International Photographer* 55, no. 10 (October 1983):15.

20. Cecile Starr, "Distaff Documentarians: Three American Pioneers," *International Documentary* 15, no. 5 (July–Aug. 1996): 12–14.

21. Estelle Kirsh, quoted in "Women and Power: Thirty-Seven Case Studies of Women in the Motion Picture and Television Industry," by Loreen Arbus, Beth Brickell, Diane Dailey, and Joelle Dobrow, ts.:1

22. Ann Oakley, "Interviewing Women: A Contradiction in Terms," in *Doing Feminist Research* ed. Helen Roberts (London: Routledge & Kegan Paul, 1981), 30–61.

23. L .L. Langness and Gelya Frank, *Lives: An Anthropological Approach to Biography* (Novato, California: Chandler & Sharp, 1981), 86.

24. Maria Mies, "Towards a Methodology for Feminist Research," in *Theories of Women's Studies*, ed. Gloria Bowles and Renate Klein, (London: Routledge & Kegan Paul, 1983), 127.

25. Haskell Wexler, quoted in "Talking with Haskell Wexler," by Jennifer Gilroy, *Behind the Lens Annual Newsmagazine* (winter 1989/90):20.

26. Figures on the sexual harassment of camerawomen are unavailable. However, "70% of female employees report experiencing some form of sexual harassment on the job, and 52% of female employees have either quit or been fired from jobs because of sexual harassment." Alexis Krasilovsky, "Interview: Attorney Gloria Allred," *Behind the Lens Annual Newsmagazine* (January 1988):1.

27. Ibid., 10.

28. *The 1987 Behind the Lens Directory* (Santa Monica, California: Behind the Lens, 1987).

29. Sally Steenland, *What's Wrong with This Picture?*, 4.

30. Geraldine Kudaka, "Union Vs. Non-Union," *Behind the Lens Newsletter*, Special Annual Issue 4, no. 1 December 1986):1.

31. Alice Guy, *Memoirs*, 128.

32. Adrienne Rich, "Conditions for Work," xvii.

33. Ibid., xxiii.

34. Judith Mayne, *The Woman at the Keyhole* (Bloomington: Indiana University Press, 1990), 1.

35. Paola Melchiori, "A Look at Female Identity," trans. Jane Dolman, in *Off-Screen: Women and Film in Italy*, eds. Giuliana Bruno and Maria Nadotti (New York: Routledge, 1988), 25.

36. Ibid., 34.

37. Shirley Clarke, quoted in "Storm De Hirsch and Shirley Clarke, A Conversation," in *Women and the Cinema*, eds. Karyn Kay and Gerald Peary 235 (abridged from *Film Culture*, no. 46 [autumn 1967]).

I

THE PIONEERS: STARTING OUT BEFORE 1970

Most pioneers are reluctant pioneers.

Emiko Omori

Whenever I would try to get into the union, I was told they weren't taking women into camera.

Brianne Murphy, ASC

There's something incredibly sexy when you put your eye in an eyepiece and you direct what is going to come into that frame.

Judy Irola, ASC

If you really want something, just keep going after it to get it.

Juliana Wang

Brianne Murphy, ASC

It is hard to believe at first glance that Brianne Murphy, a soft-spoken woman with a young, casual look, was the first camerawoman to have achieved membership in the American Society of Cinematographers.

After graduating from Brown University with a degree in journalism, Brianne went to New York to cover the theater, but soon found herself studying acting at the Neighborhood Playhouse. A combination of sheer nerve and fluke brought Brianne media exposure as a "Clown for a Day" at Ringling Brothers Circus, and with it, the sudden realization that what she most enjoyed about being interviewed and photographed was the camera itself.

Starting as a still photographer, learning on the job, Brianne moved to Hollywood, where she accumulated a myriad of job titles ranging from script supervisor to director. In 1953, she was one of the key organizers of the Associated Film Craftsmen, which in 1959 was renamed NABET 531. As the cameramen who had worked with Brianne in NABET's early days—Laszlo Kovacs, Vilmos Zsigmond, and others—left NABET to join IA, Brianne had the opportunity to fill the camera jobs that remained. Working with her husband, Ralphe Brooke, she had already shot *The Magic Tide*, which won eleven international awards. Doors began to open up to her as a cinematographer, first at NBC and, more recently, at studios such as Warner and Columbia. In 1973, after years of discrimination, Brianne Murphy was admitted to IA 659, and became the first woman director of photography in the Hollywood local, and a member of its executive board. She was also a founder of Women in Film, as well as a founding member of Behind the Lens.

Her numerous camera credits include features such as *Bermuda Triangle*; and Movies of the Week, including Emmy-nominated *There Were Times, Dear*, and Emmy Award–winner *Five Finger Discount*. Some of her numerous television series—*Highway to Heaven*, *Little House on the Prairie*, and *Breaking Away*—have also been nominated for Emmys. She received a 1982 Academy Award for technical innovation, as well as Women in Film's Crystal and Lucy Awards.

Brianne increasingly works as a director/cinematographer, on features such as *To Die to Sleep* and *Educated Heart*, and the television series *True Confessions*. She is currently President of Columbia College in Hollywood.

AK: How did you first become interested in camera work?

BM: I had a brush with the theater as an actress when I was a kid. The theater itself was magic. All I knew growing up was that I wanted to be in the theater, but I was also wise enough to know that there's nothing secure in that. So I went to school feeling that if I got teaching credentials I could always work.

I was brought up in a house full of women, with no stable man around. I didn't anticipate getting married and having someone take care of me. I went to Brown University, and when I got out, I went to White Plains to apply for a job in the newspaper there. They asked what my area of expertise was, and I told them the theater. Of course, my area of expertise was *nothing* because at this point all I'd ever been was a student. So they sent me to New York to cover the theater. And I walked into the rehearsals of *Tea and Sympathy*. I saw Elia Kazan, whom I'd known as a kid, and he greeted me with, "What're you doing?" and I said, "Writing for a newspaper." He said, "Why aren't you acting?" And I said, "I have to earn a living." He said, "You ought to be going to school," and I said, "I just got out of school." And he said, "There's a very good acting school," like he didn't hear a word I said. He told me to go to see Sandy Meisner at the Neighborhood Playhouse. He had apparently called to say that I was coming. And they took me into the Playhouse. That was the end of my newspaper career.

I got into my second year, and Ringling Brothers Circus came to town. I was living in a four-dollar-a-week room and there was a girl across the hall, Kay Mitchell, another "starving actress." I went over to the circus and I asked them for a job watering elephants. Well, I was royally kicked out of there.

I have to regress a little bit. I was born in England and I always thought that to be an American, you had to be involved with cowboys, the circus, and movies.

So I went back to my furnished room to talk to Kay, whom I didn't know very well at the time. I said, "How would you like to perform at Ringling Brothers opening night?" And she said, "How could we do that?" I said, "Why don't you go out and buy some material to make clown costumes, and I'll go to NBC to someone I know over there and borrow some clown make-up."

We got to the employees' entrance, and there was a guard sitting there, but since we were all made up it was obvious that we belonged there. A bunch of clowns all dressed alike came by and they were in very expensive outfits—tight-fitting, sequins, suits with cone hats on and white faces—and they were all marching someplace. And we followed them. We get up to this curtain and there's music going on behind it, no light coming through it, and all these clowns are lined up there. The people turn and look at us but no one says anything. All of a sudden the band changes their tune and the curtain opens, and these clowns go running in and we go running in behind them.

We stayed ringside for four solid hours, performing, signing autographs for kids, doing cartwheels, and playing leapfrog, and idolizing the stars, and sitting on the ring marker, and watching the high-wire people. Well, the ringmaster knew for sure that we shouldn't be there, but that particular night, they had celebrities and some guests, so nobody came after us. But the ringmaster would have liked to. Every time that he would start one way, we'd go another way, and we evaded him for these four hours.

In the '50s, in New York, I'd spent some time around the set of *On the Waterfront* [directed by Elia Kazan]. On the way home, we stopped by Marlon Brando's place with our makeup and clown outfits, and laughed about what we had done. He suggested that the next day we go to one of the newspapers.

So we went to *The New York Times*. We asked to go to the photo department, like we knew what we're doing, and they asked what we wanted. So we told them our story. They said, "You ought to meet Meyer Berger," who was a Pulitzer Prize–winning author at the time. They sent us up to see him and we told him our story. He said it would be in the Early Bird edition of the *Times* tomorrow morning.

No sooner had we gotten to sleep than the payphone in the hall started ringing. It was United Press, Associated Press, *Time Magazine*, and *Look*. The story just snowballed. Finally, *Movietone News* took us for an interview with John North, who interviewed us separately. In my interview, he said, "Why did you do it?" So I told him about wanting to be an American. And then Mr. North said, "Do you really want to be a clown?" And I said, "Heavens no." They had these big movie, newsreel cameras, and I was just fascinated by what was happening. And he said, "What do you want?" And I said "I want to be a photographer." I had never had a camera, never taken a picture. But at that moment I just said I wanted to be a photographer. Saying it made it happen. They sent me to see Ted Sato, who was the head of their press photography department.

So from the circus, I got to Hollywood, because the circus went to Mexico City and then to Sarasota for the winter. I looked at the map and Hollywood was about three or four inches from Mexico City, so I figured I could make it. Ted Sato asked what I was going to do during this hiatus and I said, "I'll go up to Hollywood." I said it as though I knew people there. And he said, "Great, because I'm going to Japan, and if you don't mind taking these three footlockers of equipment with you, I'll pay for their shipment, then I'll meet you on the way back from Japan and we'll go on to Sarasota together when it's that time." I said, "Fine," not realizing I didn't have a place to put them. I got to Hollywood and then wondered what to do with myself to earn a living. But here I had camera equipment and an enlarger from the circus. So I ceased using the footlockers as furniture and opened up a little business on Sunset Strip doing nightclub photography, which bombed terribly because anyone at a nightclub on Sunset Strip doesn't want to be photographed.

Every man I met was a movie producer, he said. Finally I met one who asked me to come to his office the next day. He was about to make a picture on a very, very low budget. At the time it was $30,000, which was more money than I'd ever known. He asked what I could do, and I said, "I can take your stills." He said, "On a low budget picture, we can't afford that. What else can you do?" Well, I had been on a movie set, so I knew all those jobs, so I said, "There's a lot of things I can do. Craft service. I can do script supervising." I was thinking of all the people and what their titles were. And he said, "Can you do make-up, wardrobe, script, props?" And I said, "Sure." He said, "Okay, and you'll probably take some stills, so bring your equipment, and that'll pay fifty dollars a week. And we're going on location in a couple days." So I said, "Fabulous." He'd let me do anything that I wanted to as long as I'd be there early, stay up late. Then the same producer went on to make another picture, and I was doing more and more.

I found out that the more I was willing to do and the harder I was willing to work, the more I could learn. And they always needed help running for things and following focus, changing lenses. It was often just a two-man camera crew on those things—an operator and an assistant. I spent all my spare time with it. The cameras were Mitchells and the batteries weighed a ton. They said, "There's no way you can get into camera because you can't carry the batteries." So I went out and got a little red wagon. Sometimes I would hire a local teenager who wanted to hang around the set. Nobody objected as long as the work got done. I found with each new low-budget picture, I met maybe ten new people, which would get me contacts.

Then my sister came out from Rhode Island and I taught her script supervising. She and I shared an apartment in Hollywood. Just about every weeknight after work, the gang would stop by our place and we'd all talk about if we'd heard about another show that was coming up. Networking wasn't really invented yet, but that's really what it was.

At about that time, when we were all working for very, very little money, and sometimes the money never showed up or the checks were no good, we met Sid Rose, the business rep of NABET, Local 53. He pointed out to us that Local 53, the electronic contract, had a space in it for a film unit. And we said, "What does it take to form a film union, or another union?" He said, "It takes seven interested people." And there were seven of us. That was the start of NABET in Hollywood. There were so few of us, and so many jobs.

AK: You were a film cameraperson?

BM: You could have as many positions as you could handle. So I was a script supervisor, a production manager, but I wasn't on camera yet. I was camera assistant. The person that found the job could be the cameraman or take the job of their choice, and the others came after that.

AK: Had NABET been formed in New York as a film union?

BM: No, I don't believe so. We called it AFC 531, Associated Film Craftsmen. We were doing bigger and bigger nonunion pictures as our names got to be known, and eventually I started shooting some of them.

Actually, what got me into shooting was that the IA started taking in some of the other guys. They took in Kovacs and Zsigmond and Crabe and Martin, leaving me with this world of nonunion. And whenever I would try to get into the union, I was told they weren't taking women into camera.

But it didn't really bother me too much at that time because I had an awful lot of work. I made several features a year, and I was getting to direct some of them.

These were the late '50s, early '60s. There were a lot of interesting things going on—documentaries and features and commercials, some directorial assignments.

I took a job as a production manager at a documentary studio in Hollywood, F. K. Rockett. It was the oldest documentary studio in Hollywood. Fred Rockett had died and the company had carried on, and they had advertised for a production manager. So I went to apply for it dressed pretty much as I am now, in sandals and slacks. Jack Hennessy, who was interviewing me, was very impressed with my credentials and felt that I could production manage the studio just fine, except when he called, he asked, "You mind wearing stockings and a skirt?" I said, "If you'll give me an advance I'll go out and buy some." I don't really enjoy production management and juggling figures, but I'd done enough of it to realize that the cameraman always got the biggest money. So I took the job and we did a lot of U.S. Navy pictures. I would hire the cameramen that the producers wanted and then offer them a second camera, but we didn't have the budget for two cameras. And this is where I came in. Now I was in a position to hire myself. They couldn't say no because the price was right, and the footage was indispensable. And I did some of the editing.

AK: Can you describe the resistance and the support that you've gotten from other people?

BM: There are two major men in my camera career. One was my husband, Ralph Brooke, who was a production manager that I'd worked with. We knew each other for quite a long time. We were best friends.

We'd both been working on this low-budget horror picture, and thought it would be great fun to show that we could do something of quality. So we wrote, produced, directed, and shot a picture. It was called *The Magic Tide*. It was a story about a little Mexican boy and a little American girl who meet.

When Ralph and I decided to make this picture, we went to Mexico and shot it. We formed a company that was just the two of us and my sister, Gillian. We borrowed a lot of equipment and purchased film—hundred-foot loads of 16mm. I knew incredibly little at the time. I didn't know all about filters and neutral densities and controlling the light. I was just a moviemaker. I wasn't a cameraperson yet, but that's what fascinated me the most.

We were very proud of our film. It was blown up to 35mm, and *The Magic Tide* went on to win eleven international awards.

Because of that, Ralph and I were invited to go to Chile to make a public image picture for Kennecott Copper. Ralph died at this time. I think it was the strain of working in the Andes and carrying the equipment around. The whole marriage, which was about three and a half years, was like a honeymoon. He was very supportive.

There was an old guy called Vic Fisher, who went up to cameramen's heaven last year. We were shooting a monster picture. The monster suit was too small for the man that it was built for. The producer asked me to wear the monster suit, but it was too big for me. Then the producer turned to Vic and said, "I'll pay you some extra money if you will wear the monster suit." And Vic said, "What about the camera?" The producer said, "Bri's always hanging around the camera, doesn't she know something?" And Vic took his meter belt off, came over to me and put it around my waist, and said, "That's yours now." He said, "You've picked my brain long enough. Now let's see what you can do." And that was my first operating job—in the early '60s, maybe 1960, 1961—*The Incredible Petrified World*.

During this time I also produced some pictures, because I was caught saying to a producer, "$30,000 is an awful lot of money for you to be spending on this picture." He turned out to be the banker and I didn't know it. And I turned out to be a producer. Writer, producer, director, camera, and distributor.

In 1973, I went to the union and was admitted to the 659. And then I was all for the union, really gung ho, and trying to do everything I could to see that it was an idealistic organization and for the good of the members. I worked on the executive board.

I knew when I joined that I knew no union producers, and that a woman had never worked in a major studio as a cinematographer, or anywhere else. But shortly, NBC called the union and said, "We're doing a special about women's breast cancer, but the people we're interviewing don't want a room full of guys. We need a woman to shoot this. Do you have someone?" The union notified me.

Up until now, except for the little picture that I shot with Arri S, everything that I had done was on 35mm. I go over to NBC and they have an Auricon. I had used Auricons in pictures as props, like when you have the news crew showing up. Fortunately, I went over the day before and I saw the equipment. So I went out and bought some books, and to this day I still think that buying books is the best way to get a hold of anything if there isn't somebody to tell you.

NBC liked my work. They loved it. Asked me to go on staff. But, I was so sure that my big break was coming, I couldn't go on staff. The networks hired me on a daily, which was lucrative.

News is a great place for a woman or anyone to get exposure and experience. You're your own producer and director for the most part, even though a correspondent will show up and ask the questions. You have to get there, understand the story, shoot the story. Forget words. Just make sure it's there in pictures. Get all the cutaways so that everything can be edited nicely. And you go home and you see it that night on the evening news. It's very exciting.

It was a little rough at NBC, because there was a camera room about the size of your living room here where the guys would just hang out, waiting for a call. And whenever I walked in the room, the room would go silent, giving you the impression that they're talking about you. They were probably just telling terrible dirty jokes. But it was very awkward. So I just went into one of the secretary's offices and gave the guys their space.

AK: Are there other instances of resistance or support?

BM: I've never dwelt on resistance. Even right now, this week, this month, I'm not working. And if I think of that as they're discriminating against me—it used to be I was just a woman, and now I'm an over-fifty woman. Now what do I do? I could build up a whole case and end up in a mental institution over that. I can't afford to think that way, and I don't think any of us can.

I was a founder of Women in Film. I wouldn't begin to know how to measure the good it has done for our industry. And the Crystal Award from Women in Film was very, very important to me.

AK: How did you get involved in Behind the Lens?

BM: One of the union camerawomen called me, and said, "We're all having a very hard time with discrimination on the set—the comments from the men and jokes about us. We'd like to have a rap session about how to handle it—how you've handled it and what you can tell us." I thought about the times when I was shooting news when I was not allowed into the men's locker room after a ball game. And I thought, "There's discrimination. But now we've got the Olympics coming to town, and who can go into the women's locker room? Certainly not the men. They're going to need us to do that. So maybe we should let them know we're here." The suggestion came up at the meeting to address that, rather than complaining about discrimination. The group organized to shoot the Olympics.

Up until Behind the Lens, I had often been embarrassed by women in camera who would show up on the set dressed inappropriately for their work. But if they show up in a professional mode, not flaunting sex one way or another, and just do the job, then things happen. I notice now that BTL's emphasis is on education, which is very impressive.

The work of a cinematographer is more than one thing. It's three things: it's the artistic, it's the technical, and the other is the political. If one of those elements is weak, the whole "tripod" is going to fall down. I think deportment on the set with other people comes in under the political. There's no question about the artistic because if you don't have the artistic, then you don't have the guts to even get into the field. And the technical we work on every day.

A cinematographer can be judged by his/her first day's dailies, how many hours it took to do it, how many people got upset while he did it. In other words, did he have a smooth running crew? And what does it look like? And then you know if you have a cinematographer.

With a director, it's iffy for maybe the first couple of weeks. Maybe she has something in mind. But with the camera, it's in the lab in the morning. And yet the producers seem afraid to put a woman in the position of DP. I don't know if they're afraid of a woman running the crew. They couldn't possibly be afraid that they don't know the technical and the artistic. I can understand they might be afraid of the political.

Also, a lot of men still don't know how to handle a woman when they're angry. If they want to tell a guy off, they know the words, they know how to handle it. If a man doesn't like to yell at a woman with four-letter words, he needs to find another way to do it.

AK: You must have had to take some rough jobs. Sexploitation films?

BM: I've shot soft core stuff. The first one I did was during one of those times when you don't know how you're going to pay your rent. I was using the name Brian. And once I got to the set, they were shooting already and it was too late to send me home. So this was a soft core and hard core. They made two versions. And I'm thinking I'm just going to die of embarrassment here. I said, "Can I hire the crew people that I need? I need a gaffer/grip combination as one person, and an assistant cameraman." They said, "Okay." I hired these two guys, and the grip/gaffer was a huge guy, very tall. They shot this thing on location in Apple Valley where they locked everybody up because if the girls and guys got away overnight, they might not come back, and they couldn't finish the picture. They were all such bad actors, and we were concerned about the lighting and stuff. And we realized how stupid it was to worry about a light. We ended up not saying anything, just laughing a lot. It was a dollar. Did a wonderful crane shot.

This big guy picked me up by the waist while I was handling the camera and he just floated me over the bed during a scene.

AK: What about some of the satisfactions that you've gained through your work?

BM: To this day, even though I know when I'm shooting what I'm getting, there's something so gratifying about seeing my work on the screen. In a way it's a throwback to theater, because you can really put everything into a performance, and it's gone with the wind. But when you do it on film, it's there forever. I love to see what I've shot. My vision unavoidably reflects an accumulation of my personal and professional life experiences.

The people that I've met, particularly laboratory people, have been very, very helpful and informative. There are so many people to learn from. I would suggest anyone trying to learn the business, when they can afford to, take someone with knowledge to lunch just to rap about whatever, nothing in particular. Most people will love to tell you the answer to your questions. Even without that, they're flattered to be asked, most people are. I've made a lot of good friends by asking questions and thanking them.

AK: How do you handle stress as a camerawoman?

BM: I keep it all to myself, for one thing. Few people would ever know that I was stressed on a set. The thing that saves me in the nick of time each time is a sense of humor. The other things, the smoking and drinking, sure don't help. And you can't let the people around you know that you're stressed or upset because it gives them an upper hand in a way.

It paves the way better for people who are going to come along. Otherwise it's just a suicidal situation. If you really stop and think what you're doing, and for what, you just wouldn't want to go on. It's little things . . . like watching dailies, developing the ability to express myself better in pictures. There's an outlet in seeing, really seeing.

AK: How has the industry changed in its perception of women who work behind the lens in the last several years?

BM: It used to be, "I'd never heard of a woman in camera!" That's not the case now. You still find a few cavemen who say that. But now we're accepted. I think that women are gaining respect in the business. And the fact that there are more assistants, that women are seen at equipment houses prepping equipment and handling it well—the image goes a long way.

AK: What are your ultimate goals in camera work?

BM: I want to continue shooting and directing—features, documentaries, and television. There are constant challenges and puzzles putting those together.

AK: Do you have any regrets that you haven't worked as an actress?

BM: No. As a matter of fact, working as an actress has been very, very helpful on the set. Actors seem to sense immediately that you understand where they're coming from. When you tell an actor that he missed his mark right after a take that was very emotional, there's very definitely a way to do it. Some camera crews just say, "Hey, Charlie, you didn't hit that mark when you were doing that sobbing scene over there." What you do in a case like that is feel whether he wants to go to some other mark, relight for him there, and be ready for him, without even telling him about it.

I've gotten thank you notes from actors that you wouldn't believe, just saying that they sensed something on the set. And it gets right back to the director and producer.

AK: In terms of dealing with problems and how others perceive your ability to carry heavy equipment, how have you dealt with that?

BM: Sometimes I would lift and carry things and really tear my insides out. And I wouldn't be surprised if I did damage to myself. It's just sheer endurance. And I'm aching and crying, but not on the set. Nobody would know because I just do it. Sometimes I do it out of stubbornness. If it makes more sense to get a wagon or dolly with wheels on it, then you do it. Or if there's a big burly guy and he's not doing something else, you say, "Would you mind helping me?" It makes you no less of a person to do that. And by asking him, he feels more the gentleman and he's going to treat you more like a lady, and there's nothing wrong with being a lady.

AK: Bri Murphy, American Society of Cinematographers—the highest honor a cameraperson can get. You were the first woman to have "ASC" after her name.

BM: That is a great honor. I've got to point out that it's men who gave me that honor, because the organization was a men's organization. And in order to get in you have to be recommended by men, and then it goes to the membership.

AK: Did you seek that membership?

BM: You can't really seek it, but I certainly did aspire to ASC membership. It's the highest honor that anyone can get in the professional cinematographer's ladder.

Juliana Wang

Juliana Wang was one of the first members of the newly chartered NABET in New York in the 1960s, and the first woman to belong to IA 644 as director of photography. She shot news at CBS and commercials for such companies as Film Fair, including jobs in Hollywood using Chapman cranes.

The daughter of a diplomat, Juliana Wang was born in Holland and educated in Iran. Her self-taught film career began in animation, where she was the only woman doing in-between work at an animation house in New York in the early 1960s. In response to a slow-down in the animation field, in 1966 she began to expand her still photography skills into shooting stock shots. She started a difficult career in cinematography at a time when women in general, let alone women of Asian descent, typically faced insurmountable discrimination. Her perseverance makes her a true pioneer in her profession.

Despite her challenging and successful career as one of the first female directors of photography, by the 1980s Juliana's life was burdened with financial difficulties, much of which she blamed on earlier naïveté and lack of support. Co–award winner with another camerawoman for an Emmy on *New York Illustrated* in 1978, she felt, for example, that the spotlight was on the other woman at the awards ceremony, leaving her in the dark, and, figuratively, in ensuing obscurity. In the late 1970s, when CBS switched to video, Juliana Wang was among the many film people fired. Unable to pay her union dues, she was expelled from IA 644. In the 1980s and early 1990s, Juliana ran a small video company with her sister, Smiling Cat Productions, and designed greeting cards on the side.

In 1992 Juliana underwent an operation for glaucoma. Legally blind, she struggled to pay her rent on Social Security. Urgent appeals to Behind the Lens and other women's film organizations netted negligible support; Women in Film refused to mention Juliana's predicament on the grounds that she was not a member of Women in Film (and that as an organization itself strapped for funds, it is difficult even to support those members of Women in Film who need emergency help). Juliana died in Bellevue Hospital on January 3, 1993.

It had been snowing for days at the time of her interview: the urban landscape and the freelance film scene of New York seemed equally bleak, and the bitter cold seemed to match Juliana's bitterness that despite her status as a pioneer in the industry, she had been awarded neither appropriate recognition by her peers nor sufficient opportunities for a steady income.

AK: How did you first get into camera work?

JW: They promised me at the animation company where I worked, that they were going to put me in as an assistant, but they never did. Finally they laid everybody off, so I freelanced as an assistant for animated theatrical features like *Popeye*. I just promoted myself.

I also shot with a Bolex and a Canon, for fun. Criticism, that's how I learned: people saying, "Oh, you shouldn't do this, or do this or do that." And little by little, I got jobs shooting stock shots.

I went to 644 and applied to get into the union. I said, "I don't expect you to get me work. I'll get my own work." And they still gave me all kinds of excuses. In the meantime NABET came to be organized. All the people were joining that in the 1960s, so I joined too, as camera operator. There were no women.

After a few months, 644 took whoever they thought were the best people out of NABET, trying to destroy NABET. I was in the group.

With this union card, I could go work for CBS and places like that. I did a lot of commercials with this one director at Film Fair. He took me to Hollywood to shoot with a big crew, and he had two or three Chapman cranes, one of them forty feet high. I had never used those things, so that was a lot of fun for me, shooting those commercials.

But I didn't know anybody on the crew. While we were shooting the commercial, I put my meter on the dolly. During the lunch break, the meter was smashed. Somebody stepped on it, supposedly accidentally. In a stupid, naïve little way, I thought people would never do something like this on purpose. I paid for it.

There was a bigger incident with Peter Von Schmidt on another big commercial. We were shooting with a BNC from General Camera. They've converted BNCs to reflex, so I assumed this one was reflex too. I shot the whole morning with it. The whole crew were strangers—I didn't know anybody. And while I was shooting, everything looked normal. Then some man said, "Oh, you've missed it—there's some kind of problem!" I didn't see any problem, but he kept saying that something was wrong with the camera. Maybe they switched cameras in the afternoon, but when I looked in the viewfinder, everything looked the same, and it sounded like the other one. After maybe ten rolls of film, this assistant said, "Oh, she didn't rack over!"

Again I was naïve. I thought to myself, "It's so stupid—I should know to rack over."

On a nonreflex camera, if you don't rack over and then you shoot it, it makes a noise. I didn't know that on this one, they had eliminated the noise. There was no warning! What kind of assistant doesn't look to see if I didn't rack over? He just waited until I wasted a lot of film, and then he said something. It was done on purpose, and they fired me.

I just forgot it, and went on. I did make a living doing this. In '78, I did a *New York Illustrated* documentary on lesbian mothers at NBC. I shot half and Alicia Weber shot the other half. She was on staff with NBC, I was freelance.

We won an Emmy and we shared it, she and I. I forget which hotel this affair was in, where the statue was presented. A few minutes before the thing started, they took her name, and put somebody else's name there. And put hers right across the table [*laughs*]. So when the time came to say, "For outstanding photography . . . ," the spotlight went straight to her, and a woman brought out the statue and gave it to her.

I was in total darkness. I never thought that people could do ugly things like this, so I never thought that it was done on purpose. So stupid! She took all the glory.

I didn't think of discrimination at first. But lately I've begun to think of my mistreatment as premeditated, preplanned.

AK: You weren't plugged into the women's movement?

JW: No. On the contrary, I didn't like it when this one Black woman got into the union just because she was Black and a woman.

It's very slow now. I call the Yellow Pages, from A to Z, and ask them if they use freelancers.

AK: When did you make the transition to specializing in video, and what were some of the reasons for that?

JW: It's just whatever the demand was. I was working at CBS's *Channel Two News* for a couple of years steady—freelance film work. When they switched to video, sometime in '79, '79 or '80, they fired most of the film people almost immediately.

In video, I had always freelanced. For a while there was a blank, nobody called me; they said they shot video and they thought I only shot film. Most of the jobs were not very artistic.

My sister and I have a video company, Smiling Cat Productions. If we don't need big lighting, we do everything ourselves. Industrials mostly—3/4", Beta.

AK: You were the first female director of photography in the union [IA Local 644]?

JW: Yeah. I went in first as a commercial cameraman. Then, after five years, they gave me a DP card. I was a member since 1966. All these people in the union, they don't know me now. They're all new people.

AK: When I called the union, they were so hostile. They said, "No, she was expelled," and, "No, we don't have her number."

JW: I owed them money. Three hundred and some dollars.

AK: When you were in the union, did they call you for jobs?

JW: No. I don't know if they called other people, but I never got calls, except once or twice, for work as a standby, where you stand there and do nothing. "Maybe," I said, "you should give this to some retired person who can't do anything." [*laughs*] I just hate doing nothing.

When I worked for CBS, everybody was nice. I still work with the same assistant I used to work with. He and I do gaffing, so I'm still good friends with him and a few others. But I don't know any supportive people, and I don't remember any support.

AK: So it was really your own creative vision that was your main support.

JW: Yeah. I just kept saying, "If you really want something, just keep going after it to get it. Somehow."

Estelle F. Kirsh

In 1978, Estelle F. Kirsh, a longtime independent filmmaker/cinematographer, was accepted in IA 659's Camera Assistant Training Program. Out of over fifteen hundred applicants and seventy-five interviewees, Estelle tied for first place. After successfully completing the program, she joined the union, working as an assistant primarily on network television shows, and moving up to camera operator.

In 1987, she signed an independent contractor still photographer contract on a nonunion feature. An accident on the set during the shooting left Estelle comatose and suffering from traumatic brain injury. She is seizure-prone and suffers numerous permanent physical injuries. The film company and health insurance companies denied the existence of these injuries despite medical examinations, including MRI scans, that confirm continuing brain hemorrhage.

While brain damage has made awkward and painful such motor skills as driving, typing, and ordinary physical activities, it has not destroyed her talent for outspokenness, one of her many contributions as a founder of Behind the Lens.

Estelle Kirsh recently won a class-action suit against her insurance company for gender discrimination, which will effect changes for other women. She was not awarded any damages, however; all of the money went to lawyers and to the Center for Law in the Public Interest. Six years after the accident, Estelle F. Kirsh is permanently disabled. She has been confronted by a denial of acknowledgment of the existence of her injuries and access to medical care. She has been harassed, intimidated, physically threatened by hospital bill collectors, and unable to acquire critical medical services. Estelle's inability to continue with her career in camera work has been overshadowed by personal tragedy.

AK: How did you first become interested in camera work?

EK: I saw Bergman's *Wild Strawberries*, shot by Gunnar Fischer. Seeing this film was a transcendental experience. *Wild Strawberries* is one of the most brilliantly photographed films ever made. I then became a film freak, working on film magazines, picked up a camera—and started shooting. My first public screening was at the New York Filmmakers' Cinémathèque the summer of '67.

AK: How is it different here in L.A. in terms of support, compared to New York?

EK: In New York, I made films alone, and worked on regular crews—narrative, documentary, commercials. Of course there was sexism—almost impossible to get into 644—but there was also a vibrant independent film world, parallel to the political movement of the '60s. L.A. was culture shock. There were production people and crews who honestly didn't know camerawomen existed! Movie stars, writers, etc. came up to me to chat, shake my hand . . . some out of curiosity, many, longtime women in other departments, to share in my being there.

AK: How did you handle the situation?

EK: I never saw myself as a curiosity. I saw myself as a cinematographer.

AK: Would you describe the IA 659 Camera Assistant Training Program?

EK: My experience ran from replacing the first AC on one show, to being the designated coffee server on too many others.

Too often there was an unwillingness to share knowledge, a reluctance to divulge the great secrets, as it were, of cinematography . . . religious cults with chosen acolytes. The military drill instructor mentality. I was told, several times, "I had to break my balls for thirty years to get where I am, so you'll have to do the same!"

Gentleman responsible for trainees at Paramount told me the first week, "Don't let anyone know you were in college, let alone that you got a master's degree." A later memorable quote: "Don't let anyone hear you talk, because you have a New York accent, and they hate New Yorkers here!" That, of course, was too true—a great fear of 644 DP's taking over 659. Several strikes against me—being female, Jewish, New Yorker, educated, literate, intelligent, and experienced in 16mm cinematography.

Being different, one becomes a target. One becomes a lightning rod for hostility. The misconception is that the owners are Jewish, who are oppressing all the Gentile workers. Just another vicious stereotype, yet it's believed, to an alarming degree.

By the second week of the program, I realized there was a radical difference from both what was expected, and what I was used to. Recognized the situation, realized I did not belong, could not belong. At this point, intended to leave program (as others had done).

I was dissuaded. Were I, a pioneer of sorts, to leave, I would set a disastrous example for future camerawomen, hinder any other potential female trainees. The appeal succeeded . . . I stayed.

AK: Is there more discrimination against camerawomen than in other fields?

EK: It's similar to other male-dominated professions. There is competition for a limited number of union jobs. And don't forget the queen bee syndrome—undercutting other competent women as a personal threat. As one man commented, what fun watching the women slug it out amongst themselves, to see who gets that token female position.

So—who created this situation? The men in power? Do women share/bear some of the responsibility? Some of us believed that women, especially those calling themselves feminists, would be different—and *better*! than men! We were too trusting, expecting ethics and decency and women supporting each other—where competence would be the only factor that counted in getting a job.

AK: Any specifics?

EK: Countless, too numerous to mention. Here's a "minor" one, indicative of attitude: Camera department head at major studio hiring me for new season. After first highly praising my work and attitude to the first AC, he asked, "Would you mind working with a woman?" I wonder, would the camera department head have asked, "Would you mind working with a black? Or a Mexican? Or a Jew?" Hell, the camera is not gender-sensitive.

Don't give me a job because I'm a woman.

Don't deny me a job because I'm a woman.

AK: What about sexual harassment?

EK: Sexual harassment in the film business, of *all* women, runs from inane verbal harassment (always hostile) to physical assault, to sabotage of equipment.

The casting couch puts women in a double bind. We have to deal with the expectation that women are incompetent, and will therefore do anything to be hired. All it takes is one (and unfortunately they are legion) to poison the atmosphere for the rest.

Publicly acknowledging, and attempting to end, sexual harassment is an action Behind the Lens could have done. Privately hearing from a multitude of members about individual cases of harassment; then promising never to breathe a word—as if they, the women, were the guilty ones, deserving of shame—accomplished nothing. I as a board member, having the proverbial shoulder to cry on, was sworn to secrecy by these abused women. And I do respect their confidences. But I, as an individual, as a feminist, felt caught at cross-purposes: Women, almost paralyzed by fear of being thought "controversial," not having the courage of their convictions to go public, yet asking Estelle to go fight the battle for them. And none of them supporting each other on that issue. It's the old divide and conquer. . . .

And the female power structure, such as it is, refuses to admit even privately that some of our sisters *do*, in fact, play the game getting their jobs sexually. "Sisters" in power stick their heads in the sand.

Think about it, Alexis. Without anyone fighting this stereotype, individuals like me—and you—have had to live with the dogmatic certainty that we *all* get our jobs trading "favors," and lose opportunities and jobs as a result. Of course, I resent the circumstances—the male power structure's (and the individuals') demands, the women acceding to these demands, creating the expectation that this behavior is normal. And I resent the people in power, the women especially, refusing to publicly acknowledge anything. They fear they'll be called troublemakers, so they do nothing, and instead contribute to making the situation far worse. (Remember my article in the *BTL Newsletter*, "Troublemakers"?)[1]

And fear reigns. We all remember blacklisting.

AK: Do you think your political work with Behind the Lens lowered the number of jobs you've had?

EK: I don't know. Fact is, of course, I was the first woman assistant promoted to camera operator by a director of photography. Played by the *written rules*, paid my dues, and moved up.

AK: How does one handle stress as a camerawoman?

EK: Eighteen-hour workdays require stamina, intense concentration. To do a job right, you need tools, knowledge, attitude, cooperation. My abilities at framing a shot, at composition, at working well with actors, at lighting, knowing how to use equipment—my proficiency at all the technical, artistic, craft skills—have nothing at all to do with my gender, my race, my religion, my politics. In Hollywood, expecting and seeking cooperation (believing the legends about Swiss clockwork super-efficient crews), and then, being faced by people choosing combat, who were making my gender and ethnicity paramount—I've never encountered such racism, sexism, anti-Semitism until I was on a Hollywood film set.

Let me emphasize that the cooperative crews, especially in New York, were made of disparate elements—in terms of gender/race/religion/background, it didn't matter—and these crews worked together, made a whole. Like good cooking, like a good meal.

I shot an interview with Bruce Willis for ABC. I was the DP, yet didn't give orders—I prefer working *with* people. And we had a great time. My sound mixer, Jim Tanenbaum, C.A.S. [Cinema Audio Society], said to my assistant (new in town): "Don't think Hollywood's going to be like this every day!" But it *did* work—and ABC kept giving me calls . . . too bad I was in the hospital. . . .

My own shooting was an enlightening, liberating, orgasmic experience—again the physical exhilaration of hand-holding—euphoria, a dance with the camera. Any place, with a camera in my hand, I was *alive*.

AK: Can you talk about some of the cameras and camera situations that you've worked with?

EK: I've worked diverse situations—16mm, 35mm, tape, single camera, multicamera, documentary, commercials, newsreel, Hollywood, using a variety of cameras: Auricon, Arriflex, Beaulieu, Bell & Howell, Betacam, Bolex, CP-16, Frezzolini, Hitachi, Ikegami, JVC, Mitchell, Panavision, Revere, Sony; in various formats, gauges, modifications. Technical improvements and innovations happen constantly!

Curious how some DPs swear by the lighting, others swear by certain cameras, bonding with equipment—comparable to the sensual thrill of driving a certain car to the max, or using any machinery, the natural high. . . . I went to the SMPTE Convention, and met the new Arri wheels (the Arri geared head). God, thought I'd gone to Heaven! Especially the #1 Head, which Clairmont Camera has. First time my hands were on a set of wheels since the accident. Like coming out of a trance, returning to life. Felt as natural as flying to a bird. . . .

AK: How about some thoughts relating Hollywood to the outside world?

EK: Poster in Disabled Students Center: SIGHT IS ONLY ONE OF OUR SENSES—BUT SEEING IS AN ART. I wonder about camera crews, people who can detect a quarter stop light change, but cannot see past the stereotypes and generalizations and prejudices they've been taught, and that they've grown up with. How curious—those working in the movie industry, whatever field—can see underneath the make-believe, know all the methods, every technical trick/skill/effect creating illusion on the screen, yet they still believe all the stereotypes, all the bigotry of gender and race and religion and class. To see, yet to be blind to reality, and art—not seeing past political/cultural illusions.

Remember how we were going to change the world with our films?

AK: Does Hollywood create, or merely represent, sexism?

EK: Both. The film business bears major responsibility for the culture as it is, for promulgating the consciousness, the "values" that exist in this country. The most dominant force in children's lives is television. Watch what forms every little girl's and boy's thought patterns, reality patterns. It doesn't surprise me at all that the majority of seventh graders—boys *and* girls—think rape is justified. They are indoctrinated in this perversion from TV and movies, still picturing women as objects—sex objects, servants, beautiful items to be used and then discarded in this throwaway society. And for every program which attempts, or even succeeds, at making the public aware, at raising consciousness, there are a hundred which perpetuate misogyny.

AK: Has the industry changed in its perception of camerawomen in the last several years?

EK: More than a decade later, there is more acceptance. Dozens more women—and men, for that matter!—in the union. And camerawomen are no longer oddities, rarities, curiosities. Unfortunately, closer analysis reveals too many women at the bottom, or moving to other fields. It is the veneer of progress. The second wave of feminism in the twenieth century has not achieved true integration of the genders.

How many female DPs are there in each union? How many are *working*? How many in the ASC as full members? So many camerawomen leave for positions with power, creative control, respect, all the perks. But why do they then always hire male-only crews?

AK: Has there been any improvement?

EK: Again, irony. Today's female superachievers, women in their twenties, denigrating feminists of twenty-five years ago, ignoring the possibility, if not certainty, that *their* door was opened by *those* feminists. And one should never deny today's women's achievements and success. Yet how absurd—these women are so positive that they made it *completely* on their own. They forget those who came earlier, who opened the doors, who made today's accomplishments possible through our lawsuits, demonstrations, consciousness-raising of the population as a whole.

We fought the battles to give today's women (and all women) the right to enter any school (maybe *all* schools?), certain unions (maybe *all* unions?), certain closed professions.

AK: What about discrimination of other groups in Hollywood?

EK: I don't think any ethnic or other group can or should "claim" the most oppression in Hollywood. That demeans each others' experience, and it divides us. I've heard the bitterness in Asian cameramen's voices as they remember Pearl Harbor jokes being told as a form of verbal assault.

And then I hear a camerawoman say, "But at least they're not expected to spread their legs to get a job."

So—divide and conquer, again. It *is* easier to "pass" if you're a male of any color, rather than a female—assuming of course, you're not gay. Some might say you'd have to be blind not to recognize it.

But—racism is demeaning to *all* of us. And so few realize this. There should be an alliance, with mutual support.

NOTE

1. Estelle Kirsh, "Troublemakers," *Behind the Lens Newsletter* 3, no. 4 (June 1985), 9.

Emiko Omori

One of the first camerawomen to work in news documentaries, Emiko Omori studied film at San Francisco State University, where she has recently taught in the Department of Cinema. She began her career at KQED in San Francisco in 1968. The following year, she organized NABET Local 532, becoming its first president. As a camerawoman, she helped several other camerawomen when they were getting started by employing them as her assistants, including Judy Irola, Cathy Zheutlin, Dyanna Taylor, and Leslie Hill.

Some of the films and videotapes she has shot for NBC, PBS, and independent producers include *Rivers in America, Cowboy Poets, Hopi: Songs from the Fourth World,* and *Gloria Steinem Interviews Alice Walker.* She has also directed *Tattoo City* and *The Dive,* as well as the much-acclaimed *Hot Summer Winds,* which she wrote and directed for PBS's American Playhouse. In 1995, she served as series director on *Pacific Diaries,* and won the Steve Tatsukawa Memorial Fund Award.

For the past several years, Emiko Omori has been teaching at the University of Southern California in addition to her filmmaking.

AK: How did you first become interested in camera work?

EO: When I entered college, I had no real plan about life or anything. I grew up on a truck farm in a small town in northern San Diego County, and I was also in an internment camp during the war. I found Cal State hard for me, and I switched over to San Francisco State. Some of my friends were taking film classes, so I thought I ought to, too. In fact, I was just given the Distinguished Alumni Award, the first to be given by the Department of Cinema, San Francisco State, for "an outstanding career in cinematography that has inspired others to excel."

AK: How was the atmosphere of San Francisco State for a young woman starting out?

EO: First of all, there were not many of us, and we didn't specialize—we were just taking film classes. I never, never thought I would make a living at it. I made my first little film in Super 8 in the art department, and then I had my first 16mm experience in the film department. I picked up the motion picture camera, and that's where it started for me.

School afforded me the opportunity to use equipment, which would have been impossible if I had been on my own. I also worked in the equipment cage, checking out equipment for the students. Between that and making my own little things, I learned quite a bit about equipment.

I graduated in 1967, and was managing to work at peripheral film jobs, helping a former faculty member who hired us to work on educational films. Early in the year of 1968 there was a newspaper strike in San Francisco, and they developed a program on KQED Public Television called *Newspaper of the Air.* When the strike ended in September of 1968, KQED was given a grant by the Ford Foundation to continue the show. They were looking for camerapeople and editors and whatnot who had never worked in news before. A former student and friend who was working at KQED said there are positions opening up, why don't I come to apply, so I did.

They hired me first as an editor for this new program, and in about two weeks they needed camerapeople. We'd go out and do one story each day and edit it, and it would go on live that night. That's where I think my schooling took off, because I shot and I edited five days a week.

That was from 1968 to 1972. It was a tremendously exciting thing to be working in film, and it was also a tremendously exciting time in the Bay Area. We were striking for an Ethnic Studies program at San Francisco State, there was People's Park, there was the Viet Nam antiwar movement, and the Black Panthers were organizing and becoming a force.

There were two people responsible for me getting hired. One was a very progressive white man, and the other was a very progressive black man. And the black man, Allen Willis (the white man was David Grieve), was a cameraman. My first assignment was to drive the film stock over to Berkeley for an interview with Huey Newton, who was then in jail. Shortly thereafter I started shooting a lot, people like Bobby Seale, where he described what happened to him at the Chicago trial, bound and gagged. It was exciting for me—as a woman, as a minority woman, and as a woman who had never thought that I would have a life like this.

The women's movement was just beginning then. I have always felt that I was one of the pioneers, but I didn't know that for a fact.

At that time there was another woman who was working in the department, Dorothy Littlejohn. But she was not a full-fledged cameraperson— she was learning herself, at KQED. Judy Irola came a little later, maybe a year or so. Dorothy and I would frequently appear as cutaways on other television programs.

Dorothy and I were and are great friends. I was friends with all the women. We weren't hostilely competitive. I made a rule, because it occurred a couple of times, where you wanted something desperately, and another friend of yours wanted it desperately. And I really looked at that, and what it meant—what it did to friendship. And I was determined that it would not interfere with friendship.

At that time we used to go out on two-people crews. I had guys that would help me when we would have to jockey for position at a press conference, where you would have to go and put your tripod down. The sound man would usually take the tripod and squeeze in there and get a position for us. Because I'm only five feet tall, and I weigh about a hundred, it was a lot to maneuver myself into some of these crushing situations. We used to have a sound person carry this amplifier the size of a cigar box. And we always got comments about, "How come he's carrying the small box and you're carrying the big thing?"

Because we were still using film, we would have to shoot our film and run it to the lab, which was in North Beach, across town. We'd have to get it in by a certain time, like one o'clock, and then have to go and get it around five o'clock and edit it, and our show was on at seven. It was live every night for an hour. It was quite wild—three cameras. I *love* live television.

I was at a very progressive, enlightened television station. But whenever I went out on jobs, there almost always seemed to be small remarks—usually somewhat sexist. I never got an openly racist remark. I don't fool myself into thinking that prejudice didn't exist, and within the station itself.

Being small, on top of being a woman and being Asian, people forever see you as younger than themselves. In some way it may have been an advantage. They didn't see me as much of a threat.

The way I look at pioneering, I think most pioneers are reluctant pioneers. Most pioneers were doing what they had to do, or found themselves doing something and then discovered they were pioneers because there weren't other people doing it.

AK: How was it different for you than for Asian camera*men* at that time?

EO: I don't know. I think there were a few out there already, but I know only a handful. In this business, you're better off if you are a man. If you want to put the strikes against you, probably being a woman is more of a strike than being an Asian.

AK: Has union involvement helped you with matters of discrimination, and how did you get in the union?

EO: Back in 1969, Judy Irola and I organized a NABET local at the station. And that's how we got in the union [*laughs*].

When I started at KQED, the engineers with whom I worked—the audio—belonged to NABET Local 51. Their benefits and hours were so much better than ours. We were given a charter by NABET to start our own local. We were Local 532. I was elected the first Shop Steward at KQED, and the second president. Judy Irola was the vice president. When I took a job in San Diego and left, Judy became the president.

At that time, as part of the union, we organized an apprenticeship program, and trained people as best we could. We were trying to do what we thought unions were supposed to do for workers—we were very idealistic.

I left the area and came back, and I haven't been a part of the union for a long, long time.

Let me give you some philosophical background: if you're serious about going into camera work, you should buy a camera. The reason I have been meandering through life, and through being a cameraperson, is because I never took it seriously, never thought I would go into camera work, never bought a camera. And why did I not buy a camera? I think two things: I never believed I would stay in this business. That doesn't mean I didn't think I was not capable of doing it. I kept thinking, "This is not going to last." But I have to remind everyone that my sensibilities are those of the 1950s. So the concept of getting a loan, and investing a lot in a piece of equipment, and also coming from a working-class family, it's hard for me to imagine—even today—going out and borrowing $50,000 for a piece of equipment. There was a kind of fear involved, a fear of success.

The thing about being a cameraperson, and not being another crew member, like a gaffer, where you work with a lot of different people, is that I had all this anxiety that I was not as good as all the men. I would be on a set and it would take a couple of hours, and I would think, "If so and so were doing this, I'm sure he'd have it done an hour ago." It's the vision of "the men" doing everything faster and better. What you come to find out is it takes everybody about two hours to light a set. What's nice, when I visit a set or I talk to other camerapeople, is to find out we all have the same anxieties.

When it turns out that everybody has these anxieties, it makes you feel like you're doing OK. Being insecure is the worst enemy you can have. I've really fought it, because it colors relationships. Now I can come on to a set and talk to a gaffer and say, "I don't know what I'm going to do here. You got any suggestions?"

After twenty years, I've gotten somewhere, I hope. I don't take a feature so seriously—it's just a movie. I miss documentaries, because even if you've worked just as hard and put in just as many hours on a feature or an industrial, and you're just as tired at the end of a day, you probably met somebody very interesting on that documentary, and you probably learned a few things about life that you didn't know before. And something that you shot may change the world somehow. I really prefer that to what I feel is the kind of emptiness that you get from the manufactured pressures and problems of features.

AK: How did you handle being the only woman on a crew?

EO: Well, I don't know what you mean—like harassment from the guys? Actually, I never had those problems. When you work in news, you don't have time. And as a DP or cameraperson, you're the boss of the crew, and nobody wants to fuck around with the boss, because you have the ability to fire them.

Without even knowing it, I had that power. I think that's why nobody bothered me. Because definitely ACs got hit on, sound people got hit on—I'd hear about it. Or, in fact, they might even go on a date with one of the guys [*chuckles*]. Nobody ever asked me.

My husband was very encouraging of me, by the way. I think that's one of the reasons I stuck to it. He never gave me any flack about my working independently and being in this field, traveling. So that was really great.

For me, the greatest satisfaction of my work is that it's allowed me to do a lot of things I love to do. I've worked and traveled practically all over the United States—including Hawaii—and I've traveled to Mexico, Mozambique, Liberia, Kenya, Tanzania, Tahiti, Samoa. It's allowed me into lots of people's lives that I would never have encountered. And I think it's made me a better person and broadened me in many ways.

I love being an example out in those worlds—for an African woman or an American Indian woman on a reservation to see a small Asian woman using a camera, I think it's a real statement that says something positive to her. And I love to make beautiful images, and tell stories visually.

The feminist movement has really helped. It's raised the consciousnesses of both men and women. Men are more conscious of sexist things, and they are hiring women. And women are more aware of their rights and abilities.

Personally, I don't know that it's affected me that much. What's affected me more is Reaganomics. I think it actually started around Nixon's time, but greatly so when Reagan came in. He tried to stop funding public television, and that's where most of my work comes from. In the last two or three years, I've really felt it—it's a scary time for me. That's one of the reasons I'm going into writing and directing.

I've made two personal films—one is called *Tattoo City*, about full-body Japanese-style tattooing, about a tattooist, D. E. Hardy. And ultimately, it's autobiographical, about my getting my own full-body tattoo.

The other one is called *The Departure*, which was made on an AFI grant and other grants. It's a drama about a Japanese farm family in the late '30s having to sell a set of ceremonial dolls so that the father can send money back to Japan. And *that* helped me get a grant to do *Hot Summer Winds*, about a Japanese farm family in the early '30s, based on two short stories by Hisaye Yamamoto, one of the most respected Japanese-American writers.

When I began *Hot Summer Winds* for American Playhouse, I had this fear of not wanting to get my hopes up too much—that's the way I got through it. I stopped looking at success in terms of one thing leading to another. But the film was finished to great critical acclaim. The *Chicago Tribune* talked about its "stunning images," the *New York Times* called it "haunting," and *Daily Variety* called it a "beautifully realized gem." For me, to have a movie I made with my own vision on TV, I see as success.

Judy Irola, ASC

For a woman who had served as president of a union—NABET 532 in San Francisco, which she helped to found in 1969—it was a courageous and radically different career move for Judy Irola to go inactive in IA Local Local 644 in New York in favor of shooting low-budget features as a DP.

In some ways, the magnitude of this career change was of the same scale as Judy's original move into film: after returning from a two-year stint in the Peace Corps in Niger, West Africa, in 1968, she found work as a secretary at KQED, the PBS affiliate in San Francisco. The late '60s were a heady time in the Bay Area and Judy definitely wanted to be where the action was. The film department was open to her weekend, on-the-job training plan, and soon she transferred in and was actually paid to work in film.

When KQED dismantled its film department in 1972, she joined the film collective, Cine Manifest, as its sole female member. Judy eventually did principal cinematography on the Cine Manifest film *Northern Lights*, winning the Cannes Film Festival Camera D'Or in 1979.

In 1977, when Cine Manifest disbanded, Judy moved to New York City, joined IA Local 644, and freelanced for all the New York networks. Shooting such nonunion films as *Working Girls* led her to face charges by the union. Judy went inactive in the local in 1988 and moved to Los Angeles the following year in search of nonunion assignments.

Judy's numerous DP credits include *Antigone: Rites for the Dead, Working Girls, Dead End Kids: A History of Nuclear Power, Sequin, I Love You*, filmed on location in Copenhagen, and *An Ambush of Ghosts*, which won the Grand Jury Prize for Excellence in Cinematography at the Sundance Festival in 1993. In 1995, Judy was invited into the American Society of Cinematographers, an organization whose membership currently includes 193 men and 4 women.

Judy has also continued to work in documentaries. In 1995 she traveled throughout Europe, Africa, Mexico, and the United States, shooting five hour-long films on the changing Catholic Church. Her latest narrative work was with Percy Adlon (*Bagdad Cafe*) in Berlin in December 1995.

Judy currently combines working and teaching at the University of Southern California.

AK: How did you first become interested in camera work?

JI: I was a secretary at a public television station in San Francisco, in 1968–69. I saw all these people running in and out of the building in jeans and carrying silver cases, and they looked like they were very interesting. I found out they were the film department. I proposed a couple ideas for some small films that they were doing, and they accepted them.

When they got a huge grant to do a series, a producer and a cameraman in the film department switched me over from being a secretary. They were all very nice, and they trained me to do assistant camera, assistant editing, sort of overall assistant production.

We were three-man crews. I was the camera assistant while we were out shooting, and helped the sound man with some tapes as well as loading film. Then when we came back I would sync up the film and be the assistant editor. I learned very fast, under a lot of pressure. While you're doing all that, you can decide what area of film you'd like to go into. I liked everything, but doing camera work, I could meet people and be outside, so that's really why I chose it.

For this series, they could hire five people. And they decided to hire five women. I was one of those women, although everyone else, of course, had film experience but me. I was the only one that they were training [*laughs*].

Emiko Omori was already there. And there were Christina Crowley, Pat Jackson, and Claire Ritchie.

Because of attrition and the eventual demise of this series, the film department was dismantled and people were let go.

When I left KQED in '72, together with six men, I formed a collective called Cine Manifest in San Francisco. In those days we considered ourselves a Marxist collective. We produced a number of documentaries, spots for Amnesty International, worked as crew on commercials, and made two feature films, one for *Visions* here in L.A., and another one called *Northern Lights*.

When I got into film I was in my mid-twenties. It was the beginning of the feminist movement, but I don't think there were a whole lot of feminist women in film at that point. Some of the women I met at KQED are my closest friends today, but what was important for me in '72 was to form a collective with six men. Because at that point in film, men had the power. Men still have the power.

AK: How did support from the men in the collective manifest itself?

JI: I think for the men, it was important that they had at least one woman in their group. I was the most obvious woman in San Francisco because I had been the president of the union, the NABET local there.

In most ways they felt very supportive of me, but they didn't have a clue as to what to do with me. I took care of the plants. I was the only one who would scrub the toilet.

We all worked very hard for the collective. I did what I was best at doing and could do—shoot. And I can take great credit for having been the DP on *Northern Lights*. I mean it's certainly a beautiful film. But it would have been so much better had we been three women and three men, so that we could have had real discussions about our issues instead of my being all alone.

AK: You were too isolated to bring up the subject of gender issues?

JI: I always brought it up. The problem was what happened. Men are well-trained in self-defense and rationalization for their own benefit. In terms of discussing, I brought up everything, which drove them really crazy.

One said I was the barometer for all the feelings in the entire group. I think we did the best we could. I like all those men very much. But at the same time, after my Danish experience, I started to work with a lot of women.

In 1974, I was the gaffer on an all-women's feature in Denmark. They could not find a woman gaffer in Europe, so they brought me from San Francisco. And that completely changed my life. I don't know about the East Coast, I don't know about anywhere else, but as far as I was concerned in San Francisco, European women in the film business were heads above American women in what feminism was, what it meant to be a woman, and the closeness of women. In the film business in the early '70s there was a certain isolation—we weren't in a broader struggle. American women built friendships, but not allies.

Through these Danish women I learned so much. They taught me how to talk to other women.

AK: What I'm hearing from you and so many other camerawomen is that women who are successful don't generally have, or don't focus on, much resistance in their lives. There may be resistance, but maybe you've looked the other way, and looked towards the support. Is that possible?

JI: Yes. You have to. You don't get anywhere by being angry. You only get somewhere by turning it around and making it very positive for you. And my analysis is that I've had equally good experiences with women [directors] as I've had with men. And I've had some awful women, jerks.

They're just human, exactly like men. It's more painful when it happens with a woman. In the interview, they'll tell you they're anxious to work with another woman, and they want this to be a great experience for the two of you together. You usually know more than they do because it's their first feature and you've done this for a long time. That's exactly why they hired you. You get on the set, all of a sudden, instead of being the support that they wanted, you're the competition.

I think what happens is that women become very insecure about power. All of a sudden they think, "Uh, oh, she's got more power on the set. People are listening to her!" Well, they're listening to me because they're supposed to be listening to me.

The good directors *use* me. They keep on inspiring me, and I keep on working, but the insecure ones, after a few days, can send me through torture.

AK: What about young, insecure male directors?

JI: Men are very good at hiding their insecurities. No matter how inexperienced they are, they feel they have the right to be directing, so there is no need to not be nice.

Women today amaze me. We believe that we have power because five young women are executives at Propaganda Films. Where are the women directors and cinematographers? Women have always been the best secretaries, being creative while taking good care of the boss and his interests. How is being an Executive Producer for a company owned by men any liberation? I hope to see the day when women can strive for much more and not be afraid to meet the challenge. We are still grateful for the crumbs.

AK: Could you talk about your union involvement?

JI: We organized NABET Local 532 in San Francisco in 1969, and we were the first non-IA film local. At first I was a shop steward, then I was a vice president, and then I became the president. I mean, I'm a union girl. I believe in unionism for working people. But I have a lot of problems today with the unions in general, and in particular with the film unions.

I was in NABET until '77, but when I left San Francisco and I went to New York, NABET didn't represent what I wanted to do— Local 15 represented only commercials. IATSE Local 644 was strong in New York at that time. So I filled out an application, paid New York $3,000, passed the test, and carried a commercial card.

There were other women in the local in New York—Juliana Wang, Sandi Sissel, and Alicia Weber were all camerawomen at that time, and I believe there were two or three women camera assistants as well. I free-lanced for all the networks for many years, as did Sandi and Alicia. Then, tape changed everything.

I moved into drama. I started shooting low-budget features, and I got away with *Dead-End Kids*. I got away with *The King of Prussia*, I got away with *In the King James Version*, I got away with a number of low-budget films because I didn't make a lot of money.

Then I did *Working Girls*, and it opened at the 57th Street Playhouse. The IA brought me up on charges. I was angry, because first of all, I had phoned in the job. There was a fabulous woman business agent at Local 644 at the time I worked on *Working Girls*. I called her and told her, "I'm doing this; I want you to know I'm doing it." She said, "OK, I'll put it down in my notes; I can't really approve of it, but I won't stop you."

The union ousted her. They didn't even phone me; they sent me a certified letter saying I'm being put up on trial. So I wrote a letter in my defense, and I refused to go to the trial.

I got a certified letter from the woman who was the BA [business administration] then, telling me that she had written it in the diary—it should be in the union office, you know—that I had called in the job, and what I was making. I said in the letter that this letter would stand as my defense. They found me guilty at their trial, and they charged me $4,000— just what I had made on the movie.

I decided I would fight it even further. There comes a union general body meeting after the trial, where you could plead your case. The young, new BA—Lou D'Agostino, who's also a great guy—went to the head of the International, and he got an amnesty for everyone who came under this woman BA's tenure. I was not the only person brought up on charges— there were a number of us.

But a few months later, I went to him and I said, "What am I going to do? I'm going to keep shooting low-budget features. And they're not going to have IA contracts. This is not the way the film business in New York is going anymore. This has become an anti-union country." So Lou said, "I'll have to bring you up. The union is putting a lot of pressure on me." So he advised I go inactive.

If I were a camera assistant, if I were a camera operator, if I were a script supervisor, if I were many things, as a woman, I'd probably belong to a union here. But as a low-budget DP, and as a woman, I can't see what they would do for me.

AK: Do you think if you were a man you would be shooting anything other than low-budget features at this point in your career?

JI: Yes. Of course we'd all be much further. I know fabulous women DPs, and we are up against stiff, stiff competition from guys who have done one feature, two features.

I say to myself I don't get work because I'm not the right person for the job, and I think most women do that. I don't like to talk about the rampant sexism in this business, and neither do my friends who are camerawomen. You don't want to get blacklisted. I mean, I don't want to make myself a *cause célèbre*—I want to be a working person.

Besides affirmative action and being hired by the networks and the local TV stations in the 1970s, women got their breaks independently through women's films. I shot a film years ago called *Self-Help*, which skyrocketed because it was about women doing self-exams. I've shot so many great films on women. We really needed those kinds of films.

But now I'm to the point that it drives me crazy when someone calls and says, "I'm looking for a camerawoman, and I'd really like you to call me back." Don't even tell me any more that you're only considering me for the woman's film. You know?

AK: What are some of the satisfactions that you've gained through your work?

JI: Next to the director, you're the most powerful person on the set. You can be creative, and you can be managerial and spirited.

There's something incredibly sexy when you put your eye in an eyepiece and you direct what is basically going to come into that frame. You control the lighting, you control the frame, how much air there is between their head and the top of the frame, where it stops on the left, where it stops on the right, what the colors are. . . .

And it's exciting from the very beginning, when you're working with a director and production designer, designing the film. When you have this creative dialogue before you start to shoot, you can do your best work.

Right from the beginning I understood that artists, particularly painters and still photographers, had a tremendous influence on my work. For *Northern Lights* I studied Walker Evans, Dorothea Lange, and the Depression photographers. And the films of Eisenstein, Ivens, and Flaherty. For *An Ambush of Ghosts* I was greatly influenced by Vermeer and Hopper.

Ultimately, film is a visual medium. It isn't about the camera and technology, it's about vision. Artistic vision.

II

THE PIONEERS OF SECOND-WAVE FEMINISM

My career in London was a battle, being alone. I think there was another girl, but her father owned a film company.

Madelyn Most

While you're working, you can't be afraid. Because if you're afraid, you can't work.

Lisa Seidenberg

When we finished the training program, they told us that we owed $1,800, which I did not have. I had $40 to my name when I got my first check from *American Gigolo*.

Susan Walsh

I didn't go into camera work because I wanted to be a camera technician. It was because I have a strong, visual eye and want to use it.

Kristin Glover

Leslie Hill

The first woman to be admitted to the International Alliance of Theatrical and Stage Employees-Alliance of Motion Picture and Television Producers' camera training program in 1975, and one of the first camera assistants in IA Local 659, Leslie Hill is widely regarded as a pioneer among women working in film during the 1970s. Her credits include camera assisting for Director of Photography William Fraker on *Heaven Can Wait*, *Looking for Mr. Goodbar*, *American Hot Wax*, *Exorcist II: The Heretic*, and Second Unit for *Close Encounters of the Third Kind*. She has also served as camera assistant for directors of photography John Bailey on *Silverado*, *Continental Divide*, and *American Gigolo*; Ric Waite on *Red Dawn*; Haskell Wexler on *Richard Pryor Live on Sunset Strip*; James Crabe on *China Syndome*; John Alonzo on *Blue Thunder* and *Black Sunday*; and Laszlo Kovacs on *Frances* and *Nickelodeon*; as well as camera assisted on many other features, documentaries, and commercials.

Leslie Hill worked her last camera job in May 1988, after fourteen years as a highly successful camera assistant. She had already begun to find greater satisfaction working outside of mainstream features, where she could more easily establish herself as an independent writer, director, and producer. In October 1988 a film she directed won the Lillian Gish Award for Excellence at the Women in Film Festival in Los Angeles. That award was one of a long string of awards, including two Emmies, five other Emmy nominations, a Directors Guild Award nomination, and numerous Cine Golden Eagles for network, PBS, and independent films that she wrote, directed, and/or produced, including NBC's *L.A. Law*, the pilot for ABC's *Hypernauts*, the CBS Schoolbreak Special *God, the Universe, and Hot Fudge Sundaes*, Nickelodeon's *The Secret World of Alex Mack*, reality shows such as *Rescue 911* and *I-Witness Video*, and NBC Documentary Specials *Mommy Who?* and *Living in the Fast Lane*. She also worked as associate producer of the Warner Brothers feature *First Family*, and her first screenplay, *Changes in Latitudes*, was selected for development at Robert Redford's Sundance Institute.

Leslie is currently a filmmaker-in-residence for producing and directing at the new school of filmmaking at the North Carolina School of the Arts.

In addition to her membership in IA Local 659, in 1983 Leslie helped to found Behind the Lens. For ten years, she was also an active member of Women in Film, a Hollywood-based organization of over a thousand women that has helped to change the face of the film and television industries. Leslie Hill is also a member of the Directors Guild, the Writers Guild, and the Academy of Television Arts and Sciences.

Pioneers like Leslie Hill have enabled younger women to focus on careers in cinematography and directing, rather than on their rights to such careers. What has been unusual about Leslie's personal journey has been her ability to concentrate on the positive aspects of both filmmaking and the people behind the camera during a difficult time of transition to greater filmmaking opportunities for women.

AK: Can you tell me about how you first became interested in camera work?

LH: I was always interested in camera work—I'd done black and white photography through high school, majored in motion picture production at Stanford, and started shooting student films in graduate film school at UCLA.

Then in 1975, the Hollywood camera union and the producers' association (the IA and the AMPTP) formed this joint program to bring in some fresh blood. I think they were nervous about affirmative action programs: out of the ten people they chose, two of the men were minorities and there was one woman. I was the one woman.

When I went for the selection exam, I was totally intimidated. There were 1,000 people who had applied for this opportunity and it was modeled very much after the training program for assistant directors. I was committed to going and taking the test until I got there and stood in line for an hour on this frosty morning. There were all around me hundreds of men talking. I mean, almost not a woman in sight. And the men were all talking shop. Most of them already seemed to be in the union at low-seniority levels—Group 2 or Group 3; if they got in to this program, in one year they would get Group 1 status—top seniority—which they might have to wait years for otherwise. So it was a big chance for advancement for all of them. This meant that I was in competition with guys with lots and lots of 35mm experience, many of whom had grown up in the business, whereas I had only shot student 16mm films. I got very discouraged, so I started to leave.

By sheer fate or luck, I ran into the guy who was administering the training programs. He saw me leaving, and asked me what I was doing. I said, "Well, you're never going to choose a woman anyway," and he said, "Well, you never know." He didn't know who I was, but it was just that little pat on the back, that little bit of encouragement, that reminded me, "Well, yeah, you never know." Lo and behold, I was one of the finalists.

At that point, my other experience came into play. They didn't know how to choose people, so they were trying all these strange psychological tests and things. You had to come in and do a dexterity test. Finally it came down to an interview, and the fact that I had already been shooting experimental films made a difference, I'm sure, and made me stand out. Also, I was *really* committed to it.

The only woman who I remember being in the union in 1975 when I started out was Brianne Murphy, who had just been accepted for membership; she came in laterally as a director of photography. There were also several women starting out to be assistants: Kathy Connors was working with her then-husband John; Margo Miller was working as a volunteer loader at Paramount at odd times; and another woman, who worked with Laszlo Kovacs, died tragically in the next year.

Then, in the following couple of years, several other women came into the union through the training program—Susan Walsh, whom I helped train, Pia Chamberlain, and Estelle Kirsh. Susan is the only one who I know is still working. Right around that time also an "open door" policy ensued because the camera and video unions combined. A big court action was involved, and all assistants already on either roster were converted to Group 1 status. Also, a number of members had to be admitted to the union retroactively, so through that period some other really qualified women came in—Kristin Glover and Catherine Coulson.

From when I joined the union in 1975, it took about three years until there were any other women functioning as assistants. During those first three years, I was out there alone, pioneering. It was very, very draining.

AK: What was the first year like?

LH: I remember saying to friends that the nine guys in the training program got to use 90 percent of their energy learning the job, whereas I had to use 90 percent of my energy dealing with men's attitudes.

A lot of times I was the first woman the men had ever seen, below-the-line, on a film crew, other than a woman as makeup or hairstylist or script supervisor. Their prejudice was that a woman simply couldn't *do* the job. And so I had to both *do* the job and do it in a way that had no chip on my shoulder. I tried to just be friendly and not defensive and be all "business." From the beginning, I made a very strong rule for myself that I would never flirt, other than just being friendly. And it was really hard to define that territory. Because I was teaching the men how to relate to me at the same time as they were first experiencing a woman in that role.

One of the real benefits of the ten-month camera training program was the extensive range of contacts we made. Since we were rotated among the studios every few weeks, and at each studio we were assigned to different productions (mostly TV) on an almost daily basis, by the end of the training year we had met and worked with hundreds of union members. There was rampant sexism, and many times I heard comments that would now be regarded as "harassment." A few times I was introduced to cameramen who wouldn't even shake my hand. Still, somewhere along the line you were bound to meet people who liked you and were impressed by your work—and vice-versa.

Because of this, I was lucky and already had a job offer when the program ended. Director of Photography Ric Waite asked me to work as his second assistant on some campy TV horror shows. It was a huge job, as it turned out, with four cameras and only two assistants.

That first job was memorable for the responsibility. I'd be the last one to leave the location every night, after wrapping the equipment and downloading the exposed film for the lab. I remember walking down this lovely Malibu lane at night, among blooming bougainvillea and night birds, taking the film to the driver who was waiting for me. It was a good feeling.

For some directors, getting the shot is everything. And some directors are bullies. The most extreme experience of this occurred about seven years later [after Hill's first job], when I took a two-night call to work as an extra first camera assistant on the *Twilight Zone* movie, the segment directed by

John Landis. That's when the phrase "No shot is worth a life" took on new meaning, as I witnessed three people die in a senseless movie accident. Initially, I was supposed to be stationed with a camera inside the helicopter, but at the last minute I was rotated to a cliff position from which we got somewhat singed by the huge explosions, but had a clear view of the scene after the helicopter crashed. For myself and the fourteen other camera crew members, it was unforgettable, life-changing. It was a horrible experience. I grieved for a long time, and wasn't sure I ever wanted to work in movies again. Most of the men felt the same way. But even though these stunt and crew people were being killed by accidents and carelessness, it wasn't until the *Twilight Zone* incident that the entire industry stood up and took notice.

To backtrack a little, in terms of career experience: After that first TV job with Ric Waite and another show with Chuck Arnold, I got a call to join Bill Fraker's camera crew on the Warner Brothers lot. I was only a month out of the training program. They had just started shooting *Exorcist II: The Heretic* and when the original camera operator left, everyone else moved up, so there was an opening for a second assistant. I had spent my last week of the training program working with this crew while they were doing film tests for the show, so I'd been in the right place at the right time and Fraker remembered me. It was a major career break.

I did four features in a row with him, along with some other jobs. On my very first day, Bill had me focusing for him on the extra camera, and after a couple pictures he moved me up to first assistant. It was a wonderful time: I was working with really high-caliber people, I was part of a "family," and I was treated really well. After each film I knew that I'd done a good job on a top-quality film. I didn't have to suffer any abuse at that point. And of course I was still very idealistic, and I thought *Exorcist II: The Heretic* was the greatest movie being made, because Bill Fraker did!

On location for *Exorcist II*, we had incredible views from the tops of the cliffs in Page, Arizona. Fraker's amazing key grip, Art Brooker, built a platform that extended way over the cliff's edge. We were hundreds of feet above the valley. I was the only one not afraid of heights, so I'd crawl out there and set filters, check film, and start the camera. This little Arri 2C with about three glass filters taped on the lens, and no matte box, was going to drop straight to the ground on a pulley rope, simulating the POV of a falling monk. Art fussed with the ropes, figuring out how much slack to allow, etc. Finally we did the shot. But he figured wrong. The camera came hurtling down, the ropes stretched out, and it *just* hit the ground, lens first. I was the one who recovered it. Astoundingly, only the front filters were smashed.

AK: How do you handle stress as a camerawoman?

LH: Now, when I've done other jobs, like as assistant director on independent films, or camera operating for a friend, I've discovered that camera assisting is actually one of the most stressful jobs on the set, because, if you blow it, you can blow hundreds of thousands of dollars worth of effort in one take. For instance, if you load the film wrong, or flash the film, or if you have a really crucial dolly move and the best take of the day or the actor's best performance is out of focus. Or say, it's late at night and you're filming an explosion; if you set up for it all day and then you miss it somehow. . . . This can be disastrous to a production company! I mean, if an assistant director forgets to tell the extras to cross in the background during the shot, it's usually not a disaster; they don't have to do the shot over. Also, they recognize that kind of mistake immediately, whereas a camera error often isn't known until the next day's dailies, and then it's too late. Or at least that was the case before video playback became widely used.

AK: What did you do when you felt completely pressured?

LH: Once I had developed a certain amount of experience and respect, it wasn't ever hard to ask for what I needed. But earlier on, particularly before the *Twilight Zone* disaster and some of those horrible stunt accidents that resulted in death, I was very easily pressured—particularly as a woman, I think—into doing whatever needed to be done to please everybody. I certainly was in dangerous situations way too often, and never spoke up. Men didn't speak up, and certainly as a woman, I was very reluctant to complain even when I thought I was in danger.

For instance, on the film *China Syndrome*, do you remember the scene where Jane Fonda's sound man, who's an Hispanic reporter, has found the evidence of plutonium use? Anyhow, he has the evidence in his car. He's bringing it back to meet her, he's driving a car along a mountain road, and a big van starts chasing him and finally drives him off the cliff.

Down below the cliff we spent a full day setting up camera positions for the crash. Ray Villalobos (he was still an operator) and I, as the assistant, were together at a position in a ravine very close to where they expected the car to crash when the stuntmen sent it flying off the cliff.

Finally, in the late afternoon, as we're losing light (after setting up since dawn), they're ready to do the stunt. The car comes flying off the cliff and then, everything mentally went into slow motion, because the car was coming straight at us, at my camera position. We were using a long lens—Ray was looking through a telephoto—so he couldn't judge the distance, and I remember just saying, while still focusing, you know still keeping this car sharp, "Ray, I . . . think . . . we . . . better . . . go . . . " He popped his head up, looks, his eyes about pop out of his head, and he takes off running and I take off in the other direction.

So I'm speeding down this hill, and suddenly the breath is sort of knocked out of me and I do a tuck and roll in the air, land on my feet, sort of look back and see that the car has landed all of three feet in front of our lens, then instinctively rush back to the camera. Ray sees me rush back, he rushes back, we join up at the camera and finish the shot, and it's actually used in the film. Everybody said, "Are you okay?" So I said, "Yeah, yeah," and I went on and wrapped the camera and all. But my legs ached, and my back ached. I still have back pains to this day from it. But, I never even went to a doctor then. I just went on working.

AK: Did you think of going to a lawyer?

LH: I wouldn't have wanted to call attention to myself, or to any perceived weakness. I was as into being "macho" as the *guys* who were being macho. And that was really because of my position as the first woman there: I was still being watched all the time and I felt that I had to represent *all* women. And "all women" had to be able to do the job; nobody could look like a wimp.

AK: How to be macho and a lady at the same time . . . In that case, maybe neither worked to your advantage.

LH: No, neither one worked. When Rod Mitchell, who was Brianne Murphy's key assistant, was killed in 1982—that's when everyone started sobering up about taking chances on insert cars, the need for proper precautions and safety, and that it was okay to speak up if you were concerned. It was really the men who spoke up first, to their credit. Because they were more secure with their macho identities and they didn't care if they looked like wimps. They had children and families, some of them were afraid of heights or whatever, and they would just say, "I won't do this shot, this is insane." Then came the *Twilight Zone* helicopter accident and deaths, and I think at this point in time, nobody takes those kind of chances.

AK: This is a whole other aspect of stress on a set.

LH: I probably haven't fully dealt with some of the insults and humiliations that were dished out to me the first year I was in training. My way of dealing with it then was to ignore it. Some men resented my being there because they felt it was taking a job away from a man—which is really ironic, since there was such full union employment at the time. But some guys were very open-minded, and as soon as they saw that I wasn't a threat or out to prove something, but was just there to be part of the team, they were receptive and sometimes very supportive. I took the men as individuals and made friends where I could, and that was the way I dealt with it for my own mental health.

Later on there actually were some incidents that shocked me. For instance, when I was in long-term situations working with a crew, and then a new person would come in—a man who would have some power, who would want his own lieutenants and try to get rid of me because I was a woman. And there were some situations where I was more invested in my identity and doing my job, and the "family" of guys I worked with were actually more upset about perceived discrimination than I was.

I'm afraid I should have been more confrontive, as I look back on those situations. But, it wasn't really in my personality. Now I feel it would be easier to just question the person.

AK: How did you deal with issues of strength and how others perceived your ability to carry heavy equipment on the set or on location?

LH: I just did the job. And the equipment *was* heavy. When I started, the BNCR on a gear head [a heavy 35mm camera and base] was the most widely used camera on TV series, and it took two people to move that rig off a dolly, hoisting it with poles threaded through the head. The cases and batteries were heavy, too. During my first three years as a camera assistant, when I worked *all* the time, that was my only exercise.

When I moved up from second to first assistant, that was harder because it involved more than carrying equipment cases. You had to carry, for instance, a fully loaded, very heavy, Panavision camera with a zoom lens and a thousand-foot mag on a tripod all on your shoulder—sixty to ninety pounds! That was just at the border of my strength! I could do it with a lot of willpower, but I didn't enjoy it. On the other hand, I noticed that a lot of the *men* didn't like to do it either! The way I dealt with it, was to make a quick judgment in any situation where I had to move the camera on a tripod. If I had to move it really fast, I would shoulder the whole rig. But if I didn't, I would "two-time" it, which means that I would quickly remove the camera and let my assistant grab the sticks and gear head. Without the sticks I might still be carrying forty or fifty pounds, but, in some situations, like if we had a long distance to go, a hill to climb, or a lot of stairs, I felt it was safer to move that way. I'd just cradle the camera in my arms. I usually did that if we were riding a short distance in a truck as well.

On the overall question of strength, I would never say that I was as strong as most men. So I would compensate with other strengths, for instance in areas where I *was* more efficient or more organized. There are a lot of skills required for the assistant's job, like adding up the film footage totals at night, where I was faster than many guys. I would never point it out, but I think guys just realized over time that I was making up for what I lacked in strength. As I became more secure in the job and in myself, I just asked for help whenever I needed it. I had nothing to prove anymore. I mean, I knew I was a really top assistant.

Another incredible feature to work on was *Heaven Can Wait*. First, of course, there was the infamous Warren Beatty, directing and costarring with Julie Christie, his ex. They were barely on speaking terms, so Buck Henry, the codirector, had to mediate.

We were all on location at the Filoli Mansion in the foothills outside Palo Alto, California, my home town. I had just been married there two weeks earlier. The crew was so protective of me that when Warren first came to meet with Bill Fraker, all the guys gathered around while we were being introduced and chimed in with things like "Yeah, she's just married" over and over. They were making sure that Warren wouldn't miss the point. It was like having fifteen older brothers. Except for a few embarrassing incidents when Beatty provocatively announced that he'd had an interesting dream about me (in which I was waterskiing in the air hand-holding a Panaflex!), it was an altogether nice shoot.

Julie Christie was an early feminist, very active and politically aware, and we also became friends. As I trudged up and down the stairs to my mansion darkroom, hauling equipment and countless thousand-foot magazines (I personally loaded every roll of film we shot, because Fraker didn't trust anyone else), she'd offer me a cup of tea from the makeup/hair room. What a lovely way to make a film! She also rented a spacious mediterranean house in town, and invited some of the women over on Sundays, our only day off. We'd chat and eat and lie by the pool. Nobody was complaining!

Warren was notorious for shooting multiple takes—like between fifteen and fifty takes of any given set-up! He's also notorious for being indecisive; often he couldn't make up his mind which takes to print. Given the mixed blessing of video playback, which was pretty innovative at the time, he could wait and review the takes later. We shot *at least* a case of film a day (ten thousand feet), and at one point, I had over a week's worth of exposed film standing by, waiting for him to choose his print takes. I started getting on Warren's case then, reminding him that if there was a fire or something, all the film would be lost: we *had* to get it to the lab! By the end of the shoot, I'd loaded over five hundred thousand feet of film.

After the first three years of working full-time on features, I wanted a break. Bill Fraker had me moved up to first assistant on our last complete show together, *American Hot Wax*—although I'd been assisting on extra cameras since my first week with him—and now I could go out on my own.

I wanted to work shorter jobs so I'd have time to start pursuing writing and directing again. This led to lots of opportunities to take day work with crews I already knew, working as first assistant on their extra cameras. This usually meant filming special effects and stunts, and later doing lots of documentaries and commercials. It gave me a very flexible schedule and still paid the bills.

I often worked for John Alonzo and his crew when they needed extra camera crews. I had met John during the training year, when he was shooting *Bad News Bears*, starring Tatum O'Neal. He was young and experimental, always trying new film stocks and ideas. In fact, one of the highlights of my training was being invited up in the Goodyear blimp with Alonzo, his assistants, and the Panaflex camera (which counted as one of the six passengers) when they needed to shoot a test for *Black Sunday*. Floating along in the blimp's gondola, with windows open and almost no noise, was a wonderful experience.

We often seemed to be involved in aerial events with Alonzo. For the two helicopter pictures—*Black Sunday* and *Blue Thunder*—we were always working with helicopter mounts and stunts. I remember setting up cameras with anamorphic lenses down in the dry L.A. river bed, to film a helicopter crash. I ended up assisting on the camera closest to the crash site, which often seemed to happen. In fact, the rotor blade landed only twenty-five feet from us. I remember joking with John about it, when he came around to check our positions: he was protective of me, yet I somehow always ended up in these positions of physical jeopardy. Still, when working with him I had confidence that I was safe, because he planned so carefully. John Alonzo was generally disliked by production managers because of his demands and his clout, but for the same reasons much appreciated by his crews. Also, when you worked with him, there were burrito breaks on the set. Anything to do with food and breaks is always appreciated.

I also worked on *American Gigolo* for John Bailey, with Richard Gere. One time, I had to fill in for Richard Walden, our first camera assistant, on the day we filmed a critical love scene between Gere and Lauren Hutton. The camera was mounted on an extension arm from a small crane, so that it floated above the actors, pointing straight down, as they lay seminude in bed. The shot started at their feet and traveled up to their faces, following arms, movements, etc. It was one of those really difficult focus situations, where I had no solid references because the crane might vary slightly each time in its distance from their bodies. I couldn't even reach the focus knob, and had to use a three-foot focus extension as I walked along next to the bed while the crane moved; that can add some slack and/or delay into the

Blue Thunder camera crew (1981): John Alonzo, Director of Photography in white cap, front row; Leslie Hill, Camera Assistant (and the only woman), standing next to Alonzo. Photograph courtesy of Leslie Hill.

precision of focusing. King Baggott, the operator, was perched above. As the camera drifted above these bodies making choreographed love, he had to give me verbal focus cues, such as "knee," "belly button," "freckle," "nipple," and "kiss," and I'd simultaneously eyeball it, to judge the focus differential. Even though King tried to whisper, this kind of technicality must have been really disconcerting for the actors. Thankfully, the shots turned out fine.

I also assisted on extra cameras on some wonderful outdoor films with John Bailey—*Continental Divide* and *Silverado*. On the former, we stayed at a motel way up in the Cascades in Washington, and at dawn each day we'd load ourselves and the equipment into enormous helicopters, and lift up to the top of the snowy mountain. We'd work all day without outhouses or hot meals, but the scenery made up for any hardship.

There were three women assistants on that crew—myself, Susan Walsh, and Kristin Glover—which made *Continental Divide* especially pleasant. It was so rare to get to work together. The actors were John Belushi (who was best to avoid because he was being kept on a severe diet and was very grouchy) and Blair Brown, who is the loveliest lady in the world. Blair would bring soup to a grip who was sick; she won everyone's heart. Hauling equipment around in the snow isn't easy, but the week I was on that show was a pleasure. However, Susan and the actors reported some really stressful conditions when they'd first started filming, such as accidentally being left up on a cliff after wrap was called the first night. Susan, in fact, was about the only crew member not to eventually succumb to altitude sickness, an important point in those days when most people were still convinced that a woman didn't belong on the crew. A wiry mountain climber and underwater diver, Susan more than proved the point of female fitness on many different shows.

Susan Walsh and Cindy Kurland, then second assistant, worked on *Silverado* as well. I was flown into Santa Fe to join that crew for a few days which turned into a month. It was January in New Mexico, and we were always shooting in the cold and snow.

Going to dailies on that film was a fun experience. John Bailey would boo the cattle, and eventually everyone joined in: There were endless shots of them *not* moving when they were supposed to stampede. Most of the crew had been there throughout the Thanksgiving, Christmas, and New Year's holidays along with their families, all of whom were welcome at dailies each night. I've never been on a set where there was such a democratic tenor, the tone being set by the director Larry Kasdan and his production team.

But after the big, big feature films with huge crews of men, on which I was usually the only woman, I was just worn out. I wanted to do something meaningful again. I heard about this little NBC documentary which was going to have only a four-woman crew. It was about teenage pregnancy, which was a really important topic in 1978. I fought to get on that crew, I really sold myself, I really *went* for that job! And I was hired. We four crew and the producer, who was Nancy Littlefield, had a wonderful time doing the film, because it touched all of us. Afterwards I asked Nancy Littlefield if I could come into the editing room and watch, and she said, "Sure." By the end of editing that film, Nancy and I had become indispensable to each other, and partners. We proposed three more documentaries to NBC, and they accepted two of them. We were now coproducers. She was the writer and I was going to be the director.

Three days before we were supposed to start producing these films, she sent me a special delivery letter, and sent one to NBC also, explaining that she had just accepted a staff job in New York as head of the Mayor's Film Office, which of course is a major executive job. In the subsequent years, she was responsible for bringing loads of film production back to New York City.

So the result was that I inherited the two NBC documentaries as writer/producer/director. Essentially, three years out of film school [approximately 1978], I was producing a national documentary that received

Emmy nominations. That was when I was able to start moving up, with my own crew.

AK: What about outside support?

LH: As far as outside support in the beginning, well, my boyfriend, Mark Griffiths, who became my husband for a while, and is now a feature director, was pretty supportive. He was kind of amazed that I pulled it off. We had a total role reversal at that time. I was the exhausted hard hat coming home hot and sweaty, wanting to sit down and put my feet up on the table with dinner set in front of me.

AK: And he would have the dinner in front of you?

LH: Because he was home, working as a writer, it was a refreshing change for him to cook, after a cerebral day at the typewriter. He was always eager to hear what had happened when I'd get home from a hard day. He was learning more about the industry through my experiences. It was an interesting period for both of us.

When I got into the training program, I was the first of all my UCLA graduate film school friends to get into the film industry proper. I actually experienced some jealousy and resentment, particularly from the men who'd wanted to get accepted into the training program but didn't.

AK: How did you deal with that?

LH: I didn't have much time to deal with it, but when I ran into old friends, or would occasionally work on a friend's film, I would feel that little wave of separation. There was just such a difference in our experience. I was really in the professional world, and it took years for that barrier to break down again, as the others gained their own professional film experience. Things equalized in time; now my most enduring friendships are with those same people I met in school.

AK: How did you get involved with Women in Film?

LH: Nancy Littlefield invited me to join Women in Film because she had been an early member. It was still a very small organization in 1978: there were only four hundred members when I joined, whereas now there are over twenty-five hundred.

It was more of a matronly organization when I joined—mostly women who were actresses and producers. They recruited me because they wanted to get more women members who were below-the-line and had active production experience; they wanted to get more editors and creative people. I helped bring in a lot of friends who had the qualifying minimum of three years' experience in the industry, and the interest. I saw within a few years how the group started to become very dynamic and very much younger. It became prestigious to be on the board of directors, whereas before they used to have to beg women to run for the board. So that organization became very vital in the '80s.

Then in 1983, a year before L.A. was going to host the summer Olympics, Brianne Murphy and some other women who were very active and visible in camera got together at my house, and Brianne suggested that we band together and try to promote jobs for women on the Olympic films that were going to be made—at least try to get some fair representation for women on the documentary crews. The idea for Behind the Lens grew out of that first meeting. We formed the constitution and bylaws the first year, and later became a nonprofit organization. By now, the "old guard," if you will—which would be myself, Susan Walsh (who was the first president of BTL), Catherine Coulson, Kristin Glover, and Jo Carson—we've all pulled back. A whole new group of very active, working camera assistants and videographers has carried on with newsletters, seminars, and industry outreach. These newer members, I think, are going in a terrific direction for serving their membership and continuing to increase their professionalism, their status, and technical expertise. These newer members haven't encountered the *degree* of resistance the first women in camera work did—so they may have more optimism and focused energy and be able to move much further in the field.

AK: What do you think it will take for camerawomen to be treated equally to cameramen in the industry?

LH: What it's going to take is for enough women to show they can do the job, and for enough people in power positions, men *or* women, to open those doors and give them a chance to prove themselves. I think women's efforts will primarily force the change, not men's. And I hire women cinematographers whenever I can!

I'm a member of both the Directors and Writers Guilds, and I think the Writers Guild women have maybe been the most successful in combating discrimination. They were the first group who did a study of the hiring of women, and brought the obvious discrimination against women to people's awareness in the industry. They had a women's committee in the Writers Guild before any of the other guilds or unions did.

The writers have less problem with discrimination in that there's no question of physical strength or presence on a set. In camera, the question's always, "Can this woman carry the equipment, and manage the equipment?" And in directing, it's always, "Will this woman have the authority to command a hundred people on a set?" For a woman writer, there can be no excuse like that to deny her a chance. Her writing can be neutral. She could submit it under a man's name and nobody would know the difference!

The Directors Guild's first women's committee spent years compiling statistics and doing a big study of employment. Lynne Littman spearheaded that effort. And they proved without a doubt the appalling discrimination against women directors, assistant directors, and stage managers. But increased awareness did not result in a really huge change. Women directors and ADs—especially women directors—are still very underemployed.

I think women in camera encounter the exact same problem. They're not perceived by the powers that be as having the strength or authority to carry off the job. I don't know comparison statistics, but it seems to me that many more women are holding first assistant camera jobs and even a few camera operator jobs now on TV shows, TV movies, and features than before, and at the support levels, in the Directors Guild, women are doing all right too. People will always hire women as second assistants, maybe firsts. It's just hard for women to make the move up to director, just like it's hard for women camera operators to make the move up to DP. I see the situations as very parallel.

AK: What are some of the dilemmas that faced you personally as a camerawoman?

LH: Well, I got bored. It was very gratifying to be part of the team, but it also wasn't very challenging after a while, once I'd mastered the job of camera assistant. The part of me that wanted to stretch and grow and take charge and make my own projects, and assume the risk of being in charge, didn't really get much exercise.

AK: And the creative part either?

LH: Some shots are so challenging and difficult that they require every ounce of concentration and strength you have as an assistant just to zoom and focus and finesse it all. So there would be a lot of creative challenge on some days. But I didn't see it being satisfying enough for me in the long run.

Many of the men I started with in the training program have been DPs for years now. I traded that off for the potluck chance to be a director and do my own projects, and I'm still struggling in that area and often feel underutilized. I've had a lot of successes, but I'm sure I don't have anywhere near the income I would if I'd stayed in camera. Nonetheless, I'm happy with the choice. Awards and acknowledgments have helped validate my choice.

AK: Some camerawomen have husbands and children who make demands on their time. How have you juggled your personal life with camera work? And did your male counterparts handle this situation differently?

LH: I think most of the men I worked with had a great deal more support at home than I ever had. I was in a relationship for only the first few years of my camera work. Since 1978, for the next twelve years, I was on my own. And that means when the going got rough, there would be nobody there to take care of me or to help out. I still had to do the laundry. I still had to shop for the groceries. I still had to take care of the animals. I still had to take care of the house and yard, pay the bills or whatever. Whereas most of the guys I worked with had wives or girlfriends at home who took care of many of these things. I know that *all* of my professional women friends and I lamented the fact that *we* didn't have a wife, too.

AK: What are some of the main satisfactions that you've gained from your work as a camerawoman?

LH: In 1977, when I was working regularly as an IA assistant, I took the financial aspect for granted. I was recently out of graduate film school, and suddenly I was earning a quite decent income, so I just saved most of it. It didn't change my lifestyle, except that it enabled me to help buy a house at that time. I only realized how fortunate I'd been when I lost the steady income. In 1983, I sold the house to pay for my AFI (American Film Institute) film, and started my career transition. So the IA work was really very enabling, both in the present and for my future goals, by giving me a financial start.

I think the most gratifying part of the day-to-day part of the job is the interaction with your coworkers. It's a lot of fun, a lot of the time. It's satisfying to be part of a team that does good work, and you meet great people.

I also took satisfaction from some of the routine parts of the job, particularly when I was a first assistant. I mean, I *liked* knowing that the paperwork was good and the equipment was organized and that I'd antici-pated the needs for the next day. Especially if we had extra cameras, I enjoyed ordering the equipment and organizing the crews. I think anytime I got to shoulder some responsibility, I enjoyed the work more.

And then there was the increasing gratification of having some input to the cameramen or to the operator. Or if you were operating—sometimes I got moved up on an extra camera—inputting with the director and the actors. If it was a good idea, they might incorporate it. There's a lot of diplomacy involved in that, though. I was always very careful to go through the right channels. I wouldn't just go say something to a director, but I might say something to the cameraman and let it be his idea, or he might credit me with the idea if it was worth passing on.

Later, when I got into doing commercials, I could be much more involved. It would just be the cameraman, myself, as first assistant, the director and the actors, when it came down to shooting takes and getting performances. By then, my experience as a director was useful, particularly because I'd done a lot of work with kids.

Commercials were a more absurd venue. The product was everything, and the agency folk were treated like gods. However, commercials are a cinematographer's medium, because they're able to experiment visually and take lots of time and care with every shot. Their crews are fed well and paid *very* well. As day work, it was the best, and afforded lots of quick, interesting experiences with a variety of situations and characters.

There was usually no camera operator or second assistant on commercials, so there was a higher level of responsibility for me as well. I had to both order and prep the equipment the day before, and keep ahead of him on the shooting day. One of Larry Boelens' tricks was to adhese silk or net stockings to the back of the BL's Zeiss lenses as diffusion. He much preferred that to using glass filters or front nets. This was always one of the first things I did for him while he was lighting. He had this little bag of samples—silk stockings which he'd dyed at home to all shades of neutral greys and whites and browns. He loved the look that they gave, and was always convincing directors to try them. However, they made getting eye focuses through the lenses practically impossible, because there was so much diffusion you could hardly see! On screen, it always looked great.

Sometimes when you work with a camera, the satisfaction is visual. A director comes up with an incredible shot. It's the hardest shot you've ever done, but you finally pull it off after some rehearsals and everybody is happy. That could be enormously satisfying. There's a sort of choreography of a crew doing a dolly with a rise, an actor moving, and a table being pulled out as you slide by, and all these things happening at once. Those kind of shots are like ballet, choreographed on the set.

AK: I don't think that if I were to interview a male camera assistant that word, *choreography*, would come up as much. It seems to me completely appropriate.

LH: I just love the play of light and movement. I love images. I see the world very visually, I think visually, I imagine things visually, and being any part of a visual process is really gratifying.

Another satisfaction is being part of a well-defined structure: you know your function, and you don't step outside of it. And sometimes that's just great, because you don't take the work home at night. You do your best, and you accept the paycheck, and any other gratifications. Whereas, when you have a higher level of responsibility, for instance, the director of photography—I saw a lot of guys become heavy drinkers because the responsibility weighed too heavily on them. They felt responsible for the whole crew and for keeping a director happy and pleasing producers and staying on time and budget. Of course, now that I'm directing as well, I have the same experience. I mean, you *always* take it home at night.

For the ten years that I've jumped back and forth between the two careers, that was actually one of the nice contrasts. When I did camera work, I was secure enough about my work that I really never took it home. So it gave me a break.

AK: What are your ultimate goals?

LH: I want to make films that are at least entertaining, and hopefully meaningful and of greater social value as well. I'm very concerned with women and women's issues, but I'm not driven to make films about women as much as about human beings in all their aspects.

I'm really interested in the human drama. But, of course, a writer's or director's films always reflect who they are. So my various experiences on the planet, including the experience that I've had doing camera work, are reflected in my work.

I'm directing, writing, and producing now. I did my last camera job in May 1988. Regarding the transition I've made from camera work to directing and writing, I think the one has been enormously contributive and formative for the other. The fact that I have a camera background is a big asset on the set. Because I'm completely comfortable with set procedures and the rhythm of a set. I'm not in a blind position like some new directors are, male *or* female, who don't have set experience. They're really a little lost at sea, and they have to lean heavily on the assistant director and the cameraman. I think it's a real help to know film production. And to know how to create the visuals. Then I can work really closely with the camerapersons with ideas of my own and also with an understanding of exactly what they're saying, and appreciating their contribution. I love that collaboration.

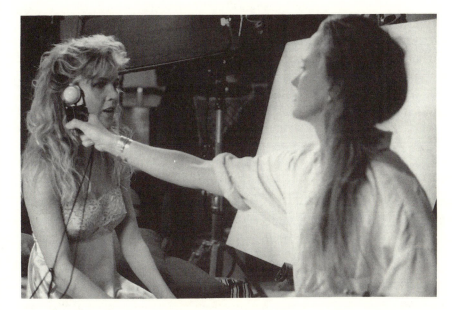

Kristin Glover

After receiving a degree in fine arts at Washington University in St. Louis, Kristin Glover moved to New York and began a career in the film industry, training on the job. In 1972, when she started working as a camera assistant in Los Angeles, the only other woman she knew of was documentarian Joan Churchill. She assisted numerous cameramen including Steve Burum and Haskell Wexler, and was the first female to work as camera assistant on a Paramount three-camera television show camera crew. In 1986, she moved up to camera operator, having switched union affiliations from NABET to IA in 1979.

Faced with the film industry's "glass ceiling" after moving up from camera assisting, she persevered and eventually made her living through camera operating. In 1991 Kristin Glover became the first woman to operate "A" camera on a major studio union picture: *Star Trek VI, The Undiscovered Country*. In addition to working as Camera Operator for Director of Photography Hiro Narita, ASC, on *Star Trek VI* and *Hocus Pocus*, she has had the pleasure of operating camera for ASC members Stephen Burum, Allen Daviau, Caleb Deschanel, and Stephen Goldblatt.

The many other features on which she has worked include: *Tombstone, Eraser, Dangerous Minds, Congo, Batman Forever, Rocketeer, Defending Your*

Life, One from the Heart, Zoot Suit, and *The Rose.* She has also worked on numerous television shows including *Taxi, Max Headroom,* and *Knott's Landing;* commercials for such companies as Volkswagen, Hallmark, and Sunkist; and, as director of photography/camera operator, on nonunion films and videotapes such as *The Legacy of the Hollywood Blacklist.*

AK: How did you get interested in camera work?

KG: We lived in Indiana across the state line from Chicago. My mother was a strong influence in my life. From 1959 to 1965, while she studied painting at the Art Institute of Chicago on Saturdays, I would go with her and study at the "junior school." We would paint in the mornings and go to foreign films in the afternoons.

My mother was a film buff. From the time I was twelve until I was eighteen, she took me to the best films that were being made in the world: Fellini's *La Dolce Vita, 8 1/2,* and all the Bergman and Truffaut films. Being from a repressed, Protestant, middle-class background, that stuff completely blew my mind. I mean, how can you compare Fellini's Rome to Valparaiso, Indiana? To know that there were other worlds out there, *that* different and *that* exotic, touched me really deeply.

I didn't realize that these films had planted a kind of seed in my unconscious. Midway through my college career I became aware that painting was not really going to "do it" for me. It was the late '60s, and everyone's consciousness was being shifted drastically. I saw filmmaking as a way to shift the consciousness further. I put it together in my mind that the cameraperson was responsible for making those visual images. In my naïve way I thought, "I'll be able to create all these wonderful images." So that's what I set out to do after I left college. I moved to New York City and tried to break into the film industry there.

AK: What were your first jobs like?

KG: [*laughs*] I worked for free with this really crazy old guy who used to shoot those *March of Time* newsreels. Then I worked as a temporary secretary at WNET in New York, and through that job I met producers Craig Gilbert and Charlotte Zwerin. They hired me as production assistant on *An American Family,* a big documentary that was being shot in Santa Barbara.

My training was mainly on the job. I also feel that my training in the fine arts was a boon in terms of how to see light and dark, and how to see color and composition. As far as the technical training, it's an ongoing thing, because technology changes all the time. Sometimes I'm just overwhelmed by it, but I figure that if I don't know something, I know someone who will know someone who will know the answer. In this town, if you want to know something, they're always there to give you that information, to help you accomplish what you need to accomplish in a given circumstance.

But it's funny, if you go in—whether you're a man or a woman—to find something out, to learn, to be a student, it's OK. But if you're going in to a production company to get a job, it's different.

I also think there is a "glass ceiling" for camerawomen. You look around you and you see a plethora of first and second assistants running around, doing lots of work and prospering. But then how many women camera operators are there who are working and successful? I certainly feel like my head has hit it. And I feel like I keep cracking my head against it all the time.

My career as a camera assistant went on much too long. As long as I was willing to be somebody's assistant, I think that was very acceptable. I spent fourteen years being a camera assistant [*laughs*].

AK: Can you describe more fully the resistance and support you've encountered in the film world?

KG: First of all, I wouldn't have made it at all as a cameraperson, operator or cinematographer, had I not had a lot of support and been given a lot of breaks, mainly by men, because they were the ones who were doing the jobs. When I started being a camera assistant in 1972, there weren't any women that I knew of, shooting. I guess there was Bri Murphy, but I had never heard of her. The only other woman I knew of was Joan Churchill, but she was busy running all over the world shooting documentaries.

The very first person who really gave me a break, and he taught me the basic rules of how to be a good camera assistant and what cameras were all about, was Joe Steuben. That was back in the old NABET days, when you could take a test and get into a union, which is really the way it should be, I think. I had met Joe on a commercial through friends. He was the camera assistant, I was just hanging out, watching him work, and we got to talking. I told him I wanted to be a camera assistant, and would he please teach me how to do that? I mean, I had so much innocence and so much chutzpah without even knowing it.

Joe took me down to Armistead [a camera rental house] and taught me how to load mags. The guys at Armistead were really wonderful. Their doors were always open, so I would go down and practice loading mags and cameras, practice putting lenses on, and learned bit by bit. I started working on small jobs and moved up to more complicated jobs.

I got into the union by good fortune. I just happened to hear that it was being forced to open its doors. There was a year-long period in '77 or '78 during which, as a result of a lawsuit by some directors of photography who were suing to get in, the government forced the union to open its doors to people who were qualified and could prove that they had worked in the L.A. area for thirty days with one company, or one hundred days with varied companies. And I had proof of the work I had done as camera assistant for six years. It was that simple. I joined IA in 1979. When I finally made the move up in the union, I was primarily a camera assistant by trade. That's how I made my living until 1986.

It's been a roller coaster ride all the way. Doors will fly open and there'll be lots of support, and then suddenly it seems as if they all shut, and there's this tremendous resistance.

AK: As you've gotten closer to expressing yourself creatively through the camera, what kind of resistance have you gotten?

KG: I think it boils down to something really, really simple. I think they would rather give the job to a man than to a woman. I've been building a reel since 1977. I started shooting dramatic shorts and this and that in 1977, for free, because I could see, at that time, that the system was not going to teach me how to shoot. The system was created to keep people down, and to keep them from moving up. I volunteered my services for AFI films, UCLA films, friends' films. I've been shooting for twelve years!

A friend, who is a very successful cameraman (ten years younger than I am, and he's shooting all the time), looked at my reel a couple of years ago, and said to me, "You know, Kristin, if you were a man, you would have been a DP a long time ago." And it's true. I don't really hold any malice towards any particular people over it. I just think that it's the system. It's our society. The men are as much victims of it as the women, you know. So resistance has been really subtle, and it's hard sometimes to figure out where it's coming from.

AK: That can make resistance more insidious, because if it's overt, you can label it for what it is and externalize it. But otherwise, you're wondering if it's you.

KG: Exactly.

I was probably the first woman on a lot of camera crews, on a lot of studio lots. I tried very hard not to show my angst on the set. That was the main goal that I kept in mind.

I worked with Haskell Wexler for a while in 1977 and 1978. He was wonderful to work with. When I was assisting Haskell in '77, we were working on a commercial for Great Western Banks, and John Wayne was the spokesman.

At that time I had brought with me Bonnie Parker, whom I was training as my second assistant. So, we're on location the first day and, as the first camera assistant, I had to measure out to where Mr. Wayne was standing, and he completely ignored me. I just let that go by.

We were working with Haskell's cameras, and it was raining. Haskell, being very protective of his equipment, decided he was going to carry his camera across this very muddy stretch of land.

So, segue to that night. Haskell and his crew are invited to dinner by John Wayne and his entourage. I am the first one to walk in, and there stands John Wayne. He looks at me and he says, "Well, I see that you can't carry the camera. So what *are* ya good for?" And I said, "Why, Mr. Wayne. How rude!" [*laughs*]

And then we all sit down to have dinner, and it's common knowledge that Haskell is very propeace and a pretty left-wing guy, and is pretty public about it. And John Wayne, of course, was a hawk, and always very, very right wing.

So here we are seated at dinner, and Wayne was going on and on about "what we need in America is another good war." And of course Haskell's company was producing the commercial, so he was trying not to get into a confrontation with Wayne.

So when the Duke wasn't able to incite an argument with that, he started in on Bonnie and me—as the women. He went on and on about, how did we ever get hired to do men's jobs, and we were obviously not capable of doing it, and we shouldn't be taking men's jobs away from them. I was quaking in my boots, but I didn't want to let it pass, so I said to him, "Mr. Wayne, you know, Bonnie and I were hired because we're capable of doing the job. The only reason that Haskell hired me is that I'm a good camera assistant, and I'm here because of that." And then I think my voice kind of cracked. I was feeling very emotional, I was overwrought, and I said, "Besides, you're hurting our feelings." [*laughs*] Whereupon, he melted. His whole attitude just changed and his face sort of dropped and he looked at me and said, "Why ahmm sorry, Ah didn't mean to hurt your feelin's." The next day he comes out to the set. He walks right up to me, puts his arm around me, and looks down at me and says, "Ah hope you're still not mad at me." [*laughs*] I mean, how you could you be mad at John Wayne?

AK: Was he acting?

KG: I think that he was really sincere. I think that what he liked to do was to spar with people, and that he liked to push you to see how far you'd go. If you pushed back, he thought that was sort of good.

I really wish the union would push for more women being hired. Anybody who moves up to operator finds it's a very difficult transition. Most guys that I've talked to say, "Oh, my God, it was terrible. You know, I didn't work for a year and a half." Sometimes people make the move very easily, and they continue working and it's all fine, but sometimes it's difficult. I accepted that it might be difficult and I also accepted that there was no way that I was going to be a perfect operator immediately. That takes time. I think that in that area it's probably no different for me than it is for a guy. However, I have seen that it's just much more difficult for a woman to get hired as operator than for the guys of parallel experience.

I have to say that when I read interviews with people who seem to have a perfect life, I feel like I missed it. They've got everything: wealth and fame and success in their careers and children and a great husband. And you think, "She can do it, why can't I?" I think I'm buying the commercials that I work on, buying the American image of what life should be.

But if you're a camerawoman, you're not a "run of the mill" kind of woman. There's no way that you can fit into that mold. There are times when I think that by missing having a more normal domestic life, I've missed having children. That's been a conscious and painful sacrifice that I've made. Sometimes I look at my life and I look at how hard it has been to even make it this far, and I question it sometimes.

One time I was working on a feature in Paris as an assistant. I went to France with a tremendous amount of trepidation since I expected it to be very chauvinist. What I found was exactly the opposite. I found that in France there is a much greater acceptance of women as creative, intelligent beings than there is here. They *expect* you to be intelligent. They *expect* that you're going to be talented. They *expect* that if you've got the job you know how to do it. Whereas here in L.A., there's still a hugely predominant attitude that if you're a woman and you have the job, that somehow you've screwed someone to get it, or you're somebody's daughter or somebody's wife, or somebody's sister. It's moronic [*laughs*].

I think that even in the first ten years of being a camera assistant, I was very proud of the accomplishment. I forget to give myself that pat on the back. There weren't many women who were even attempting it, and to succeed at it was an accomplishment. I was proud of being able to figure things out mechanically, because I wasn't sure that I would be able to. I found I had a pretty good aptitude for those things.

AK: How have you dealt with problems of strength, and how others have perceived your ability to carry heavy equipment on the set or on location?

KG: As a camera assistant, I made it my business to learn how to carry heavy stuff. I suffered a back injury, but so do a lot of guys.

I have very strong feelings about this sort of macho prerequisite for camera assistants. I think it's ludicrous. The most important job that a good camera assistant can do is to pull focus with accuracy and zoom with gentle finesse. The job of camera assistant is a very, very demanding job, physically and mentally. You have to be on your toes technically and mathematically speaking. You have to have sensitivity to be able to follow focus and zoom. You can't just be a stupid lug.

So I resent it that that is thrown up in women's faces as they're trying to meet the challenge of becoming a cinematographer. But anyway, the way I've dealt with it is, by sheer willpower I'd heave that stuff most of the time. And toward the end of my career as a camera assistant, I learned how to split things up. I would pull the camera off the tripod if it was a Panaflex with a thousand-foot load and a five-to-one zoom and carry it separately.

As a camera operator, there still are issues of strength in hand-held work. I find when I'm on the set and a hand-held shot comes up, a lot of times they'll be afraid that I can't do it, but I really like doing hand-held work, and I think I'm good at it.

AK: Could you describe some of your independent work?

KG: I have to say that the most deeply creative experience I've had so far has been working with a guy named Max Aguilera-Hellweg, whom I met in 1977. Max was a young still photographer, working at that time for *Rolling Stone.* He called me up and asked if I would be interested in shooting something for him. He was trying to make his first film. It was right about that time that I realized that I had better start shooting, otherwise I wasn't going to learn how. I ended up shooting Max's first film short, and then, several years after that, in 1984, I shot another picture for Max in New York City, a fifteen-minute film short called *The Perfect Couple.* And it was the best experience I've had. It's just one of those things of creative chemistry. Even though there were difficult moments, Max and I have a similar vision of the world. That's my favorite film to date that I've shot.

That was the one place so far, that I've been allowed to express myself, visually, in a way that I felt was really me. I was able to come through and make a creative statement. There were others that were good—but working with Max was the best.

I also really love working in black and white. I think if I had my choice, I would work in black and white at least 75 percent of the time. It's so much more interesting than shooting color—there's a certain depth to it, and a certain kind of reality that feels more real than color.

I worked on a film last summer about the Dalai Lama of Tibet, because I've always been interested in Tibet. Out of the blue they said, "We need people who will work for free," and so I gave my time. It was one of the most gratifying experiences I've ever had in my entire life. And that's one of the things that being a camerawoman gave me the opportunity to do—I was really glad that I had the capability to be able to offer my services to them because it bought me a ticket to get close to a world figure that I've always wanted to see and meet. So, [*laughs*] I get the most gratification from the pictures I work on for free. That makes it hard to earn a living.

The flip side of my spiritual side is that I really enjoy working on commercials. There are several reasons. One is that commercials are now what great cathedrals used to be in centuries past. The large multinational corporations are the patrons of the art of the twentieth century—through commercials, the commercial form being the art, and the only art, right? So that's where all the money gets poured in. So when you're working on a commercial, you can do something visually incredible. I like that. And I also like being paid a lot of money [*laughs*]. As a result, you can also take a long time off to travel or research or write or do something else.

I like being freelance. I like personal freedom. That's wonderful. But it was easy to become distracted by a little bit of success, and to forget what my original intention was. I didn't go into camera work because I wanted to be a camera technician. It was because I have a strong, visual eye and want to use it. Operating is a satisfaction when I'm allowed to do it.

I thought operating camera was going to be this creative statement—sometimes it is, but not always. Most of the time, it's executing somebody else's vision—which can be inspiring or boring, depending on the people and the project.

AK: What are some of your negotiating tricks to be able to assert your talent?

KG: Most of the time, I try to carry out the wishes of the director and the DP, and that's really what I have to do. The miracle is when those two coincide with my own vision.

I don't do that many commercials, although frankly, I would like to do more. My dilemma is that while I don't believe that all the products are bad, I believe that a lot of them are. People don't need these things thrust at them through the television.

AK: It's a moral dilemma.

KG: I recently found out that the Mazda Corporation is part of a larger conglomerate that's cutting down the rain forests in Malaysia and in Japan. I bought a Mazda in 1983, but if someone called me up, would I go out and shoot a Mazda commercial? I don't know. That becomes a real dilemma. Practically every corporation [that advertises] is connected to some kind of evil. So do we all become whores? Is that what we have to do in order to make a living or in order to do anything that's of artistic merit? That's why I'm trying to move toward doing my own work.

AK: You've been working in this area for a number of years. And you feel it's taking a kind of psychic toll?

KG: I don't feel tortured by it. I just feel like it's a questionable endeavor. I would prefer not to sell my soul down the river. I think karmically there's a lot to pay.

AK: Did you feel that way when you began making commercials?

KG: I don't think I even thought about it. It didn't occur to me. But I think that it's a tragedy that a lot of the world's greatest talent is focused there.

My ultimate goal is to direct the scripts that I've written, but I also intend to continue shooting. I love shooting and operating. I love working on a movie set. Obviously I wouldn't keep going back to do it unless I had some fun doing it.

I've found lately great satisfaction working with different actors and directors and directors of photography. I get to meet a lot of really great people. That is a wonderful aspect of this industry. It's constantly changing and you get to meet different personalities, and if you're lucky, you get to work with really good actors.

I love that almost everybody that's working on a film set is there because they love movies, and they have a dream. It's that common dream that makes us love doing it so much, and that makes us keep doing it. We keep hoping that we'll be able to create that magic moment.

And there is magic in the actual process, especially, I think, with film, as opposed to video. I've felt that way for a long time. There's a visual quality to what happens on the emulsion with the silver halides that can't happen with video. To me, it's something tactile about film emulsion.

I think in many ways we have not yet begun to plumb the depths of what film can really do. And I mean that on several levels: psychologically, spiritually, and certainly visually. Most of the time, we tend to tell very flat stories, both emotionally and visually. But film is not a flat medium. It involves time, and the manipulation of time. And although film is projected onto a flat screen, it is an incredibly sculptural and three-dimensional medium.

I think one of the saddest outcomes of formula filmmaking is shooting according to formula: i.e., establishing shot, long shot, waist shot, close-up, over the shoulder, and matching shots. For the most part, we've ceased to think originally, because we're in such a hurry to meet a production schedule. We grind out movie after TV episode after MOW after miniseries, that most of the time look exactly the same. The fault does not lie with the cinematographer necessarily, but the system, which has become more and more like a factory every day.

I don't mean to imply that incredible, powerful work hasn't been done. Great talents have graced the screen both in front of and behind the camera. But so much more is waiting to be done. We haven't as yet begun to scratch the surface of what film and filmmaking will become. We hold in our hands such a treasure: glimmering silver halides, and light projected through them, creating something potentially powerful and magical.

I'm in love with films and filmmaking. I'll never give up working—trying to get a chance to do something that will perhaps challenge the way I look at things, that might expand someone else's vision as well.

Lisa Seidenberg

After working with portable video equipment at the University of Wisconsin, Madison, where she was studying to become a foreign correspondent, Lisa Seidenberg went to New York and began a career in television, first as a video engineer at WPLX, and then as one of the first camerawomen at WNET-13. Lisa joined IBEW in the late 1970s, working for Channel 11 and United Nations Television. In 1980, she joined NABET 15, when she went to work shooting news for ABC, and started her own company, Metro Video, in 1981. Today she is an independent television producer as well as a journalist and camerawoman, working with Betacam and Video-8, as well as film.

Lisa has shot news, documentaries, and industrials in Southeast Asia, the Soviet Union/Russia, the Middle East, China, and Europe. She covered the Vietnamese troop withdrawal for *Wall Street Journal Reports* (CBS) and *World Monitor* (The Discovery Channel); traveled to Siberia and Central Asia for Pepsi, and covered news events in the Soviet Union/Russia since the early days of "glasnost."

After working as a producer/director/camerawoman for *Roving Reports*, an internationally distributed magazine show from Worldwide Television News, producing "Amerasians in the U.S.," and a story on Cambodian dance, she gave birth to a daughter, Rebeka, in December 1991. Thus far, Rebeka has accompanied her mother on location to Cuba, New Mexico, and Spain.

In 1995, Lisa traveled to Mongolia with Cheryl Collins to shoot and direct a documentary essay about the changes in Mongolia since the 1990 democracy movement. She is currently planning to do a series on Mongolia.

AK: How did you first get interested in camera work?

LS: Actually, I didn't start out to be a camerawoman. I wanted to be a foreign correspondent, and got involved in portable video as a way of covering events. I was in journalism school in 1971 at the University of Wisconsin at Madison. I wandered over to the public access facility one day, and they were playing around with portable video cameras, and it was just a lot more fun.

I was very lucky, because I got involved with video when portable video first came out. At that time it was something that people who were in the antiwar movement, involved in politics and women's stuff were using, as part of the public access movement. So I learned to use cameras, and recorders, and a fair amount of electronics at a time when none of this equipment was thought to be professional. Nobody ever thought that it was something that people in the real world were going to use. Of course, everything changed, and video replaced film. And when I went to apply for jobs professionally, all of a sudden I was one of the few who knew how to use this equipment.

AK: For many of the camerapeople that I talk to—especially Hollywood first assistants, as opposed to second assistants—it's a very stratified thing, where you know the technical equipment, like the inner workings of a Porsche. For you, I think, that's not the point. The point is, if your thrust is journalism, how do you use this equipment effectively to make a particular statement?

LS: It was very definitely both. Video equipment was very unreliable when it first came out, so people with my kind of experience, who had both the technical background and either visual or journalistic background, were definitely needed. And I kind of knew that in the back of my mind. I wouldn't be traveling around the world unless I really had confidence in my ability to keep the equipment working.

I got my first job in television at Synapse and the Alternative Media Center in Syracuse, New York, where I was postproduction supervisor. I had just graduated from college. I also had a dozen people under me running programming for Public Access System.

In 1977 I went to New York and applied for a job at a television station. They asked what I could do, and I said, "Well, I can produce, and write, and shoot, and solder cables," and of course, all they heard was the last thing. So I was first a video engineer at WPLX. I was the first woman who was a video engineer. Not the first camerawoman. Then I went to UN Television for half a year, covering general sessions as a camerawoman. I was sometimes a camerawoman at the PBS station, Channel 13, in 1978–79.

AK: Were you the only woman working as a camerawoman on your first shows?

LS: No. Usually. It's perhaps a little different than the film industry—we were assigned to different positions, not just camera. Out of the staff of perhaps sixty of what were called video engineers, which includes camerapeople, there might be one other woman. Usually, the other one was black. If they could find a black woman, they usually hired her permanently, because then she could fill two minority positions. I'm sure it's incredibly difficult for minority women to get into the industry. There are very few of them. They got in for the same reason I got in. When Carter was president, the networks and all the stations who were getting government money were very worried about having a proportion of their staff being women and minorities, so they were looking to hire all of us.

The most sad and disappointing thing about those days is that there wasn't a lot of camaraderie. I've since made friends with a lot of other camerawomen, but not usually camerawomen that I was working with. It just seemed that we were always competing for the same position. I don't think that it was either of our faults; I think it was the way it was constructed.

Equal opportunity was always a guideline. The stations were afraid that they would lose certain tax benefits and funding if they didn't have women and minorities, or they would be subject to lawsuits. It seems that there's a change in perception—that those laws aren't going to be enforced under the Bush administration, so they're not as worried anymore. I see fewer women at the stations today, and certainly in the freelance world, I know of almost no black women.

My last desk job was for ABC News. I covered all the national network news, like the Republican and Democratic conventions. I left ABC in 1981 to go freelance, bought my own Beaulieu camera in 1983, and set up a company called Metro Video.

AK: How is it different to own equipment from renting equipment?

LS: Owning equipment made my image as a camerawoman legitimate in the world. I bought my first camera when I was still struggling freelance, and it made all the difference in my career because people began to take me seriously. They figured if I owned a camera, then I must be a camerawoman. I think it's less true for men. If men look like a cameraman, then people think they are.

When people gave me jobs in the early days, they put me through the wringer a lot more. They wanted to know all my credentials, or else they thought they were taking a chance because they were hiring a woman. Most of my fellow camerapeople and engineers were men, and they were usually older men. They were very threatened by me, either very openly, or they would do things like sabotage. They would give me equipment that didn't work, or they would manipulate the camera controls so that they were way out. I didn't always know this. I would think that it was an accident, but it would happen over and over again. Then I'd talk to other women and they'd say the same thing happened to them.

AK: Right. I remember shooting the nuclear disarmament rally in Central Park, with the park full of thousands of people. I was on an Hitachi 40–SS. And since I was not the engineer, I was the cameraperson, when it turned out that every control was wrong, all it meant was that they put the other camera on. If I hadn't screamed about it, they wouldn't have done anything about my camera. They would have just let it sit.

LS: At the beginning of my career, I was afraid to say anything. Everything was supposed to be perfect.

AK: How do you deal with the stress, especially in a live situation?

LS: I guess you either crack up—which a couple of my women friends did, and left the business—or for some crazy reason, you keep on going. And that's essentially what I did. I guess I wanted to prove to myself and to other people that I really could do it.

After a while I got to have allies. Sometimes I'd find somebody nice who'd say I'd been given something that didn't work, and would help me out. It's not that all men were awful.

I must say that women were not always that supportive, either. When they suddenly started hiring women and minorities in the late '70s, we were all competing against each other for those little minority-and-women spots. I knew if there was another camerawoman at the station, it was going to be her or me each time on a show, so of course, she wasn't very friendly to me. I don't think other women were sabotaging me, but it was just an ally I didn't have and a friend that I didn't have.

AK: Do you think people have seen all-male crews as a norm?

LS: Well, that's true, but I think they can handle a mixed crew better than they can an all-female crew. It takes time to change the way people think. It took a while before there were enough of us camerawomen who were as good as men and who had the professional background and experience to compete. But the problem is, when you walk in the room with a camera and you're a woman, it's still an event, and you're still unusual.

In the early days I think everybody was kind of insecure, but now it's not so negative. Now most women are very eager to make friends and be supportive, because we're all realizing that we've all been through similar situations, and that only other camerawomen really understand it.

It's still unusual for a woman to do the specialization that I do, which is location shooting, traveling around the world to exotic places by myself. I've done at least half a dozen projects in the Soviet Union. In the early days of *glasnost* I shot *Rockin' Russia*, an hour-long special for MTV. I shot Billy Joel and John Denver and Paul Simon's tour of the Soviet Union. I shot a lot in Europe, I was in the Middle East, I've shot around Asia, and I just returned from Eastern Europe.

People in official positions may take a female independent camerawoman producer less seriously than, you know, a big guy from CBS, with a crew behind them. But actually it works to my advantage when I'm shooting documentaries. It allows me to get into a lot of situations where maybe I would be refused, because people don't think that I'm doing something that they should necessarily bother with.

It's changing, of course, but there are so many places, especially in Communist countries, where you're not supposed to wander in with your camera. The way I work is I just make sure there's a minimum of people, and I think that's a much less threatening presence than your eight-person CBS crew.

I get different reactions from women than from men. Women always seem to be curious. They always ask, one, "Are you married?"; two, "How much money do you make?"; [*laughs*] and three, "How heavy is your camera?"

AK: How do you deal with problems of strength and how others perceive your ability to carry heavy equipment on location?

LS: Well, first of all, I think the problem of strength is not such a big one. The cameras and the equipment are heavy, but they're certainly not that heavy, and they're heavy for men, too.

My Betacam, with a light and a battery ready to shoot, weighs about 45 pounds.

AK: Have you been in any particularly dangerous situations?

LS: I just came back from Viet Nam and Cambodia, shooting for *World Monitor*. There were a few days I went out on patrol with the militia. The day before, I had shot in the hospital where there were all these mine victims who had walked around the area I was shooting in [*laughs*]. So I was a little bit nervous that morning.

I was also in Beirut three weeks ago. There was fighting in the hills. My most nervous moments are always in the quiet moments. It's the anticipation. It's never when I'm shooting. Maybe a little of that is experience. I was more nervous years ago when I was in a safer situation. And now I do a lot of news, and I'm better at telling more dangerous situations from less dangerous situations. So you pick and choose. While you're working, you can't be afraid. Because if you're afraid, you can't work. And probably I'm trying to prove that I'm a little macho, so I don't back away.

AK: Although, it's possible to be a brave, female warrior with a camera, isn't it?

LS: Yeah. I like that image. Of course, I would always tell people that I could do anything and everything, and ended up with a lot more than I could actually deal with. I guess it was some sort of personal survival instinct. I'm sure a lot of women did the same thing, all trying to prove that we could lift five hundred pounds with one finger and it didn't bother us.

When I was hired as a cameraperson on ABC Network News in New York, I was originally interviewed for a management job. When I said, "I really want to be on a crew," they thought I was crazy.

In the beginning, of course, I didn't have that much experience—I was 25 when I started at ABC. And I didn't shoot right away. Instead of making me a camera person and giving me what was at that time a twenty-pound camera, I was put in lighting, and I was carrying around lighting cases which were three times as heavy [*laughs*]. And then they made me a sound person, and at that time it was 3/4 inch, so I was carrying around a video recorder which was very, very heavy, too.

No matter where I go, anywhere in the world, people still ask me, "How heavy is that camera? How do you lift it?" But the weight of the camera really isn't a problem, although I wish there were lighter cameras. It's everything else.

AK: Could you describe the resistance and the support you've had in the different areas in your career?

LS: I got a great deal of emotional support from my family. Both my parents are feminists. I guess they were only emotionally supportive, but I knew that they'd help me out if I really needed it. When adverse things would happen, I knew that my family was behind what I was doing. And that really helped a lot.

A lot of the stress had to do with the hostility that I had to face every day. Now I can pick and choose a little bit who I work for, and I'm not in contact all the time with people who are hostile to me. People call me because they want to work with me, so it's a much better situation. It's taken a long time to get there, and it's part of why I am now functioning as an independent producer and camerawoman.

I was forced into it in a lot of ways, because I really didn't feel I could go very far, nor did I feel very comfortable, working in stations and for big companies. So it forced me to organize productions on my own, because I could hire myself. A lot of male cameramen do not produce because they get more work than women do.

I used to think I only wanted to produce. There's probably more prestige in being only a producer, but I know I'd like to continue to do both camera work and producing. They're very different kinds of things. I don't see why one has to have just one thing. Doing camera work is actually an advantage in documentaries, because you can realize your own ideas without having to translate them through another person.

Essentially, I make a living as a camerawoman and DP. I don't make a living as an independent documentary producer. I don't know how you do it unless you're [*laughs*] tied into—you know—the inner circle of PBS.

The unions have never helped me in any way whatsoever. When I was freelance, and became part of the freelance union, I never got any work from the union. I never thought that they had the least little interest in anything that could help me.

AK: Do you know anybody who has been helped by the union?

LS: Yeah. I know a lot of men who get a lot of union jobs. I get hired because people like me—or my work. I don't work on union jobs now, I'm not hired for union jobs, and though I'm still in the freelance union, I am never called for union jobs. It has absolutely no relevance to my life.

AK: How do you feel that the industry has changed in its perception of women who work behind the lens in the last several years, if at all, and how has this affected you?

LS: I've gotten to the point where I'm known to some degree, and so I get work. Having said that, I think the situation's getting worse. I see fewer and fewer camerawomen doing what I do—I travel and do documentaries. I think there may be more women in feature production in studios, but there certainly aren't women traveling around.

Ten years ago there were a lot more women. I got into it because of the women's movement. Maybe women who came after our generation don't have a need to be that independent. I don't know. Cathy Zheutlin is the only other documentary camerawoman I know. I met Cathy through the *AIVF Newsletter* [Association of Independent Video and Filmmakers], and we got to be good friends. There was a period of about three years in my life that I became a *glasnost* news camerawoman, along with Cathy. Russians were going to think all American camerapeople were women, the way the two of us kept running into each other in Moscow.

I'm a member of Women in Film, and I'm a member of Behind the Lens. In both I've met a few really wonderful women who have been very supportive, and I tried to be supportive of them. I was very surprised that there wasn't a BTL chapter in New York, and I tried to start one.

WIF in New York is very large. But I didn't join it for a number of years because I was a defiantly below-the-line DP camerawoman, and I didn't think they were particularly receptive to women who were what they called technicians, or below-the-line people. But I think it's changed a great deal, which is one of the reasons I finally joined. They asked me to speak on a panel on "Women on the Front Lines." Then I started meeting all these women, and they kept saying, "What you do is so interesting," and, "How do I get into that?" or, "I have a project you might be interested in."

There used to be no money in shooting international news. The money is in making commercials and features here. So the men get hired to do that, and they miss out on traveling Russia. Which is not the glamorous stuff, in general. Now there's starting to be some money in it. My early trips to Russia were always very low budget. I'd meet underground rock and roll bands and travel around Siberia and go into churches that were forbidden. Much more interesting than to be in a New York production studio [*laughs*].

But it's difficult on a lot of levels, and there are a lot of things that haven't been worked out. It's been much, much harder than I ever imagined. The difficulties, the stress, the competition, all of it, and I thought that at this age I would be a lot farther along than I am. Even with all the changes in society, it just seems that it's forever an uphill struggle. I'm happy with it. I don't have any regrets. But I certainly wouldn't recommend anybody to do it because it's glamorous or fun.

It's only in the last couple of years that I've gotten to work on topics that have meaning to me. I suggest feature stories to news programs which are my own ideas, and I go out and shoot them as a producer and camerawoman. And I've gotten some grant money to do my own documentaries. But when I tried to cover the Decade for Women Conference in Africa in 1986, I was turned down by three different women's groups who hired male crews to cover it. I've made ten trips to the Soviet Union, mostly doing documentaries for PBS and for other people. I got a grant a couple years ago for something on Russian children. But I wanted to do a documentary on Russian women, and I'm still unable to get any funding for it.

I don't particularly want to do women and children's issues all the time, either. I guess it sounds contradictory, but I am interested in doing some women's-oriented stories, because I am interested in them, and they don't get enough attention. I don't think that women should always be assigned to just women's issues.

AK: Of course. You don't want to be ghettoized.

LS: Exactly.

Susan Walsh

Susan Walsh, despite her petite looks, has carried a Panaflex with a thousand-foot mag and a zoom lens—nearly 100 pounds—at fourteen thousand foot in the Andes. A fervent outdoorswoman, she has prepped cameras at seven degrees Fahrenheit; worked six-day weeks, fourteen hours a day, back and forth on helicopters; and filmed 65mm underwater off the northern coast of Vancouver Island. Her specialization in underwater cinematography has won her industry respect as well as provided a host of exciting experiences.

Susan Walsh has been at the forefront of women who have gained respect for their pioneering efforts in the film industry. She was elected to the Executive Board of IA Local 659 in 1982–84 as well as serving as a representative to the Motion Picture Industry Safety Committee. A founding member of Behind the Lens, she helped to organize camerawomen in Los Angeles in 1983 when the Olympics were being planned, and worked on the feature documentary of the 1984 Olympics, *Sixteen Days of Glory*. She served as Behind the Lens' first president in 1984–85.

Her numerous feature film credits as camera assistant include *Silverado*, *Continental Divide*, and *Vibes* with John Bailey; *Personal Best* and other underwater units for Alan Gornick; and *Richard Prior Live on Sunset Strip* with Haskell Wexler. She has also served as cinematographer on *Legends of the Old West* and underwater cinematographer on *A Cry in the Wild*, and as videographer on a segment for *Psychology, the Study of Human Behavior* for KCET in Los Angeles.

After twelve years as a union camera assistant (eight of them as first camera assistant), Susan undertook a graduate program in psychology, and currently counsels victims of crime, as well as continuing her work in the film industry. Expanding on her film background as well as on her additional roles as counselor and women's self-defense instructor, she is planning to produce educational videos on interpersonal communication.

AK: How did you first become interested in camera work?

SW: I actually started in still photography. My mother had been involved in still photography before she was married, and had worked for a photography studio.

While I was growing up I wanted to be an M.D. I started college in premed, but then began to shift the focus and ended up with a literature minor, and majors in psychology and art history.

I actually got started in photography when I was at NYU. One of the patients in the psychiatric hospital where I was working had some of his photographs on display at some show. He gave me my basic photography lessons.

I did a little traveling in Colorado and California after I quit that job and finished school, and started taking more photographs while I was traveling. When I got back to New York, I decided that I wanted to try to get work in still photography. A friend of my father's said, "Well, here are the names of some of the top photographers in New York. Call them up and get a job." When I tried to call one of them, a woman answered the phone. We got to talking, and she was interested in going to Colorado; I had just come back from there. So we talked a long time, and she gave me a hot tip. She told me about a far less successful photographer who was desperately in need of help in his studio.

It lasted about six months. In exchange for doing whatever letter writing and billing needed to be done, I would be able to use the studio, all the equipment, and his studio manager would teach me to print.

I was there as much as I could be, although it was during the recession in 1971, and we didn't have much work going on. For the most part I supported myself working as a bartender and a cocktail waitress in Connecticut. I'd go back to Connecticut on weekends, then return to New York and hang out at the studio during the week.

After he folded up, I went to the Caribbean through a connection that I had made through the studio, and ended up staying in Miami. There, I met a commercial still photographer who needed an assistant. He was impressed that I'd worked for a photographer in New York—people in Miami were very impressed with New York—but he said to me, "Well, I don't know. I've never met a girl who was a good printer, but I guess there's no reason why you couldn't be." This was a man of thirty-one, who had graduated from the Art Center in L.A. Within a couple of months I was doing all of his black and white printing, including his portfolio. Within a year, he was getting feedback from retouchers asking if he was sending his work to New York to be printed.

After I left, he hired another woman, and continued to hire women [*laughs*]. And his best friend, who's also a photographer, hired a woman friend of mine.

AK: So basically, the way you handled the resistance, was just to be patient and let your work speak for itself.

SW: Yes. Over time. And luckily, there was the opportunity. I was assisting him, and as you know, assisting is a great opportunity to learn. I was able to go out with him on jobs, see how he set up his lights and see how he handled the client and actors and models, and be involved in the whole process. After about a year, he told me he didn't want to have me assisting him anymore, that he wanted me to work strictly in the darkroom. I told him I wasn't happy with that situation, and the compromise that was reached was that he started giving me some of the smaller accounts to shoot myself. If he got a double booking, he'd send me out on one of those shoots also.

I felt like I really wasn't ready to give up assisting, and yet it did work in my favor. It got me out shooting my own jobs.

AK: How did this lead to motion picture camera work?

SW: I chose to get into film because I was really dissatisfied with commercial photography. I have always been so impressed with film as a powerful medium of communication. I came out here to L.A. specifically to put myself in touch with the film world, with the idea that I might go back to school in the field if it were necessary.

I had one contact through a friend of a friend. This man and his brother put me in touch with a woman who had a theatrical organization, for which I worked for the first six or eight months that I was in town, shooting models' and actors' portfolios and head shots. I would also train the models to work with the photographer. My having had commercial experience was helpful, because I basically knew what was needed.

At the end of that first year in L.A., 1978, I took the test for the Camera Assistant Training Program along with close to two thousand others: half the alphabet on Saturday and half the alphabet on Sunday. When I saw the number of people, I was overwhelmed. Basically, I went into the test feeling like, "Well, have a good time." [*laughs*]

Fortunately, I have always been a good test taker. They narrowed it down to maybe fifty people that they actually interviewed, and out of that they took the people into the program. They asked me some technical questions, and some questions about what I wanted to do. It wasn't a particularly challenging situation—I got the impression they were more interested in drawing out people's personalities. They did ask me a question I didn't know the answer to, and I said, "I don't know that." It turned out it was a very exotic piece of equipment called the DynaLens. I found out later there are only about three of them in existence [*laughs*]

AK: So they were testing your cool. But the pressure must have been intense.

SW: I saw a lot of people walk out during the test. But I always try to keep in my mind that my life doesn't depend on a single issue. And I don't think I was even aware of what a wonderful opportunity it was until I actually got into the program.

Being selected was a marvelous surprise. Once I got started, it put me in contact with all the major studios, where we spent time in the loading rooms and equipment rooms, becoming familiar with the equipment, and becoming familiar with the loading procedures. Not just how to load the magazines, but the procedural operations of the loading rooms and of the camera departments of the major studios.

We got to know our way around the lots. We got to know how things function, so it wasn't such a foreign world. And we got to know people. Then they sent us for a day to several major rental houses around town—and they broke us up into small groups of two or three at a time to do this. Also we went to an animation house and to a special effects house; they covered the bases pretty well in terms of giving us an overview behind the scenes.

Then they started assigning us to shows. We were paid $125 a week by Contract Services, which is funded by a trust fund, and placed as trainees with various camera crews. The understanding was that the camera crew could give us as much or as little responsibility as they felt comfortable doing. My experience was that people gave me quite a bit of responsibility in most cases. I was fortunate, because some people did not have that kind of experience.

There was one situation when I was on *White Shadow* and one of the other trainees was on *Lou Grant*. We were supposed to switch off after five weeks. I ended up being kept on *White Shadow* for another five weeks and he stayed on *Lou Grant* for a second five weeks. I found out later that the DP on *Lou Grant* had said that he would not have a female on his camera crew. So, that was the one major stumbling block that I ran into. Well, I felt that it was my good fortune, that I was able to spend ten weeks with Chuck Arnold, Peter Hapke, and David Diano, people who trusted me and who were willing to share information with me. I was much happier doing that, than going into a situation where I was going to be shut out.

Actually, as a trainee, I had to push to get on features, because they were wanting to pretty much keep people just on TV shows. I also asked, because I'm a diver, and I had underwater photography experience, to get onto underwater films. When I was working on *Fantasy Island*, I went into the camera department and I said, "I know they're going to do an underwater unit. Please try to let me go on the underwater unit," and I was able to do that. I took my equipment along, just in case—figuring they were all crewed, and they wouldn't want a trainee in the water. Much to my surprise, it turned out that neither of the assistants that were along were divers, and so the cameraman, J. Barry Herron, said, "Come on, get into your gear and come on with me." I ended up working in the water with them. It was a great boost, too, that he was that accepting of me.

I was a trainee on *American Gigolo*. I had met Richard Walden and Kristin Glover; they were the assistants. They put in a request for me, and managed to get me on the show. Kristin, unfortunately, was injured during that time and had to leave the show. John Bailey told me that when I finished the training program, he didn't want me to take another job. He wanted me to take over Kristin's job for her. And in the meantime, Leslie Hill was filling in as second assistant. So I was on *Gigolo* as trainee, had one day off for our graduation ceremony, and then I went back on as an official assistant.

Leslie Hill had gotten in on the first training program. The second year Pia Chamberlain got in, and the year I was in we had three women: Estelle Kirsh, Candy Foster, and myself. I don't know what happened to Candy. I kept in touch with her for a while—I know she had a lot of difficulties. Part of it was that her husband also wanted to get into film, and Candy was the one that was successful.

Towards the end of the training program, I asked Jerry Smith, who was then the business agent, and Eileen Leonard, who was in charge of Contract Services administering the training program, "What do I have to do when

I get out of this training program? How much money will I have to pay?"
And they said, "You'll find out about all that in due time."

When we finished the training program, they told us that we owed
$1,800, which I did not have. I had $40 to my name when I got my first
check from *American Gigolo*. I wrote a letter to the Executive Board saying
that I would like to work out some kind of plan to pay them when I could
afford it. I got a letter back from Jerry Smith saying that I should have made
arrangements to take care of my obligations during the course of my
training.

I decided that it was best to keep a low profile. They told me that if I
worked without a union card I could be thrown off the job. I just went
ahead and worked. When I saved the money, I called them up and said,
"I'd like to be initiated," and I got initiated.

Candy Foster, on the other hand, got the same kind of letter, and took
a temporary job doing office work, trying to save enough money to pay her
initiation fee. There's no way you can save enough money at an office job
when you have four children and an unemployed husband. When I finally
saw her six, eight months after I finished the training program, and she told
me what she'd been doing, I encouraged her to do what I had done. But at
that point, she had already lost a lot of contacts.

AK: Do you think racism played a part in it?

SW: Well, I certainly wouldn't be surprised. It's hard for me to say, really,
what was going on. I know that during the training program, her husband
lost his job and her father died. She had tremendous difficulties to deal
with, supporting a family on $125 a week, and she didn't have an easy time
in the training program. Nothing is ever simple: nothing is ever just racism
or just sexism or just a death in the family, but it's all of these many, many
influences, some of them large, and some of them small, that can build up
at inopportune times and really undermine you.

AK: How did you get involved in Behind the Lens?

SW: The initial gathering of Behind the Lens was prompted by Patricia
Hill's interest in meeting some of the other women in the union. Patricia's
an operator now. Patricia started going through the membership roster of
the union and pulling out what she thought were female names—some
names were difficult to determine, and they used to be very secretive about
the membership roster. She then phoned up a reasonable number of people
and invited them to a gathering that Leslie Hill (they're not related) had
volunteered her house for.

We had lot of common problems, interests, and goals, like functioning
as a support group. Someone said, "Maybe it's worth thinking about making

this an official group, instead of just an ad hoc committee to discuss the Olympics." We began meeting to define what the group would be, to start writing a constitution and bylaws, to agree on a name, design stationery, the whole thing. And we elected the first board of directors.

One of the strong feelings that came across from most of the women in the group during this formation period, was they didn't want the typical, hierarchical structure that you see in most male organizations. So we tried to define who and what we were and agree upon leadership for the sake of being able to have the organization exist and operate effectively, and yet to keep it as egalitarian as possible, and to try to encourage people to be as involved as possible.

While I was involved, I was bringing women together to give each support in a field where it's difficult for women to get support and be taken seriously. I found, like in the case of *American Gigolo*, I got on that show because Richard Walden and Kristin Glover requested and pushed for me, and made a number of phone calls. Richard Walden has always been very, very consistent in his efforts to hire and help women and minorities. He was very supportive of Kristin, of me, of Leslie, and of many other women. He deserves to be recognized. I think it's important to put our biggest emphasis on acknowledging what is positive for us, because how we think and what we believe determines the direction our lives will go.

At the same time as I was involved so heavily in the presidency of BTL, I did one term on the Executive Board of 659, and I also did two or three years on the Motion Picture Industry Safety Committee. I think I was doing too much at one time, but all of those were fascinating experiences.

AK: What are some of the satisfactions that you've gotten out of being a camera assistant?

SW: Being an assistant has opened doors to different and fascinating worlds that probably would not have been opened to me otherwise.

One of the most outstanding jobs I've had was an underwater job off the northern coast of Vancouver Island in Canada. We did a Showscan film in 65mm, for Expo '86 for the Canadian government. I worked with Chuck Barbee—he's someone else who has been incredibly supportive of women, and always hires women. The first time I worked with him, he called me up out of the blue to go on a job as an assistant to the Gulf of Mexico where we were working at two hundred feet on an oil rig. And we had never worked together before. He had read my articles in the *International Photographer* on underwater work, and I guess he also heard from some other people about my underwater assisting, so he called me and hired me. I think it said a lot about him, because that is a very demanding job, working at two hundred feet in open water.

I was assisting Chuck again on a Showscan film called *Deep Water Rescue*. We were working with five deep submersibles, hi-tech submarines, two of which were operated by people inside them, and three of them were remote operated. With my interest in the underwater world, in underwater film, it's the equivalent to someone who's interested in the space program being invited to film a shuttle mission. It was a wonderful opportunity, an opportunity I would not have had, had I not been in the film business.

AK: What changes or improvements have you seen while a member of IA 659, especially while on the Executive Board?

SW: Well I've got to tell you that I haven't been very active lately, so I'm not terribly well-informed at the moment. I have seen that the effort to keep people out of the union has been considerably relaxed. I think that's important, but unfortunately, it's come very late. Of course unions are being undermined throughout the country at this time. It's a result of where we are politically as a nation. And having had the experience of being a member of the union, I recognize the necessity for workers to be able to act and speak collectively, and not have to each negotiate their own terms, and then each individually and personally try to fight to hold onto these terms. It's an impossible task. Because the person who has the work to give, who's in a position to hire, has basically all the control, unless you have a strong labor organization. Only with that can the worker in any way hope to meet the employer eye to eye and begin to hold their own. Without that, it's guaranteed exploitation. There's enough exploitation with unions. A very good example is the kinds of hours and conditions that you do end up with. You can go twenty hours without a meal, or work a twenty-hour day—even with a union.

I'm an outdoors person. I'm a rock climber, I'm a diver, I love working outside. I have the gear for being out working at nine degrees early in the morning. Those kinds of things don't bother me, the snow, the sleet, the hail, the rain—in themselves. It's when it's six days a week, fourteen hours a day without a break, and you get sick and you just keep working and you get all run down, and everybody's sick and everybody passes it around. It just gets to be dehumanizing. The entire four months I was away on *Silverado*, I never slept more than five hours, even on Sundays when I could have.

Luckily, most of the jobs that are very difficult experiences are short. Usually the difficulties are political. They have to do with interpersonal relationships and communications. That's where the problems lie. If the difficulties are, say, weather or logistics, or something of that nature, usually as a group you can get together and overcome these difficulties; and they're treated more as challenges, often pulling the crew closer together. But when the problems are with the crew, the producers, the production, or the problem is disorganization, that's when it becomes undermining, and really difficult.

AK: How do you handle stress as a camerawoman?

SW: That's one of the most difficult things to deal with in the industry, because what you really need to deal with stress is rest and relaxation. And that's the very thing that you're denied when you're working—particularly on location. So it becomes almost an impossible problem; you just end up living it more and more. I should emphasize that this is not the film industry alone, but the way industry in general in this country is organized. It's organized to be very compulsive and oppressive, and there's very little concern for anything beyond the job. And I disagree with this. I think it's a very unhealthy and ultimately unproductive attitude on a personal level. It's productive for the gross national product, and for the few at the top who make the big profit. The rest of us pay a very big price.

AK: How do you handle it, in terms of not being able to change it?

SW: I've been doing yoga for over twenty-two years now—every morning, since I've gotten into the film industry. Also, I'm involved in Buddhist meditation, and have been doing that actively for thirteen years since I arrived in L.A. I go on periodic retreats. I feel that this has been of major importance to me in my life for my own stability, for my own personal growth, and certainly for dealing with the stress, not just of work, but of life.

AK: What will it take for camerawomen to be treated equally to cameramen in the industry?

SW: Frankly, I don't see it happening in the foreseeable future. It would require a basic change in our cultural structure and cultural assumptions. We are dealing with something that isn't just part of the film industry. I ran across an article several years ago in the *L.A. Weekly* about a woman director who was researching a screenplay that she was writing. It had to do with cops. She was interviewing police officers, and asked, "How do you feel about the fact that there are more women getting jobs on the police force?" A male officer's very candid and revealing response was, "The trouble with women on the police force is that it devalues my job." I think he zeroed in on the very thing that's a problem here. If the basic assumption is that women are inferior, and if women can do this work, then the men who are doing the same work feel that their work is devalued.

It's very unusual for me to find that there's another woman working on a camera crew, although it has happened. When I've had the opportunity, I've drawn other women in. Other women have hired me. But typically I will be the only woman on the camera crew.

I thoroughly enjoy working with other women. It always irritates me when I hear men—and I hear it from women too—say that the women can't work together. I absolutely disagree with this. My personal experience has been that there have certainly been individual women that I haven't gotten along with, just like there are individual men that I haven't gotten along with, or prefer not to work with. In both cases, that is rare.

Brianne Murphy has been very supportive, and certainly been an inspiration. She is a very dear and wonderful person. Of course, people like Kristin Glover and Catherine Coulson are very dear friends. I've known Kristin since before I got into the film industry. Catherine I've known for a long time also. We refer each other for jobs, and we help each other prep equipment.

If I can't take a job, I try to pass it on to another woman if I can, because I know it is, indeed, harder for women to get work. When there's plenty of work, it's fine, but when the work gets thin, it's harder, because there's still the attitude that men need to work because they need to make a living. Women need to make a living. It must be kept in mind that we all don't have sugar daddies, and we don't necessarily have husbands that are supporting us.

AK: Some camerawomen have husbands or lovers and/or children who make demands on their time. How do you juggle your personal life and camera work, and do your male counterparts handle this differently, and if so, how?

SW: What people need is a traditional "wife" who's going to take care of every aspect of their life for them. Without that, it's extremely stressful. I don't think I can work a full schedule—show after show, all the year around, like some of the men do who are married—because I don't have anybody to take the car in to be fixed, I don't have anybody to take the cat to the vet, I don't have anybody to take care of all the little aspects of life that have to be dealt with. When I was working as a second assistant, one show after the other, for most of the year, my life fell apart.

I remember at one point, somebody put a dent in my car. I looked at it, and I didn't even bother to take his license number because I thought, "I do not have time to deal with it." I ate in restaurants constantly, I never invited anybody over, it was pretty much of a nonlife. As a result, I do not work constantly anymore [laughs].

Even if I had somebody to fill that role of picking up all the pieces of my life, I have too many other interests and would not choose to give them all up. For example, teaching self-defense for women has become more and more important to me over time. What I'm hoping to do is expand on the work I am doing in self-defense and utilize my film experience to make instructional videos.

What drew me to film is its power as a medium of communication. It's a medium that can be used for teaching, for communicating values in a more conscious and socially responsible way. I think I'll probably find my way into social psychology. The very issues that I've seen create the biggest problems on a film set, on a film location, in any working environment, involve the breakdown of communications between people. I want to help people to communicate more effectively, to let people know what they really want from them and what their limits are through assertiveness training, conflict resolution, issues of this sort—and to use my film training to make videos and films in this field as well.

AK: Is your work in self-defense related in any way to your thinking about sexual harassment in the industry?

SW: Sexual harassment is an issue that has to be dealt with, not just in the film industry, but also in every aspect of our lives. When I am trying to relate to someone as a professional, and he is relating to the size of my breasts, or the shape of my derrière, or the eye makeup that I have on, or the cut of my clothing, he is basically not confirming and relating to me as a professional. He's paying attention to irrelevant and marginal details. It is damaging when you encounter this, time and again. It's very undermining, as is indifference. Often women are treated as irrelevant, particularly in professional settings, but also in personal settings.

One solution is to find people who will confirm you, and find ways to confirm yourself. As much as possible, seek out opportunities with people who want you with them, assuming there are situations where you *are* wanted. If there are no such situations, then we're stuck. Then we need to force our way in, like the first women and people of color in this or any field. Then we need to look for allies, to let those allies know that they are our allies, and give them some reinforcement, and thanks, and be loyal to them if they continue to be supportive of us. We do not, however, owe anyone permission to exploit us, not even our supporters.

Some of our best allies are other women. I have to at least mention Elizabeth Barbee, who was once an assistant herself, and Aimee Gornick. They are both wives of cameramen with whom I have worked a lot. They have not only been supportive of me professionally, but have also invited me into their homes for dinner, parties, Thanksgiving. They have accepted me as a whole person.

This is significant because as women working with male peers and bosses, we do not have the same opportunity to establish friendships or camaraderie with our male counterparts. That relationship can become more complicated because of the possibility of developing into a sexual relationship, or at least the possibility raises questions that most of the men in the same position do not have to deal with. When the wife of a coworker accepts me personally and professionally, it at the same time clarifies the relationship I have with her husband. In such a situation many of those questions regarding the relationship between myself and my male coworkers don't come up. It is already clear. I am thus free to do my job and be a professional associate, and am freed of the necessity to invest time and energy in defining or limiting the nature of this relationship. And it can take a lot of energy that I would prefer to allocate to doing my job. Needless to say I am very careful to make a distinction in my own mind between professional associates and playmates.

AK: How have you dealt with problems of strength?

SW: I have always been remarkably strong. People are always shocked at what I'm able to do, in terms of handling the equipment, carrying the camera, and the ease with which I've been able to do it, taking into account my physical size. The BL [a 35mm Arriflex camera] is probably about a hundred pounds—I've been told it's over, actually. And I weigh a hundred twelve pounds.

I think it's unfortunate that more men don't take the gamble of hiring women, and aren't open-minded. The situation might be different from what they expect.

We were shooting *Continental Divide* in Colorado. It was late October, early November. We were trying to stay ahead of the snowfall because, according to the script, these scenes were to take place prior to the first snowfall. We were shooting at altitudes anywhere from ten thousand to fourteen thousand feet.

There had been a lot of resistance to taking me on the crew as second assistant because I'm small and female, and this was going to be a rugged show. Richard Walden, in one of many struggles, managed to be successful in keeping me on the show. As it turned out, there were only two other women working at the high altitudes and we were on our feet all the time. It was some of the men who were vomiting, or lightheaded, or experiencing other problems with altitude.

One of the lead actors, Blair Brown, and I both love the outdoors. The higher we went, the happier we were [*laughs*]. Richard Walden used to comment, "Everybody gets out of the helicopters like the troops returning from the wars, and you look like you've just been on a vacation."

On our last day in Colorado, the weather turned very bad. If we had to walk out, it would have taken a very long time, and we didn't have the supplies to do that. So the climbing instructor said, "I'm really concerned that if the weather gets worse and the helicopters can't take off, that some of these people won't make it, because they're having such a bad time with the altitude to begin with." At this dinner in Chicago, one of the people who had not been at the high location asked, "Who wouldn't have made it?" The camera operator was silent for a moment, then he said, "Uh—the women!" A knee-jerk reaction, because the women were the ones who were most likely to make it, judging by the way we'd been handling it up until then. It so floored me that I didn't even say anything. It was such a denial of the obvious.

I feel very strongly about not wasting a lot of energy in fruitless arguments. My investment is not in yelling louder than somebody else or trying to make a point. My investment is in being able to do what I really want to do, and ultimately changing attitudes. I don't think that's always best done through direct confrontation. I think that we have to be clear with people, that we have to directly challenge some things at appropriate times. There are other times when what we're confronted with is best handled with humor—or best ignored. In reacting to it, and fighting it, we can lose precious energy that we could be putting into going in the direction we really want to go.

Liz Bailey

Liz Bailey started her career in camera at the ABC affiliate, WBRZ, in Baton Rouge, as the first camerawoman in Louisiana. As a result of working in Coppola's then groundbreaking Electronic Cinema Division on *One From the Heart,* she received a professional boost with mentions in *Time* and *Newsweek,* and joined the union. A member of IA 600 and IBEW 45, Liz is a two-term vice president of the Society of Operating Cameramen as well as a former president of Behind the Lens.

Liz has worked on numerous films and television shows, including *Innerspace, The Right Stuff, Star Trek: The Series, Alfred Hitchcock Theater,* and *Murder, She Wrote.* She has also shot numerous commercials and industrials for such companies as Arco, Dupont, and Reebok.

As camera operator, Liz continued to work on ShotMaker and Chapman cranes through her seventh month of pregnancy, and gave birth to her son David at the Upland Birthing Center, where she had recently filmed a birth in water for Japanese television. While she and her husband, Mark D'Antoni, have been raising their son, Liz has worked as camera operator on numerous television shows, including *Murphy Brown, Home Improvement,* and *Anything But Love,* and on the features *Sidewalk Motel, Fearless,* and *Independence Day.*

AK: You were the first camerawoman in Louisiana. When you were first studying film, at Louisiana State University, were the teachers supportive?

LB: No, the teachers were extremely unsupportive. My independent study project, a still-to-tape transfer with voice-over, talking about what I learned during an internship with the news department of WBRZ, showing really dramatic shots of the cameraman hanging out of helicopters and on top of flaming buildings getting shots, was received wholeheartedly. They still use it as a promotion on the station.

But the professor I did this for had been coming on to me sexually. I had just met the man who is now my husband, and didn't want to date anyone else. This didn't go over well with this guy, and he gave me a D. So I fought it. I had to be extremely persistent. I'm a little Southern girl—I was taught to say "Yes, ma'am," and "No, ma'am," and not to be aggressive. So it was very much out of character to pursue that.

One of the things that made me want to go into the field of camera work, when I was working at that first station, was a cameraman who said, "Well, we'll never hire a girl in our camera department," and the professor who said, "Why should I teach you how to work the camera, because you're a girl, and you're never going to get hired anyway." Those very challenges are what made me go for it.

I get really angry when I hear some of the younger women say that they really aren't feminist, and they're working in nontraditional jobs, such as camera work. They wouldn't have those jobs if their sisters, the founders of feminism, had not spilled their blood to break the ground, to pioneer the industry so that they could be in those positions.

AK: How did you first get involved with Behind the Lens?

LB: I was first drawn to Behind the Lens because being a camerawoman was always so insular. Whenever I found another technical woman, it was a cause for celebration, to be able to talk over the problems and fears and successes we had in common. It was exciting to find out what makes these other women tick; what makes them get into camera work; and what makes them put up with all the heartache and underemployment.

I want the industry to be opened up to all camerawomen, including minorities. It's been pretty much a closed club, and although it's opening up, it's certainly not going very fast. Even with the numbers of women we have in the guild, we are still very poorly represented.

AK: There are two issues I'd like to talk about. One of them is camaraderie. The other is the lack of it—the isolation on the set.

LB: Most of the time I am the only woman on the crew except for maybe hair or makeup. Sometimes there is the "script girl." Even then I form bonds with those women very often. On the film I just finished this summer, the script woman and I were constantly getting sexist comments, being talked down to, yelled at—things like that. In a professional situation, you can't talk back, because there are two million other people waiting to take your job. We were able to form bonds and warn each other of potential hazards.

I'm always trying to please, and constantly trying to overcompensate. Every job is a new job, every crew is a new crew. I'm constantly put in the position of being the teacher and the new student, too. I can do a lighting set-up in no time, but most of the time, my energy on productions is spent dealing with the obstacles of a hostile First AD or disgruntled assistant or a director who has never worked with women before.

A lot of men today don't want to be seen as the "sexist," the bad guy. The ones I have trouble with are the ones who act friendly and say, "Let's have lunch," and the phone never rings. Those are the guys who absolutely kill me.

AK: Because they waste your time in a busy town.

LB: And also, they seem supportive on the set. They are all nice, and say, "How are you? How was your weekend?" And then I find out later that they are scratching my film, or they are making fun of my techniques, or analyzing the way I dress, instead of working towards what we need. If everyone is happy, and focused on the issue or subject at hand, you are going to have a richer film.

The idea of visual communication is what I get off on. You have an idea and you are able to express it without words, but with an image. That's what makes me excited. That's what keeps me doing what I do. Motion pictures and video have brought it a step farther by including the synchronicity of the subject. So not only can I express what I'm trying to show in my mind's eye, but I can do it with movement.

It's joyful being on a Titan crane with a Panahead and a Golden Panaflex, with a top-notch assistant, following the motion of a fine actor like Anthony Newly, whom I worked with on *The Garbage Pail Kids*. The whole thing moved over an area of maybe fifty square yards, an extension of thirty feet all the way down to the ground level. It was moving constantly, and balancing all those components within the frame by the wheels in my hands, by my dolly grip moving the Titan crane, by the height of it going up and down. Just the synchronicity of it was very exciting. I felt very alive, very plugged into my craft. It was a feeling like flying, a complete freedom, where I felt very much at one with what I was shooting.

I think that being a woman has helped me very much in expressing my mind's eye. I took dance from age three all the way into college. That helped me in the synchronicity of movement. So many big cameramen, who are three times my size and can hold the camera up with one pinky finger, don't have half the balance. I can waltz around the room and have a steady shot. I can bury the weight of the camera into my pelvis.

AK: When people say, "How can you carry that camera?" what do you say back to them?

LB: It depends. When people say, "What's a little ol' girl like you carrying a big ol' camera?" what I normally say is, "Oh, it's not that heavy," or "Well, this isn't any bigger than a small child, you know."

I was at Lorimar one month ago, on the MGM studio lot. I was speaking directly to the UPM [Unit Production Manager] of *Full House*. I was telling her how, it was funny, but one of the first things that people always say is, "What's a little ol' girl like you carrying a big ol' camera?" On cue, her producer walks in, she introduces me to him, and he says, "What's a little ol' girl like you carrying a big ol' camera?" We both had to laugh. You just have to be good-natured. Attitudes are as important as being able to carry the camera.

AK: How has it felt to combine camera operating with motherhood?

LB: I worked up until my seventh month as a camera operator, on a variety of programs. I do the L.A. marathon every year on a ShotMaker crane, which is a camera car with a huge, thirty-foot arm on it. When I was four months' pregnant, I was on top of the crane, pregnant. I wasn't really showing, and it actually kept me off my feet. When you're pregnant, you kinda don't like to stand up a lot, so that was actually good.

In my fifth month, I got a couple of multiple-camera comedy shows for TV, and again I was on a crane, so it worked out really well. I didn't have any problems, and I found the crews to be real supportive. Everybody's got a baby or grandson or nephew or niece or something, so although I expected a lot of discrimination on the set, I got just the opposite. Grips were telling me what the best diaper was, and giving me child-rearing tips.

AK: Would you recommend continuing to work through the pregnancy for most camerawomen choosing to have a baby?

LB: Well, I don't know how it would be for an assistant. It might be tough, because their job is more laborious—more physical. My last camera job during pregnancy was at seven months; I produced and shot a documentary. What I did was hire myself a real good assistant. Because I was producing it, it gave me the freedom to pace myself, and to make the schedule work for me. It ended up being a nice long project. The editing took me into the final weeks of pregnancy, and it gave me something to do besides bounce off the walls.

AK: What happened as your due date approached?

LB: Well, I was offered two features which I had to turn down. One was with an old director of photography friend of mine named Harry Genkins. I'd shot a number of pictures with him, and over the years, I'd been trying to encourage him to hire more camerawomen. He'd always said, "No, no, y'all would talk too much. I don't want to hire any other camerawomen." I ended up getting both Kelly McGowen and Marie Pedersen on the show as camera assistants.

The Gum Shoe Kid was his last picture, and I wanted to shoot it for him—I was the operator, but it kept getting postponed. I kept saying, "Hey, let's do it. I can do it right now!" The show finally started two weeks before my due date. That was probably the hardest thing to swallow, in terms of being disappointed in work by pregnancy.

AK: You chose the birthing center because you had done some camera work there, right?

LB: When I was four months pregnant, I was contacted to shoot a birth for Japanese television in Hong Kong. They wanted to document a birth in water, and the only place at that time in North America was a place called the Upland Family Birthing Center run by Dr. Michael Rosenthal. One of the few times that camerawomen get the calls is when they need someone to shoot a birth [*laughs*].

AK: How did you begin your company, Video Births?

LB: I found that a lot of people want a camerawoman to shoot a birth. It's a very intimate, personal event, and most women feel a little awkward with having a strange man there, shooting their most private moment. When I started Video Births, I got some calls from some cameramen who were teasing me, saying, "Oh, what's next? Video funerals? Video wills?" I thought, "You just obviously don't understand, do you?" [*laughs*] It's more than just business. I can't think of anything I'd rather witness.

Jane Brenner, a camerawoman from Behind the Lens, just covered me for a birth. I couldn't be there—I was working on a new pilot for Grant Tinker. It was nice having the network of BTL to call upon.

Video Births is going well. It's just a little cottage industry; most camerapeople I know have something to tide them through the peaks and valleys of the film industry. It's ideal in that respect, because there are many times when I have time to be with my son, whereas if I were a full-time working mother in an office, I would not be free to be with him as much.

AK: What about child care? If you get a call that you've got to go shoot a birth at two in the morning . . . ?

LB: My husband is *perfectly* capable. It would be more difficult for a single parent, if they didn't have some sort of familial support. There have been a few times when it was difficult for me. One concern that I had during pregnancy, and even after I had David, was that I'm very dedicated to nursing. I came across a wonderful book, called *Breastfeeding and the Working Mother*,[1] that offered all kinds of tips for women working all kinds of different jobs.

The breast pump I got a hold of when my son was about six months old was called the "Lactina." It fit into a case that also included a styrofoam insert with little blue ice compartments with plastic container bottles. It looked like a little VHS camera case. You put it into super vac, and you could pump both breasts at the same time, and in ten minutes you could be back on the set. It was fantastic!

AK: Were the directors sympathetic to your taking a few breaks?

LB: I had nothing but support. For example, on the *Murphy Brown Show*, I'm an on-camera camera operator on the news set of the TV news show that Candice Bergen was the star of. I actually work camera during that show. I just finished my second season, and I started the show when David was three weeks old. They would always provide me with a trailer, an extra dressing room or something, and I could either pump, or my husband would bring David and I could nurse. Of course, the producer, Diane English, is a female, and very woman-conscious.

I can't say it wasn't tough. But with some planning, the right equipment, and a halfway humane shooting schedule, I had no problem.

AK: You just went on location. Did you bring your baby?

LB: Yes. I brought my baby. If my husband can't come with me on a location job, I bring his caregiver, a woman I hired when David was very young to look after him when I wasn't home. Just recently I went to San Diego to do a commercial with Mickey Rooney, and I mentioned to the cameramen that I had to bring my nanny and my son, because I was still nursing [*laughs*]. They ended up giving me a better room than the cameramen—a suite with a kitchen and the whole thing. I mean, people just bend over backwards.

AK: What a success story! Is there a gloomy downside?

LB: Yeah. There have been a few fifteen-hour days. It's a disruption in his pattern. He hasn't always been happy, but for the most part he's had more than a good dose of good, stable parenting from both of us, so I don't think the occasional disruption has hurt him.

Last summer, on *Sidewalk Motel*, a featurette about the homeless, the producer said, "There's a spot in the script for a baby." So my child, at seven months of age, ended up being in a movie. And the kid's always looking at

Liz Bailey and son, David D'Antoni, on the set of *Sidewalk Motel*.

the camera, because Mama's on the camera. It was nice, too, because I could be with my baby all day on the set. When I was not working, I could go play with him. That was the only time I've ever been able to bring him full-time on the set. I guess some actresses have that luxury, but as camerapeople we don't.

I've been in full-tilt hustle as a camerawoman for fifteen years, and I have to say that when I became a mother, I would have never believed it, but all of a sudden I learned that there was more to life than just being a working woman. Now, if I don't get that call from that cameraman, if I miss that show, if I don't get that job, it's just not the end of the world anymore. I mean, I still want to be a camerawoman, I still *am* a camerawoman, and I will *be* a camerawoman till the end of my last breath, but in perspective, being a mother is more important.

NOTE

1. Diane Mason, *Breastfeeding and the Working Mother* (New York: St. Martin's Press, 1986).

Laurel Klick

After studying in California and Sweden, Laurel Klick embarked on a dual career of performance art and optical effects camera work. She worked for Rob Blaylock on *Star Wars*, and went on to do special effects on *Predator*, *Terminator*, *Wolfen*, *Nine to Five*, and *Incredible Shrinking Woman*, among other features, as a member of IA 659 in Los Angeles and IA 644 in New York, for such companies as Industrial Light and Magic, Fantasy II, and Praxis Film Works, among others. She won an Emmy for outstanding individual achievement in special visual effects on *Winds of War*. In addition to optical and animation line-up and camera, Laurel Klick has also worked as a blue screen director.

I interviewed a congenial Laurel Klick on a treacherously icy evening in New York. She had put in a long day at R. Greenberg and Associates doing optical line-up, which is lonely and tedious, but technically reward-ing work. Laurel was more open than many of the other camerawomen I interviewed regarding the effects of subtle and not-so-subtle discrimination on her well-being, and her needs for continued growth and camaraderie seemed to be going largely unmet at that period in her career.

Shortly after the interview, Laurel became a digital video effects editor, and left Greenberg's to explore a burgeoning video job market at a time when film work—her first love—had become increasingly scarce on the East Coast.

AK: How did you first get interested in camera work?

LK: It wasn't a direct path. I was a performance artist, doing anything to make a living. Rob Blaylock was working on *Star Wars* at that time, and living with a friend of mine who was another performing artist. He said, "You know, there's a film cleaning job coming up. Do you want to do it?" I said fine.

I had never done anything in film. My whole background was in art. So I went to work for the last three months on *Star Wars*, cleaning film for twelve hours a day. I saw what people were making moneywise doing what they were doing, and I was amazed. So I decided to learn the optical camera and get work that way. When Rob started his own business a little while later, he hired me.

Although I'd started by cleaning film, Rob threw me in the optical department, and in the beginning, I was the only one in there. He showed me the optical printer and how it ran. I had absolutely no idea what all these technical things were, but I learned very fast. Rob gave me a good technical foundation. I learned a lot from him.

AK: What other kinds of support and resistance to your work have you had from people?

LK: On one job, the man hired a lot of women. The thing about us women was that we worked for a lot less money. We asked for much less. He would put this in the guise of "I'm giving all you women this opportunity," but he was making out on the deal.

That he hired a few women actually turned out to be a real plus. Because the optical department was run by women. Animation was run by women. There wasn't that kind of man influence like, "Here, let me show you what to do on this." We just did it. Also a lot of very strong friendships formed. We've all helped each other as far as jobs and also in our own work. That's one reason I pushed to get women I knew from the West Coast out here working, even if it was for a short while. After working with Rob for quite a few years, I worked with Fantasy II and with Jean Warren and Leslie Huntley. Working there was not like getting hired for a job. It was more like getting adopted. When they called me back to work on *Terminator* after a brief period of unemployment, they got me in the union—659. They were strong believers in the union.

Boyfriends? I didn't involve them in my life. I basically went to bed with them or I was involved sexually and that's about it. Alan, my husband, has been very supportive. I feel that where I work now is much more difficult because I am working with all men. There has been very heavy competition with different people. It's like the boys' club. When I go home, I go, "Am I crazy? I don't understand these guys." He'll let me know that this is the way boys are, and this is the way they think.

They don't see as many women in technical fields in New York. Maybe it's because the film business is not as big here. Because it is a smaller business, there are fewer women. But I miss having women working with me in technical positions—if the camaraderie is missing, I feel very alone.

If men I work with see me cry, they don't know what to do about it. The first time I cried on the job I work at now, three different guys came up to me. They didn't offer me a shoulder to cry on, which is what I needed. They just wanted to give me some drugs. It's very difficult to not be intimidated into thinking that I don't know what I know.

AK: What do you enjoy the most about your work?

LK: I think it's a sense of accomplishment. A sense of being able to take a lot of different information, using it and transforming it into something. The sense of mastery over something—making something do something that doesn't happen in nature—is probably the most satisfying.

When I first came to New York, I was checking out places and interviewing. This one small optical place had one printer and the man saw my résumé. He shows me his printer and says "Now is this what you know how to run?" It doesn't take a genius to do this. It doesn't take balls to do this. I couldn't believe that he was in such doubt of my ability, that I would lie or be confused about something like running an optical printer.

AK: Have you encountered other types of discrimination?

LK: Well, where I am now, it's indirect. It's like them not seeing me being more capable, or giving me more. Part of this stuff I feed into. It's very hard for me to be the one to push myself forward.

AK: What is your job title now?

LK: I don't really know. I do optical layout, called layout line-up on the West Coast. Here the people that are lining up are the people that give the directions, not the cameraperson. Here I'm basically given the shots, and I figure out what needs to be done on them. I don't do the actual shooting on them anymore. I give that to someone else to do.

AK: Do you feel you have more responsibility now?

LK: Yes.

AK: Have you been able to make a living consistently as a camerawoman?

LK: Yes, I have. In Los Angeles it would be on-again, off-again on projects. But I made a living, and the only time it was really discouraging was when I first moved to New York. Then I was hired at Greenberg and Associates. As far as my union classification goes, I'm doing just fine. I'm not being held back there at all.

I think what hasn't happened, though, is getting significant advancements or making certain big jobs where you make this amount, you make that amount. I would like to be doing more than what I'm doing, and given more responsibility, like directing blue screen on stage. I'd rather do effects directing than be a camerawoman. There's a lot of optical camera work that I've done over and over again that actually I'm a little bored with.

AK: Has the union been supportive?

LK: I had to join the union, because I was working at a union shop. I was more than happy to join, but I couldn't believe the initiation. It was around $5,000 when I joined.

I would have liked to participate in some of the camera workshops that they made available through 659. About one and a half years ago I went to a camera workshop here in New York. It was mainly men, and it was the first time in a long, long time that I felt overwhelmed. It was a real eye-opener and an odd experience in that way. I really had to be aggressive in order to get my turn in the hands-on equipment part of the workshop.

I still think I have that typical female problem of selling myself short. I have seen so many guys come into places that I've been working at, knowing very little, but coming off as if they're the hottest thing since sync sound. I find that almost impossible to do, and I must admit I am somewhat envious of their ability to present themselves with some bravado. I think that even with all the advances that women have made, there are still some very deep-seated perceptions and feelings about women that have remained unchanged. I think that women are still seen as Other, and that our place in the working world was not a birthright, but rather, a right we have had to fight for.

Madelyn Most

Madelyn Most received her camera training in London, England, by apprenticing herself to a cameraman after studying at the London Film School and, prior to this, at the University of California, Berkeley, and the American University of Paris, France. Her original ambition was to be a painter (and a lawyer) and she was proud to work in Britain on large productions with the top crews, where technical standards of quality and excellence were demanded. She remembers surviving the early years as an isolated female with no other women colleagues on British camera crews.

From London, where she was a member of the British film industry trade union, A.C.T.T., Madelyn Most moved first to New York, joining NABET 15 in 1980 and IA 644 in 1982. She then relocated to Los Angeles for the 1984 official Olympic film, transferred to NABET 531 in 1985, and was finally admitted to IA 659 in 1987. She was involved in the early meetings of Behind the Lens in 1984, which was organizing around the issue of how few women were asked to work on the official Olympic film in Los Angeles. She worked as camera assistant on feature films such as *Star Wars*, *Superman*, *The Empire Strikes Back*, and *Sunset*, and in 1987 moved up to operator, while continuing to photograph documentaries.

In 1989, Madelyn moved to Germany, working as lighting camera-woman on commercials. Through her company, Most Films, she is producing and directing opera, theater, and dance films. In 1993 she moved to Paris, as her production of *Le Train Fantôme* demanded that she be closer to the survivors of the Ghost Train, the very last deportation convoy from France, trapped on the railway lines for two months in the summer of 1944. She is currently working in London and Paris.

AK: How did you become interested in camera work?

MM: I wanted to become a painter, and somehow I was able to live in beautiful places: Denmark, Switzerland, and France. While in art school in London, I visited a set. When I walked up to the camera and looked through the lens, it was like painting with light, printmaking, sculpting, and life drawing. It was lighting, acting, drama. And it was ideas, and working with people—when you're an artist, you spend hours and hours alone in your studio.

So suddenly this bolt of lightning hit me, looking down this lens—you have a very technical, active, creative job which actually communicates with people. I was immediately hooked.

In England, it wasn't even respectable to go to film school to get into the camera department. Most of the guys I knew had fathers who dragged them in at a tender age as tea boys, and they worked their way up. I did get technical lectures and some practical experience at London Film School, but my real training came from working as a camera assistant with different cameramen.

The BBC had a written rule: You couldn't be a girl camera assistant. So of course I had to break that straightaway. I went for an interview, and the guy started asking all kinds of questions: What if I wanted babies, what if I had my period, what would my boyfriend say if I were sent on location.

First I got asked on documentaries as an assistant. People in London that do documentaries are top feature guys. You have to understand, in Europe, cinematographers are people who for some reason have gotten into it as a lifelong commitment. In England it takes a long, slow gestation period to make your way up through the grades—the four stages of the hierarchy—to arrive at the position of lighting cameraman. When I was first starting, the directors of photography were in their sixties or seventies, the operators were in their fifties, the focus pullers were in their forties. And they had spent ten, twenty, thirty, forty years respectively, learning their craft. I run up against people here in America who get a little degree from a film school, who do half a year or something, and they say, "I'm a cameraperson." In America, one can move up very quickly.

My very first job as clapper loader on a big feature was on the first *Star Wars*. The director of photography was known as an old-regime dinosaur. Well, nobody spoke to me for two days. I found out later that he tried to get me removed from the picture, because it wasn't "proper" for the camera department in Britain to have a girl assistant. It never happened before. They took a vote, and it was George and Marcia [Lucas] who said, "Well, she does her job, so she stays."

Now the next thing was to try not to fall as I climbed the ladder sixty feet in the air with thirty-pound Vistavision magazines on my shoulder. I remember thinking over and over as I climbed that flimsy ladder, if I fall and go splat on this stage at Elstree Studios, that's gonna be it for girls in the camera department in England. I was the testing ground.

I was so proud to be there knowing that they didn't allow very many women in. It was me and the script supervisor. We'd meet each other in the bathroom. Maybe there was a makeup woman for Carrie Fisher. And all the rest of nine hundred people on *Star Wars* were men.

Of course, I did the usual dressing down—like a boy, wearing leotards to flatten any bumps that might show, wearing no makeup, mandatory pony-tail, and denying my sexuality. The last thing you wanted was for someone to say you got your job because you were pretty. I never smiled.

It is not a job about lifting weights. You can hire somebody to lift weight for you like a beast of burden, and that's not what cameramen are. They're thinking people, and they use their minds the whole day.

I remember trying to explain that cinematography was my goal; the job involved a sensitivity to light and shadows, an ability to solve problems quickly, be flexible and experiment, take risks, push the limits sometimes, create new images and communicate well with the rest of the team, not to hump weights. I saw these guys in L.A. twirling the camera around like it was some army rifle.

The assistant gets much more involved with the cameraman in Europe. John Alcott was a great teacher who shared his knowledge and experience, not only with his own crew, but with the rest of the industry. Directors of photography are constantly teaching their crew one way or another, sharing special filters, special nets. If you're invited to that team, you're expected to contribute, too. I have a focus puller friend in Paris, and to prepare for the next picture, he and the cameraman went to Amsterdam to look at the paintings of Rembrandt, Van Eyck, and Vermeer. They studied the lighting on those canvases to discuss the mood, style, and approach they would use to photograph the movie.

Here in L.A., the director is god, and if you make a suggestion, they'll fire you. But if you are determined about something—it doesn't matter what sex or shape or color or what form of humanity you are—there's nobody that can stop you.

Smart people, intelligent people, creative people, competent people, people that are secure in what *they* do, and who are good, will always encourage you. They may train you very severely, they may make strong rules at what you have to do, and they're hard and demanding. Only because they want you to be great.

The assistants who took me under their wing were very strict and severe, a lot like my father was: expecting excellence, almost perfection, and not accepting less. I am grateful for that, actually. When I'm training people that I feel have potential and stamina, I'm very hard on them. Because it's like training somebody to run in the Olympics if you are a sports trainer. My teachers tried to get me to think clearly, to be focused and orderly, to select priorities, and concentrate on the task at hand. I learned how to work out problems in a linear way, methodically attacking things.

A lot of females are afraid if something breaks down, and are threatened if they have to repair it. Women don't have enough mechanical training. Nuts and bolts weren't part of our education, so repairing motors, engines, camera gears, or cams is alien. I watch guys bluff their ignorance when they didn't know a particular camera-lacing pattern. But the male technicians in the camera houses talk to them simply and directly, while I've watched them talk to women in a childish gibberish, as if they were talking to someone mentally handicapped.

You shouldn't let somebody cry on your shoulder. One woman—her father's a cameraman—kept complaining that I was being too hard on her. She ended up in tears, and I said, "You have to act properly. You can't resort to the women tactics." Another woman came on a job wearing these sexy clothes and flirting with all the actors. She spent the afternoon in the actor's Winnebago, and I was just totally appalled. You can't use advantages like being pretty or being sociable if you want to be taken seriously.

Camera assisting, however you divide it—"second" or "first" here, or "clapper loader" and "focus puller" in England—that has nothing to do with operating. And operating has nothing to do with lighting. It's four separate parts of your brain that are used in different ways.

In London I had instructions coming at me from forty different directions. I had to carry a little book on me to remind myself of all the minutiae, all the phone calls to wives and girlfriends, making tea for the camera crew, mixed in with the important stuff like loading a reverse-load magazine, changing the camera shutter from 180 to 200 degrees, ordering up the reprints from the day's rushes, and ordering extra cameras for tomorrow's special effects shots, etc. The great thing of moving up is that you leave that behind. You can start thinking about the photography, and you start seeing your work on the screen.

I don't know if it's good or bad, but my father said, if something is worth doing, it has to be done well, the best you can. You try to work with the best directors, with the most interesting ideas, making the best stories for humanity. I can't work on certain movies—specifically violent or gory horror or exploitative films. As that is the Hollywood main staple, it's a good thing I left!

I never thought about support. I always thought there was that world out there that I was having to conquer. My career in London was a battle, being alone. I think there was another girl, but her father owned a film company or commercial company, so she had automatic work. I was totally isolated. I had no women colleagues—women that did the same job as me. There were only male friends that I would ring up when I had problems.

It has been said that women starting in the early to mid-seventies in London—the women that were directors for the BBC, in their 40s—it was so tough on them, that they started making women's committees, like the London Women's Film Group. The first time I ran into a women's camera group was here in L.A. I realized, talking to other women, how stressful it was being a freelancer.

If you go to those Women in Film meetings, they come in dressed like very high-class hookers. And it's very hard as a schleppy technician, to come in from a day's work and look at these people in stiletto heels. They have a lot of power. Being attached as an assistant to somebody very powerful has gotten them to be presidents of film companies. And that's a very hard thing for me to deal with. The women I know in London are intellectuals: they're frumpy and they're old, and they're very successful producers.

AK: What do you think it will take for camerawomen to be treated equally as cameramen in this industry?

MM: They're never going to be treated equally. I'm not so positive about the camerawomen in this town, because I see how cameramen are treated. The greatest directors of photography and cameramen I knew in London died of heart attacks and strokes. One was a suicide. It's very stressful.

There is so much pressure on the cameraman, more than the director. Because the director has some kind of magical aura, and everybody believes, no matter how badly he's doing, or how terrible he is, he's the director. But the cameraman's responsible for problems, and the quietest people, who internalize the stress—this really gets to them.

Cameramen, camera operators in L.A. are common fodder. Many get killed on the job in film accidents every year.

AK: Can you describe the process by which you got into the various unions, here and abroad?

MM: London used to have a powerful trade union, one big umbrella over everyone's head, the Alliance of Cinematographic and Television Technicians. It was in their interest to have 100 percent membership to represent everyone. They legislated rates, contracts, hours, overtime payments, safety standards and hazard pay, accident and maternity leave, health benefits, penalty meals, antidiscrimination policy, the whole gambit.

In New York, I joined NABET in 1980, and IA in 1982. I joined NABET and IA out here in '85 and '87. The IA gave a fifty-page multiple choice test and then a practical test that lasted ten hours. I passed all the tests with very high scores, and I had good credits, but people said, "You won't get into IA—your father's not a cameraman." Miraculously, they let me in, because when I got in, it was father to son.

American unions are country clubs. I paid over $10,000 in initiation fees in America: $3,500 to IATSE—New York and L.A.— and $1,500 to NABET—New York and L.A. And then, my accountant yelled at me the other day about $3,000 a year in subs. For that, I have gotten nothing. No help, no health insurance, pension, welfare benefits, no *nothing* to take care of you. Your producer puts in pension and welfare and things like that. So I am totally dissatisfied.

Working on nonunion in this town is like working with a bunch of clowns in a circus. I mean, people are very well-meaning, but it's so chaotic, and so dangerous. People have been hired because they're cheap and will accept anything: no food, no sleep, no sanitary conditions. But everything is turning nonunion.

It's called "the product." It is not a movie, it is not a work of art, it is not something to give to humanity. It's a can of dog food. It is already presold. Producers in this town do not care. They've made their distribution deal. The deal is more important than making the film or the end result.

I care so much, and so does the guy I work with, his heart's gonna burst. Because he cares so much about the lighting, and he lights actors and actresses individually, for their features, the mood of the scene. He personally lights them, he sculpts their faces. Especially women. He sculpts their faces with light. We give them marks, because there's usually a light shining for their eyes and a light coming down the side of their face and a backlight of their hair—sculpting, carving out on a negative that person's figure and how you want them to look.

A brilliant director, at breakfast on the last day of one film, said, "You know, this film looks so beautiful. The cinematography is so gorgeous, and you two have worked so hard. Too bad the script is such shit." And that's what it is, it's violence, people killing each other, people raping each other. Malicious, evil, destructive ideas that I truly believe are having a corrosive effect on this country and the people that watch it on a daily basis.

You can get a cameraman in this town to work for nothing, just to have the privilege and the honor of making their slash movies. Producers have people paying them to do their movies, for the privilege. Every country on this planet comes to Hollywood begging, begging for work.

On the other hand, the whole union thing just doesn't work for choosing a cinematographer. The Italians are great painters. And if you want the work of Vittorio Storaro, you can't have Joe Surfer, who grew up in L.A. and never went to a museum in his life, just because he's a [union] member and he's paid his money. When you work with Storaro, or Sven Nykvist, or somebody like that, they bring in their ideas, their experience, their vision, their culture, their "knowledge," their sensitivity about humanity—they bring in everything.

There are brilliant British and American guys, too, but you can't say, "I need a British person in the British union to do my movie," or, "A New York person has to shoot my movie." You can't. This is a different job. You're painting pictures, and you need people who understand and communicate and feel things and tell stories with their pictures.

I want to work my way up to features, lighting as a camerawoman, seeing as a painter. Maybe on some of the pictures I'll do in Europe, I'll be lighting and operating in a smaller world again where the quality is very high.

The dilemma with everybody, I think, is the moving up. Every time you move up, you work less. I don't know whether I can go through that, because I'm too involved, and I want too much. I'm a person that loves working.

AK: How do you juggle your personal life with camera work?

MM: I must say that my career and the fact that I love what I do made me forget to have children. Well, maybe I didn't. I just didn't act on it, because I knew I'd be put out to pasture for a few years (perhaps I'd like it and then never get back in), and the image of me in an apron, changing diapers, frightened the living daylights out of me. But I am jealous of the men who get all the strokes, love and hugs from their kids, and just walk out the door, jump on the plane, and resume work. They just get the good times.

I think I have seen that, because the competition is so fierce and unrelenting in America, only the most ambitious, selfish, and egocentric achieve the kind of success everyone aspires to. I want a quality of life, a rich life: not material wealth, fame, or fortune, but a life full of adventure and experiences.

AK: What are some of the satisfactions that you have gained from your work?

MM: Working with Blake Edwards on *Sunset* was interesting. I learned so much every day, watching the way he'd visualize what was in his mind. And the people Blake surrounds himself with are at the top of their field.

I remember one day they spent three hours lighting a scene, and he came back after lunch, and he had in mind a different camera angle composition. We stopped and did it over differently, traveling through five rooms in one long take. The lighting was a nightmare, through two rooms and a corridor, ending outside in the California sun by a swimming pool. And he used the entire scene in the film: one full roll of film, ten minutes long.

But *Hotel Terminus: The Life and Times of Klaus Barbie*, Marcel Ophüls' film about the butcher of Lyons, really affected my life. It made me want to go back to doing documentaries, to use films not only to help people, but in a healing way psychologically.

I was second camera, and assisted when we had one camera. I found people talking before the camera about concentration camp experiences, about torture, and about the decisions they made in their life to obey orders or not obey orders—there's some magical experience, that when you put them in front of the camera and you ask questions, they're almost talking to another self. They're resolving something in their mind that they never dared expose. After they've said something, they look at you, and they're either brought to tears or to incredible crisis because it lifted the horror or the revelation out of their memories that they themselves didn't want to bring up. And there's a huge release. So many times you end up crying with them—you've put them through such periods of sadness and remembrance that they would never hit on with a psychiatrist, you feel responsible for having asked them to bring up all that pain. And you ask yourself if you have a right to do this. Yet once that's come out, like a deep stone inside of them, they can finally let go.

I remember traveling overnight by train and driving through the snow, high up into the Alps. We finally arrived at an apartment of an old crippled woman in a wheelchair. This was Lise Lefèvre, who had been tortured by Barbie while interrogating her about fellow resistance members. He used *le baignoire* technique, which was to hang the victim upside down with a strap and dunk them into the ice cold bath, until they either started talking or drowned.

What hit me most was that these were only boys and girls in their teens or early twenties when they watched their mothers and fathers beaten or murdered in front of their eyes, when they were beaten and tortured for information, and then deported half-conscious, to concentration camps where their closest friends died in their sleep up against their bodies. I realized that up until that moment, I had no real understanding of pain, suffering, and loss. Now my heart had a new feeling that was so deep and of such overwhelming sorrow, I was never going to be the same.

III

THE SECOND WAVE:
STARTING OUT IN
INDEPENDENT FILM

I thought, "I've got to learn how to make films, how to make videos, basically to change the image of women."

Cathy Zheutlin

Nobody can look at a DP doing a feature and say, "Well, she's not strong enough physically." I think it comes down to, "Is she strong enough mentally?" and "Is she able to make decisions?" and "Can she move it along quick enough?" and in many ways, those battles are still being fought.

Sandi Sissel

Is there a particular vision I have because I am a woman?

Geraldine Kudaka

Cathy Zheutlin

A freelance camerawoman with her own Betacam and CP-16, Cathy Zheutlin has filmed and taped documentaries all over the world. Her documentary feature *Just One Step: The Great Peace March* won first place for social-issue documentaries at the Anthropos Film Festival in Los Angeles, as well as a Cine Golden Eagle.

When Cathy appeared on a Media and Peace panel at California State University, Northridge, in 1989, her fellow panelist, a former programming director for NBC, told Cathy that she was just at the beginning of her career. "It's odd how it's taken me eighteen years to get to the 'beginning,' " she replied. "Yet, historically this year is the beginning of camerawomen expressing their cinematographic, photographic and filmic visions . . . throughout the world. With few exceptions, our history only encompasses fifteen to twenty years. It isn't very much unless you are one of the people who has been at it that long."[1]

Her comments reflect a social and political context in which Cathy has triumphed. Her numerous camera credits include many films about women's issues, including the award-winning *Rosie the Riveter*, and many other political and social issues, including Nicaragua, AIDS, the deaf community, children's issues, and Soviet-American peace. An outstanding spokeswoman, her leadership among camerawomen ranges from founding and serving as president of Iris Films, an all-woman's film collective, to serving as the vice president of NABET 532 and of Behind the Lens.

While filming *The Great Peace March*, Cathy met a Soviet cameraman, and married him, *glasnost*-style. In 1990, she brought her new baby to the Soviet Union with her to shoot a documentary about healers, as well as working in Los Angeles on *Murphy Brown* as Camera Operator. In 1991, Cathy and her new family moved to Portland, Oregon, after completing *Voice of the Planet*, a ten-hour series about global ecology for TBS and CNN.

Currently she teaches 16mm cinematography and film production at the Northwest Film Center, as well as shooting birth videos and occasional documentaries. Her primary work, however, is as a licensed massage therapist which she feels is more compatible with motherhood than the high-pressured travels connected with documentary filmmaking.

AK: How did you first become interested in camera work?

CZ: I got interested in making films primarily from being involved in the women's movement in the early '70s. In those days, we either worked in the health care movement or we worked in the cultural part of the movement. I saw myself as a culture worker, and I thought, "I've got to learn how to make films, how to make videos, basically to change the image of women." I specialized in camera later because the industry required people to have specialties, but initially I just wanted to make films.

I joined a project that was organized by one woman, who asked other women to be technicians on her crew. Those were the days of experimenting with rearranging the power structure. We formed what we called the Santa Cruz Women's Film Collective. We made one film together, which we cowrote, coshot, and acted in ourselves, called *Wish Fulfilming*. It was a very idealistic film, promoting the concept of collective filming.

I dropped out of school without telling the AV Department, so I could still check out equipment. They liked me there because I was interested in technology and I was good with the equipment, so they allowed me to have access to all the audiovisual equipment. I was able to be one of the main forces of the collective. I didn't have to go to school, and I had a small stipend for living, so I was pretty well committed to doing the media work, which was totally unpaid.

Then an opportunity came up in San Diego. There was a woman who decided she wanted to hire a women's crew for her film about women and psychology that she was going to present at a convention. I thought, "Okay, now's my chance to really make a commitment in filmmaking: if I actually pick up and move to another town to make a movie, that's really a commitment!"

I went to San Diego, ready to make what was going to be my first color film—up until then I'd only worked in video and black and white film. We had presented ourselves very honestly to the producer. We told her, "This is how much experience we have, this is how much experience we don't have." But she got cold feet, and hired a group of men. We were so pissed off because she wouldn't have faith in us.

Meanwhile, I was at loose ends, because I had moved to San Diego. I'd grown up in L.A. where my parents were living, so I came back to L.A. not knowing what to do.

My father had just invested money in a feature film. So he called up the producer and said, "My daughter's interested in filmmaking, can you give her a job?" I got a job on their crew as an extra for $20 a day, so that gave me a lot of free time on a movie set.

I went over to the camera department and started hanging out with the camerapeople. To them it was really great, because—you know how a second assistant can get overburdened with too much work? Well, he saw me as free labor. "You want to load magazines? Here, this is how you load magazines."

Since I had an interest in the camera, that job led to another. For a while I had very low-level jobs on feature films. As a production assistant, I used my position of being somebody on the set to go learn more about the camera. I started to go to rental houses saying, "Well, I want to practice with a Mitchell now." I found the ones who were receptive. Not everybody was in 1974, but you could, in those days, find people who were.

I remember walking into a camera rental house wearing cowboy boots, and without looking up they would just automatically assume that I was a man, because women didn't do camera work, and call me "guy" or "mister" or "sir." I experienced this big culture shock because I had lived and learned about filmmaking in a women's film collective, and then I came to L.A. and started living and learning feature films in a totally male-dominated world.

I didn't have a concept of it being pioneering. In L.A., it really sank in that women didn't do it, and that there were no role models, so there were nobody's footsteps to follow in. I started to try and find out, aren't there other women?

I knew about a few women who had been involved with camera work before myself. There was Judy Irola, there was Dyanna Taylor, I think, in those days. Everyone knew there was this one woman, Brianne Murphy. I started doing a serious search to find the other women who were working in films. I found this one woman named Frances Reid who had been doing sound. I talked to her about the situation, and she said she'd been living in L.A. awhile and she knew of several other women involved in filmmaking. We decided to hold a conference for women in film here in L.A. at the Women's Building [in 1975], and we called it "The Feminist Eye." While we were organizing that, we discovered that there was [*sic*] some people on the East Coast coincidentally organizing a national conference for women in film, in New York City. They managed to have a conference of women's film organizations like Kartemquin, and Women Make Movies. Kartemquin wasn't only a women's organization, but there were a lot of women involved in it and they made political films.

On the West Coast, all we could garner were individuals for a gathering. But in the course of organizing the West Coast conference and going to the East Coast one, I formed a new film company with Fran Reid, Elizabeth Stephens, Joan Biren, and Mary Farmer. The purpose of our company was to produce and promote films by women. We decided to organize a national film circuit of films made by and for women, and kicked it off with a film festival in Washington, D.C. Out of that film festival, we chose two hours of films made by women. We found women in twenty different cities around the country who would sponsor that two-hour package in their city.

Iris Films was a national company, because two people were on the East Coast, and three of us were on the West Coast. We'd all had a lot of history of working collectively, so we skipped some of the important steps of getting to know each other, building trust, and learning each other's styles of work. As a result of that, we ended up in these terrible fights with each other. By the time we pulled off the festival, we could barely talk to each other. We decided to split up, the East Coast keeping the film circuit and the West Coast keeping the name, Iris Films.

Iris Films had already started research on a film about lesbian mothers and child custody, *In the Best Interests of the Children*, so we decided to go ahead and make the film.

I wasn't yet trying to be a camera assistant. I did investigate the camera union, but I still believed that I was a filmmaker. It was hard for me to narrow myself down to one thing, just camera work. So when I heard that you could take this test and become a union camera assistant and work your way up over a period of eight or ten years, I was basically too haughty to pursue it. I pursued Iris Films instead. I was really naïve. I didn't understand the power of the "system." While in postproduction on *In the Best Interests of the Children*, I found an inexpensive place to edit in San Francisco. There was some resistance, but we moved Iris Films up to San Francisco, where the work was cheaper for us. We were also escaping the Hollywood syndrome. You could say the words "16mm" in L.A., and people laughed. In San Francisco, there was a thriving independent filmmaking community that worked with 16mm film.

By the time we finished *In the Best Interests of the Children*, I started to look for something else to do, and that's when I started being a camera assistant. Over the years I graduated, I suppose, to 35mm for commercials, but there were a lot of smaller, 16mm projects being done in San Francisco. It was a small community and I managed to get a good reputation as a camera assistant, so I got a lot of work.

On practically my first job as a camera assistant in 1976 or 1977, I assisted the president of NABET 532. I learned a lot about the union from him, and I learned about the process of getting in the union from him as well. IA 659 was closed, with iron doors surrounding it, but all I had to do was study camera assisting in order to get into NABET. If you had the intelligence and the persistence and you were interested enough, you could just study and pass a test; and if you passed an oral test and a practical test, NABET was accessible.

It was a pretty thorough test for camera assisting. The criteria that we used in NABET, because I became very active in NABET, was you gave a test to somebody, and you passed a person based on the fact that if you couldn't show up for work one day, you'd feel comfortable sending that person in your place. It was a real trade union in that sense. That's how we guarded our reputations, by making sure we all were very professional in our work.

I assisted for a while and then I wanted to shoot. I had shot *In the Best Interests of the Children*, after recommending to our collective that we, in fact, learn from Hollywood and specialize. Even though my background had been "everybody can do everything and everybody's equally competent," as I got more training, I'd begun to see that if you specialized, you really could excel in a certain area.

A couple of my friends were able to freelance in the live theatre community by owning theatre lights. I thought, "Maybe I'll be able to freelance in shooting films if I own a camera." So I went out and purchased a used CP-16 camera.

Owning the means of production is definitely a good way to become one of the producers. I started out shooting social issue documentaries for people who didn't have any money but needed a crew. I wanted the experience and they wanted the crew. So that's how it worked out. I learned by shooting. I'd assisted enough to see how other people shot, so I pretty much knew what to do.

When I first worked on *Rosie The Riveter*, I worked as an assistant to Emiko Omori. By the next time I worked on it I had already had some camera experience shooting, so I got to shoot it. Emiko was one of the few women role models that I had, because she lived up in San Francisco, she worked as a camerawoman, and she made it independently.

Some of the other early films on my résumé are only relevant in the sense that they gave me practice. The basic things you have to practice when you're doing camera work are the lighting—being able to light in all the different unusual situations you might encounter—and the actual camera operation.

AK: Did you have your own lights also, or did you just rent them?

CZ: I got my own lights later on.

When I'm able to do lighting that I really think is good, there's a lot of creative satisfaction. When I'm able to cover an event as a documentary cameraperson and I feel like I've actually communicated that event with pictures, there's a lot of creative satisfaction in that. It's like dancing with the world, because you are channeling the world through pictures to other people.

You have all these choices, you know. When something's happening in front of you, are you going to stand far away or up close? Are you going to frame right or left, or make the person big or small? And you have to make those choices instinctively, because if you thought about it, you'd be making a feature. In a documentary, you're capturing it in real time.

The combination of camera and lights made me really mobile in terms of being able to go around and shoot documentaries, so then it just slowly happened where I shot more and more documentaries and got better at it as I went along.

At a certain point I got a teaching position at San Francisco Art Institute. They were hiring one person to teach how to make documentaries, and another one to teach how to do lighting. Phil Green and I were both hired. They thought they would put me to teach documentaries and him to teach lighting. I talked to him and I said, you know, I'd rather teach the lighting class, and he said he had no problem with that, so I got to teach the lighting class. I really didn't know that much about lighting when I went into teaching that class. But I set it up as a series of experiments for the students and I kept myself about a jump ahead of them in terms of what outcomes we could expect, and we would run through any number of things, like experiments on exposure ratios shot with 35mm slide film. We would evaluate the slides and talk about the effects: Did this make it look more like night, more like day, more dramatic, less dramatic?

In 1981 I decided to make my own ten-minute comedy, *Lost Love*, because you're never allowed to make a move in this industry without having already made the move somehow, and I had mostly been shooting documentaries. *Lost Love* was a lot of fun to make and it did, indeed, help me down the line to eventually get camera jobs.

I think another thing that helped me get camera-shooting jobs was moving to L.A. I didn't have any work, but I also didn't have any history here, so I could eventually start as a cameraperson. I wasn't typecast as an assistant.

Definitely, I wanted a camera career. But I wasn't able to find one. Someone told me about a job as script supervisor on a low-budget feature, so I thought, "Well, I've never done it, but it'll give me something to do." About two days into the shoot, the cameraman quit and I said, "You know, I can be the cameraperson here," so they let me.

There's something about the mystique of the DP. I think that that mystique is promoted in order keep the pool of people small, and to maintain high salaries for those people. If you're going to become a really good cameraperson, there's a lot to learn, but I think it's all quite learnable. It's unfortunate that some of what people need to learn is mystified. I would love to see that changed, because mystification is one of the reasons why women have stayed away.

When I was twenty-one, I was just starting to learn the mechanics of a camera. How does the pull-down claw work? I didn't have a childhood where somebody brought me up taking things apart and putting them back together, because only boys did that. I felt like a twelve-year-old boy taking something apart and putting it back together, seeing how it worked, for the first time. It was fascinating to me, but I also felt like I had to catch up to where the guys are.

AK: Could you describe the resistance and the support that you've gotten from other people?

CZ: I've had a lot of both. The resistance is in the mainstream industry. On the other hand, people in San Francisco actually took pride in hiring women. They wanted to prove that they were changing. Along with the women who were out there making the changes, there were men who supported us and hired us as camera assistants. But they're still the minority.

I started to push very hard on the IA in 1986—in other words, I filed a complaint of discrimination against them and against all the major movie studios. The IA sent me another letter saying that they would accept me into their training program without a test, as a camera assistant. It felt insulting. I understand that system and how it works, yet I think that they need to learn flexibility.

I still feel prounion, because I think that workers are often subject to exploitation, and you need unions to protect you. Yet I was never so naïve about the IA as to think that they were the answer for the film industry, because they were too discriminatory, not just against women but against all nonwhites as well.

I got involved in Behind the Lens in the very early days, when it was getting organized. Having come from a whole background of organizing women in the film industry, of course I was interested in organizing camerawomen, because that meant a big, historical change from the days where we could count the camerawomen on one hand. A lot more women have also gotten into the field of camera work through the advent of video.

I brought up my complaint against the union anonymously at a Behind the Lens meeting. We had invited the EEOC guys to the BTL meeting and they said, "Look, one of your members has filed a complaint against the union and the studios for discrimination against women and we need affidavits of support for her. You can be anonymous in your affidavit—the only thing is, if it ever did go to court, we might need to call on you to support this case." The people in Behind the Lens that just so happened to be at that particular meeting were so afraid for their jobs, for their careers, that they were not willing to support the case.

It's important for women to support each other while there's a change going on, because you've got to take care of each other. A lot of women are now working as assistants, and if they just keep at it, they're going to move up naturally, the way men have over the years.

After freelancing for years, I got a job as a staff cameraperson shooting video for a magazine show. For the first time, I had what I'd been striving for, which was constant, daily practice with a camera and lights. That's the only way I knew to get better. It was also a steady income.

At the same time, I was trying to get a job on the documentary of the Great Peace March. I was pursuing all the big names who I heard were supposedly going to produce this documentary or movie of the week. I thought, "Well, if I'm lucky, maybe I can get hired on one of these crews as a camera person." Meanwhile I had access to these Betacams from the magazine show that had just closed shop, and I said to them, "Can I borrow a camera and go shoot the beginnings of the Peace March? Because whoever's doing it hasn't got their act together and they're not shooting the beginnings." [*Chuckles*] They said, "Yeah, fine, go borrow a camera." So

I started documenting this Peace March on my own. I discovered that there was no big company coming forth. But a small company had given Pro-Peace a hundred and fifty thousand dollars to tie up the media rights based on a rumor that Sting was going to be at the sendoff for the Peace March. I went to that small company and said, "Can I shoot the documentary? To make your lives easier and cheaper, I'll direct and shoot simultaneously."

I really considered directing and shooting a documentary practically synonymous. I didn't think that there was going to be such a big difference from what I'd been doing for years of shooting documentaries to shooting and directing. But I was wrong. And shooting and directing simultaneously is a lot more work. On *The Great Peace March*, I took on not only directing, but producing and production managing and shooting and fund-raising. My work load increased dramatically. I think I handled it well given the situation, but I was surprised at the amount of things I hadn't thought about from a directing point of view, and that I hadn't had to think about from a camera point of view. For instance, who are the main characters? That had never really been my problem. The main characters were always given to me.

And point of view. Even though it was always up to me to choose a point of view when I was covering an event, it wasn't always up to me to choose the point of view of what the overall message of a movie was. Directing added a whole different arena of thoughts. Out of my insecurity, I overshot, because I didn't know when to start and when to stop. So I just shot everything: one hundred thirty hours of half-inch Betacam—four hundred tapes.

What happened to me on the Peace March is, for the first time, I had to take camera work as a given. I had to assume that my camera work was fine, because I was so busy learning how to manage all these new roles: directing and producing. It gave me confidence about my camera work that I hadn't had up until then, because suddenly the camera became the thing I knew.

Another thing that happened to me on the Peace March was that I got so passionately involved in what it was about that I forgot about pursuing a camera career. Because if you're pursuing a camera career, you don't take two years off to do a political documentary.

One of the things that became apparent was that I could handle shooting, traveling, and low budgets. So I got hired to do just that, and this time it was around the world: I went to India, Bangladesh, China, Japan, Italy, Greece, Turkey, and Russia. So in an odd sort of way, even though I wasn't looking at my career, my career kept going in this new direction, of shooting and directing documentaries.

It took me two years to make a one-and-a-half-hour feature documentary, and now we're spending two years making a ten-hour docudrama for TBS about ecology, history, philosophy, and human impact on the planet Earth. There's a bigger staff, and there's funding, but nonetheless, it's a lot of work in a short amount of time.

AK: What are some of the dilemmas which face you personally in the camera world?

CZ: There's a camerawomen dilemma. It's only come up recently, since I've gotten married and started to think about my family.

AK: You married a Soviet cameraperson?

CZ: Yeah.

AK: Do you plan to work with your husband, coshooting?

CZ: I hope so. I'd love to.

AK: Can you both work and live in either country?

CZ: We'll see how it works out, you know. It should work out. Our friendship formed while shooting together. So it's such a joy to work with him. I have fantasies about me being a producer-director and he being a cameraperson, and if we needed a second camera, then of course I could shoot. I also fantasize about the two of us going off on adventures, like *National Geographic* type of things, where they might need a team to go and live somewhere for a long time.

My career was very much based on being able to pick up and go anywhere, and having a family, it's not as easy to just traipse off. Recently someone called and asked, did I want to go shoot this documentary in Ireland? And, of course I want to, but it's a much bigger consideration— where does that leave the rest of the family when I pick up and go? That's a current dilemma, and I don't know how it will unfold. I married a cameraman, and we're both going to have offers to pick up and go places, and we'll have to balance it out: Who goes when, and who stays home with the children.

I've got to figure out how to make the transition out of these low-budget, interesting independent jobs into high-budget things to support the family and support babysitters.

POSTSCRIPT

CZ: Ever since my pregnancy with Teresa, I've been faced with choosing between motherhood and my career. When I was pregnant, I couldn't shoot a documentary in Israel, for fear of tear gas. When Teresa was three months old, I did manage to take her along to Russia and shoot a documentary about healers. And I had that cushy job as video camera operator on *Murphy Brown* while she was quite young, though it was only two days a week.

In 1991 we left Los Angeles, and I started teaching 16mm cinematography and 16mm production classes at the Northwest Film Center. I also started shooting birth videos with my High-8 camera. But I never fully pursued camera work here in Portland.

The big shift has been that I went to massage school in 1993, and now work regularly as a licensed massage therapist doing massage and polarity therapy—a very simple and effective way of allowing someone's life force to heal themselves.

Whereas I went into filmmaking as a way to change the world, and particularly to make it a better place for women, I now do healing work with the intention of making the world a better place. Filmmaking took me on many outward journeys, and massage is taking me into inner journeys.

I still imagine that someday I will return to filmmaking, and perhaps produce or direct rather than return to camera work—because I'm not keeping up with the technology, and I never developed the skills in lighting that I so admire in others.

What I hope is that all women who want to do camera work will do so with passion and persistence.

NOTE

1. Cathy Zheutlin, "Just One Step: The Great Peace March," in *Behind the Lens Newsmagazine* 4, no. 5 (May 1989):1.

Dyanna Taylor

Granddaughter of the great photographer Dorothea Lange, Dyanna Taylor changed her career emphasis from photography to film as a Film/Aesthetic Studies major at the University of California, Santa Cruz. After leaving school, she made her first film, *Harmon Summer*, with Warren Franklin in the Bay Area. In 1972, they formed Taylor-Franklin Films, making documentaries, industrials and commercials for three and a half years.

At the age of twenty-four, Dyanna joined NABET in San Francisco as a cinematographer, transferring to NABET Local 15 in 1979, when she moved to New York. She joined IA in New York in 1981.

Dyanna Taylor is renowned for filming news and documentaries throughout the world, including extensive work in Japan and film assignments in Egypt, Malaysia, Morocco, Mali, and the Brazilian Amazon. She was part of the first all-woman crew to film a mountaineering expedition, to Annapurna I in Nepal in 1978. She was also the videographer for director Jonathan Demme's *Haiti: Dream of Democracy*, and shot film and video in France, Spain, and Germany for *The Exiles*.

In the United States, Dyanna has worked as director of photography on theatrical features including *Pumping Iron II: The Women*, and as "B" camera operator on *Married to the Mob* and *Over Her Dead Body*. Her television specials include the Academy Award–winning *Common Threads: Stories from the Quilt*, and the CBS miniseries *500 Nations*, hosted by Kevin Costner.

Most recently, she has worked as director of photography on the feature film *Fresh Paint*.

AK: How did you get interested in camera work?

DT: I came from an extremely formal background in black and white photography, because of my grandmother, Dorothea Lange. She influenced me enormously. I was around when the printing took place, and when she was organizing work for her shows, including one of her big shows for the Museum of Modern Art. My perception was that all grandmothers were like this.

The most important thing, when I look back, is that she was a very rigorous kind of person, and in many ways difficult to be around. My grandmother expected me to understand that there was something more to seeing than seeing. Once, at our rustic cabin by the sea, where we often went together, I collected a handful of rocks and shells and thrust them toward her in my open palm. She looked at my upturned hand and then rather sternly at me, and said, "Yes, I see them. But do you see them?" I had expected a warm, "Oh, how nice." Instead, I was perplexed, and walked away. That weekend, I looked a lot at my hand and the things around me without any further prompting from her.

Slowly, I began to get that she saw more. I watched her, too, always photographing or arranging something on the old wooden table. She'd point out the light playing on the curtains in the breeze, or the gray light of the overcast on the water. Ultimately, she taught me about space, rooms, intriguing objects, and light. I learned by her example, by exposure, and finally by seeing. "Seeing" for me now is simply an extension of what I began to learn then. There is always something to gain from looking twice. The layers under the obvious are what intrigue me. But, I am to this day always pleased by an upturned child's palm.

At sixteen, I was judgmental about my work. My printing techniques were unsophisticated, and none of it had the profundity of Dorothea's. I was frozen, choked, and miserable. But in college, I stumbled upon a film course. When I was allowed to hold the camera, the "instant" became less important than the series of instants. Subjects could move, and light could change within the composition. Celluloid, color, and motion allowed me to begin my real work.

Through my camera, I could respond effectively and instinctually. I learned to play with light and composition in a domain different than Dorothea's, where I didn't compare myself with her. And I could express myself freely, without demanding instant perfection from myself.

Cathy Zheutlin was one of the few women besides myself in that tiny, fledgling film department at UC Santa Cruz. And both of us fled the university. Talking about film and theory was interesting, but it really had nothing to do with what I was interested in, which was to *do* it.

I collaborated on my first film with Warren Franklin, who is now general manager of George Lucas's Entertainment Group. *Harmon Summer* was a film for the Easter Seal Society—a half-hour color documentary promoting the concept that handicapped children and adults can go camping in the wilderness and have an enriching time. As filmmakers, we did everything: I shot, he shot, we did the scripts, we shared direction, I edited, he did the graphics, he did the animation, I did the negative cutting.

Our first film led us to form a small company, called Taylor-Franklin Films, in 1972. We had our own editing space, and we did a lot of local commercials and little industrials and little documentaries. We were very, very lucky, and one job led to the next. For the next three or four years we tried to teach ourselves what filmmaking really was—not what theory is, or the offscreen glance, but what it means to have a camera in your hand, and applying what we knew about light to jobs for clients.

I learned by stumbling a lot. I remember in two or three films, sitting somewhere away from everyone and weeping, because I thought, "I can't stand the pressure of this, and I've taken on too much, and I don't know what I'm doing." But I discovered that in the cinematography itself, in each case, there was something natural and right for me. By 1976, we both were going in different directions, Warren toward special effects, and I decided that I wanted to specialize in camera work exclusively.

As a woman in a field that is typically male-oriented, it's easy to blame men. But San Francisco was a very supportive environment in those days. No one there said, "You can't do that." The biggest resistance came from inside me. I was enormously intimidated by technical things, despite the fact that my grandmother proved that women *can* work professionally—competently and technically.

I wanted to enter the union as a camera assistant, because I thought maybe I was not good enough to be a cinematographer. The fact was that I had an entire reel of work. But I thought, "Gosh, if I enter the union, it's serious business." When NABET tested me, they said I had no clue what it was to be a camera assistant, "But you definitely know what it means to be a cinematographer."

So, at twenty-four, they entered me as a cinematographer. I went back and discovered what an assistant does, so I could begin to utilize one myself, and decided to work as an assistant as well, so I could broaden my experience with other cinematographers. I also bought my own 16mm rig, which took quite a while to pay off. I never regretted it.

AK: Can you describe the process by which you got into IA?

DT: I had been a real NABET union person in San Francisco—a real believer in the union. I'd done a lot of political films, films about union workers. But when I arrived in New York in 1979, and transferred to NABET Local 15, I discovered that a lot of doors were closed to me. The work I wanted was network-based and feature-based, and the only way I could do it was to join the IA.

It was a completely different environment than San Francisco had been, where men in the community had given me enormous support. IA made me feel like a nothing. When I finally got to the testing process, which was showing my work and my reel, I was in a smoky room with over twenty cameramen. Only a few were even close to my age, and they were actually the ones most rigorously opposed to my being in the union. I finally got into the IA in September 1981. But the whole process took about two years.

AK: The Directors Guild (until they dropped their suit) and the Writers Guild have been active in fighting discrimination. What do you think it will take for camerawomen to be treated equally to cameramen in the industry? And can Women in Film help, specifically?

DT: We have to get our work out there so someone can see it. That's the first thing. Women in Film can help a lot.

Women in Film in New York is a very sophisticated, wonderful organization. There must be some one thousand women. I get a lot of referrals from women who know that I'm in the organization and who call for advice, or who call to see if I'm available for work. Not only that, but the organization is taken very seriously in New York. It's because the women who are in it are very powerful. There are a lot of very powerful producers, directors, and some great thinkers. So it's exciting. The meetings and seminars are always invigorating and interesting. Alicia Weber's done a cinematography workshop. John Bailey, the cinematographer, came and spoke. We had a four-part series, "The Documentary," with interesting directors coming to show their clips. Women in Film also helps members with health insurance and insurance plans. It's a great resource.

AK: What are some of the satisfactions that you've gotten from your camera career?

DT: I've enjoyed working for the directors I've worked for: Jonathan Demme and Nigel Noble. I've loved working with DPs Tak Fujimoto and Alfonso Beato.

Jonathan Demme will take a chance on anyone that's interesting. He did with me, and I really appreciate it. I shot a film for him in '87, in Haiti, and he subsequently picked me up on *Married to the Mob*. Tak is very understated, but quietly supportive. And Alfonso Beato, the Brazilian cameraman who shot *Great Balls of Fire*, is just spectacular.

Feature films—studio pictures with union contracts—are very, very different from a feature documentary or an independent feature. In these, you're much more involved with the world. I've enjoyed working on big pictures. I think the DP has a lot of freedom, but people below that don't [*laughs*]. As second unit or "B" camera, you're just below the DP, which is the case for me. I've also shot an independent feature as the DP. Because it had a lower budget, I didn't have the facilities that I had on the bigger picture, but I had more flexibility and a little more cooperation on the set.

Pumping Iron and *In the Blood* were both feature documentaries over which I had a lot of control, as a DP might on a regular feature. And in both cases, I worked for at least three or four months on each project, as Second Unit DP, and again that was like a feature, in the commitment to a long-term process. In both cases I hired other men to work for and with me, when I needed extra cameras on various subjects.

In the Blood was incredibly physically taxing. This was George Butler's study of men, fathers and sons, and big-game hunting—all shot in Africa. I was hired, on some level, because he wanted the perspective of a woman in viewing these animals and men.

As a woman, I've found a number of men who were spectacular, informed, open, unthreatened human beings who have loved working with me and have been great collaborators and supporters. I also have a couple of women assistants I work with. I've worked with sound women whom I adore—less frequently, though, simply because they're not available and there are not as many of them.

I think Marie Ashton (sound and coproducer) and I broke a record in 1978 as the first women's team to shoot a major mountaineering expedition in Nepal when we made the *Annapurna Women's Expedition Film*. It was the first time Americans or women had stood on the summit of Annapurna I, and the first time an all-women's crew had shot an expedition.

I had no assistant on that job. And we had six cases of equipment. We had Sherpa and porter support to get to base camp, but after that we carried everything.

I've done a lot of work in Africa, in the Alps, and in the Brazilian jungle. For instance, for the most recent hunting film, we had to trek for days across swamps. And that's a lot of weight.

In Africa, the women want to know if I have a baby. That's the main question. They touch my breasts and then they say, "Baby." And when I say I don't have a baby, they no longer view me as a woman like them. That doesn't mean that they shut me out in any way. In fact I'm an object of curiosity. Not a woman or a man—somehow different. I'm of lesser status [*laughs*] because I haven't borne children yet.

Show me the camerawoman who works as much as I do who has a family too, and I'll be thrilled to talk to her. Every producer wants a hundred percent of you. My male film colleagues have their families because they have wonderful women at home who cooperate. And it's made me frustrated and angry for years.

I remember standing in the middle of some African desert. We'd been out for some time working, and we came to some town large enough to have a phone. All the guys immediately rushed to the phone to call their wives and families and to have these conversations, and when they got off the phone they were glowing. And I stood there feeling barren and alone, in a very profound way.

On the film features I've been on, there have been wonderful single mothers, but they're making a lot of money. The actresses, the production designers, the costume designers keep their babies on location, and their nannies with them. It certainly wouldn't work on any documentary work.

I love my work. First of all, it's given me the college education that I walked away from when I was eighteen or nineteen years old. It's been restored thousands of times over, in that I've walked into more complex live situations than I ever had at the university. And I've walked into these situations at critical moments, straight to the center, so I've learned the essence of something. It's been the best series of seminars on life that you could possibly want, on every subject imaginable.

From a village in Zimbabwe or the heart of the Brazilian jungle to Temples in Kyoto, from striking cotton workers to families with AIDS, from swimming with dolphins to climbing in Nepal. From Mahler's *First* with the Berlin Philharmonic to recording sessions with Elvis Costello. From Australia's Great Barrier reef to hanging out of a helicopter over the Rockies. And I love the people I've met.

The skill that documentaries require, many feature people don't understand at all. They think documentaries are just a messy form of shooting, and it's really so much more sophisticated than that to make a good one.

The "moment of the frame," I call it. That's my aesthetic moment. The expressive moment. When I'm inside the frame in the moment and time stops, that's cinematography for me.

Each of us has an essential need to express and create. When I'm framed up and the camera whirrs reassuringly next to my ear, the action begins, the composition forms, the clouds move, and the light changes—there my magic occurs, instinctively framing, selectively containing the moment as it unfolds. It is also the moment when, after all the collaboration so required in this medium has culminated, I am alone. For me, it is the moment of my art.

I want to deal with emulsion and light for the rest of my life. My ultimate goal, I think, is to be able to continue being a DP and be able to have a family. I refuse to think I would have to leave my work for years to do that. I'll have to count on terrific, open-minded producers.

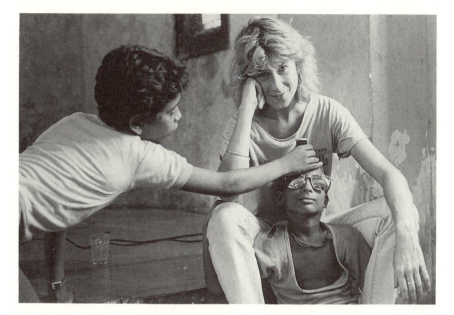

Sandi Sissel, ASC

One of only a small handful of women currently listed in IA 600 as directors of photography, Sandi Sissel credits Haskell Wexler, Robbie Müller, Ed Bianchi, and Geraldo Rivera for their support in helping her up the cinematographer's ladder from working on documentaries to commercials to movies of the week to features.

While I was interviewing Sandi Sissel, her low, authoritative voice with its hard-driving, logical cadence struck me as an unusual, yet superb negotiating asset for an otherwise feminine camerawoman working in today's industry.

As a documentary camerawoman, Sandi Sissel filmed the wars in Lebanon, Viet Nam, El Salvador, and other countries, as well as filming with a hidden camera in illegal abortion clinics and on the streets, impersonating prostitutes. Later, as camera operator, she braved an accident in which a crane collapsed above her.

Throughout her career, her mental strength and realistic sense of timing have helped her to survive and move forward in her career. When it was rare for camerawomen to find employment, she got her master's at the University of Wisconsin, and taught film. When the IA was looking for qualified women to shoot newsreel footage in 1974, she applied and was accepted.

Some of Sandi Sissel's numerous credits as director of photography include *Salaam Bombay*, which won the Camera D'Or at the 1988 Cannes Film Festival, and *Mother Teresa*, winner of a 1987 Emmy. Sandi also shot the miniseries *Drug Wars: The Camerena Story*; commercials for NASA, American Airlines and Mattel; and documentaries on Jane Goodall, Aretha Franklin, Alice Walker, and Lily Tomlin. Her numerous television credits include eight episodes of *Class of '96*.

At the time of our interview, Sandi was working as director of photography on a $12 million studio feature—*The People under the Stairs*, with Wes Craven. Her recent credits include the HBO feature *The Soul of the Game*; the ABC television movie *Radiant City*; the documentary *Colors* for Michael Jackson; and the feature film *Camp Nowhere*. She is currently in Prague, filming *The Reef*.

AK: How did you first get interested in camera work?

SS: My father was a still photographer. I used to spend a lot of time with him, going to work with him and doing darkroom work with him. When I got to college—SMU [Southern Methodist University], in Dallas, Texas—I entered the television department, thinking at first that I wanted to be a reporter. Then I started some of the classes, and I decided I liked being on the other side of the camera much better.

Around 1969, I started working as an intern at the local ABC affiliate, WFAA, getting credit for the time I was working. As an intern, I was doing a little bit of shooting, but mostly working as an assistant.

Women weren't allowed to wear pants to work in Texas in those days. So here I was doing all this menial work, carrying all this heavy equipment around, wearing a skirt the entire time. I used to wear a pair of shorts under my skirt, so that when I climbed ladders, it'd be OK. One day, I read some women at the station had worn pantsuits to work, so I wore them. Some of the news crews actually filmed us going to work. It became a big deal, and some of the people that worked at the station thought that we were being very rebellious.

In 1971, I started working for the University of Wisconsin. I began teaching "Intro to Film" and also making educational films for the university system. I did that for about three years while I got a master's degree and began working toward a doctorate. I think a lot of women, Blacks, and Hispanics did the same thing in those days. One way to get ahead in the workplace, certainly at that time, was if we couldn't actually compete, many of us were going back and getting higher education. Within the university system, it was possible to advance.

As I had been teaching and making some films, I had a small reel of my work put together that was basically some political documentaries and some educational films. When my husband and I split up in 1974, I moved to New York to stay with some filmmakers who had been guest lecturers in my classes.

In 1974, the IATSE local 644 was being sued by NBC, ABC, and CBS in New York because there were no women available to be put on shooting. The IA put out the word they were looking for qualified women to come in and show reels and go through the testing and try to join the IA. A number of my friends who were then prominent independent filmmakers—people like Jill Godmilow, Ira Wohl, and Ken Locker—suggested that I go in and join the union. I was at that point transferring dailies at Duart Film Laboratory, trying to do odd jobs to make money, and I thought, "Well, I'll give it a shot."

Walking into the hallowed halls of the IA seemed like an overwhelming experience. There were about ten or fifteen guys sitting around—older men, you know, who were intimidating. To be honest, they were just looking for *anybody* who knew *anything*. They asked very simple things. Nothing like I thought it would be.

Anyway, I got a call the next day that they accepted me. Then that afternoon I got a call from NBC asking me to go on staff. They accepted me as what was called "newsreel camerawoman." They accepted two other women at the same time: Alicia Weber and Risa Corliff.

We all went on staff at various and sundry networks, and I did that for about two or three years. On weekends I continued to do independent films, but my finances improved dramatically. It was very hard being a woman shooting newsreel in New York at the networks, because there had never been any. But it was also a time when some of the older guys in the union learned that we knew what we were doing. Eventually we became sort of like uncles and nieces.

I'm a very small person, and in those days, I was lucky if I weighed ninety pounds. So I think that that was something in the early days that people used as an excuse, you know, "How could somebody so small like you do this kind of work?" But I used to always laugh it off, because a 16mm camera is no more than about twenty pounds, and any pregnant woman's carrying that kind of weight. Mentally, what we all had to go through was much more difficult.

AK: Could you describe the resistance and the support you've gotten from other people?

SS: Haskell Wexler hired me as a camera operator, and I've been a DP on a couple commercials that he's directed, so that was *extremely* important, because he's such a visible person in the industry. Once he hired me, then other people took notice.

The same is true with Robbie Müller. He shoots all of Wim Wender's films. When he insisted on me in New York as his operator, people took notice. Ed Bianchi, a commercial director in New York, insisted on me. He really got me into commercials.

Geraldo Rivera was extremely important to my career in the early days, because we did a lot of work for ABC that was very political in nature, and that got a lot of notice.

I had a lot of support, there's no question. To be honest with you, it's come from men more than it's come from women, because I think that women have been put into very competitive situations with each other.

The people I've been involved with personally throughout my life have been supportive, but anyone's feelings get hurt when they feel that your job is more important than the time you have for them. And I think that's a constant struggle—for anyone who has loved me to deal with that issue. When you're working eighty hours a week, someone feels neglected. Certainly in the past, it was very difficult for a man to see me making more money than he was, and this is a very high-paying business.

It's a very difficult and stressful business. On the film that I'm doing now, I have an enormous crew—six cameras. I'm also in charge of the lighting department and the grip department. So right now, I'm directly in charge of probably forty people. As productions grow in size, working your way up from documentaries that cost $100,000, to independent features, and then to studio features, it's the same issue that it was in 1974, when I was one of the first women shooting newsreel at one of the networks. You have to keep improving.

When I did *Salaam Bombay*, I had $700,000. When I did *Wonder Years*, I had a $1.5 million per episode. Then on the miniseries *Drug Wars*, I had $24 million dollars for a six-hour program. And then I started doing movies of the week, where the budget for each one was about $4 million.

Now I'm doing a film where I have $12 million. For me the difference in the money means that I get more Steadicams, more operators, more equipment, more cranes, and I can design shots that are more interesting. I can use bigger lights for better lighting. Each time I do a project, it's going to look better. It's not necessarily going to be better, as far as the directing or the story goes. But it's going to look better because I have more to work with. If things look better, my reel is going to improve, and the next time

I go in to do a film, people are going to say, "Wow, this is a great reel!" and they're not going to question whether I'm a woman or not. That's not going to be the issue. The reason that it still is an issue is because virtually no women have had the opportunity to have that kind of reel. Brianne's done a lot of work, I've gotten to do a lot of work, there are literally a handful of women around the world who have had the opportunity.

In the mid-to-late '70s, I got a lot of work because I was a camerawoman. Certain people came to me because they felt there were some subjects where a woman would be better doing the camera work than a man. By the late '70s, early '80s, there were enough really good, qualified women shooting that it became less of an issue. Frankly, when I was living in New York, some of the documentary camerawomen like Joan Churchill, Alicia Weber, Dyanna Taylor, Judy Irola, and I were equal to our competition in the city, and we were all called in equally for each job.

They look at my reel of work next to any cameraman's reel of work, depending on the budget of the film. Working in Hollywood as a DP, you're competing with anyone who does camera work from all over the world. Now if the director and producer decide they want me, then it's up to the executives to decide whether they can deal with it or not. When they're finally doing the actual contract with my agent, then it comes down to, "Oh my God, do we really think we can hire a woman to do this?"

When you get down to it, when you talk about high-budget pictures, "Can a woman run a crew on a large production?" becomes the same issue: "Can a woman be prime minister of England?"

My agent is able to get for me the kind of money they're able to get for any man in my position. I've been lucky enough to get to a certain level, but at this point it has absolutely nothing to do with being a woman.

AK: How did you get involved in Behind the Lens, Women in Film, or other women's support groups in the industry?

SS: I've never really been involved with any of those organizations. I've been working nonstop in this industry since 1971, and although I've always been at the forefront of women doing it, I've never had a problem getting work.

But other camerawomen and camera assistants and I were constantly thrown into competitive situations with each other for work. Even though I consider two of my best friends women who at one point were certainly my direct competition in documentaries, we had to work very hard at remaining close friends. Joan Churchill and Chris Burrill are like my sisters.

Some women who moved to executive positions were put into so much stress, in fact they were not always that kind to the women that worked with them. Certainly for me, I've had some wonderful experiences working with women. I did a film called *Mother Teresa*, which was a wonderful experience working with a woman director—Ann Petrie. And I've had many other wonderful experiences, where people were very supportive of each other.

AK: What about the union out here?

SS: I'm in all the unions. I'm in the IA here and in New York, and I'm in IBEW and NABET. And in each particular case, I've joined the union to be able to do a film that I was up for. I'm still only one of two female DPs in Local 659. The other one is Brianne Murphy.

The things that I have been doing for the last few years have basically been nonunion. The miniseries, and the movies of the week that I've shot in L.A., have been nonunion.

I did take a status out of the IA called "financial core status," which was a Supreme Court decision a few years ago based on a Disney strike that allows union members to work on both union and nonunion productions. It's actually a technical term that allows funding organizations to feel that they're not putting themselves in financial jeopardy, hiring a union person who's going to cause pickets when it begins. Now, I would prefer to work on union films because I think it's easier on the crew, and I think that everyone deserves Health and Welfare. But because the business has shifted, largely because of what Reagan did during his administration, there's not been enough union work for people to be employed.

Frankly, my salary is exactly the same whether I'm working on a union film or nonunion film. The difference is that I have a larger crew, and a crew that makes better wages and benefits. It just makes it a more pleasant work experience if you can work within a union environment.

AK: Now that you're in a position of having forty or more people working for you, how do you convey a sense of calm to them?

SS: Well, I hire the best people I can to make me look good.

When I did *Salaam Bombay*, it was a very stressful situation, working in India with very little money, with a non-English-speaking crew and a first-time director, and there was only so much money and so much time. That was the lowest budget thing I've ever done, and yet in many ways I had the most control, because although we had no money, we had a lot of preproduction, so we were able to predesign every shot in the film before we shot it.

I think now, I have a lot of money and no time. I have a lot of experience on the crew, but we have to do in thirty minutes what we had four hours to do on *Salaam Bombay*, and that's a big difference. Preproduction is the most important thing in this business, so you have the time to plan out what you're doing.

AK: Have there been any special, challenging situations in your career as a cinematographer?

SS: When I was doing documentaries, I worked a lot in wars. I became well known for getting war footage. I've been in the wars in Lebanon, Viet Nam, the Philippines, Haiti, El Salvador, Guatemala. That was very challenging, very difficult, and very exciting.

In the mid-seventies I did a lot of hidden camera work, where I impersonated prostitutes and women getting abortions and drug busts with my camera hidden in a bag. Long before there was home video, 16mm cameras were the smallest cameras available. So I designed a hidden camera bag that had a piece of black mesh in front of the lens, and a little strap that I could use to turn the camera on and off. I was hired by all the networks and a lot of independent productions to do hidden camera work to try and bust people. There were illegal abortion clinics, there were a lot of doctors giving out drugs illegally, there were a lot of welfare institutions that were doing illegal business. I went with Geraldo Rivera to do a lot of very difficult assignments, busting various institutions. I became more of an actress than a camerawoman. Because I was young and very small, no one suspected me of being a cinematographer or a reporter.

Even with the camera on my shoulder in Haiti and the Philippines, when you wear a pair of shorts and run around with a small Aaton, people thought I was a tourist. So there were a lot of things I could do that my male counterparts could not do.

Later on, I bought a Steadicam, and that was very challenging to learn to do that well. As I became a camera operator, just technically learning to use cranes and Steadicams and large cameras was in itself a challenge.

I was in a crane accident once—I landed underneath a crane that collapsed, and broke my elbow. For a while I didn't know if I could ever hand-hold again. I think you'd talk to a lot of people like me: I have tennis elbows, and bursitis in my knee, and cuts all over, and broken limbs from doing the actual physical part of the business, which is a whole different thing from the mental part of the business.

AK: What has given you the inner strength to have a broken arm and say, "OK, I'm going to get it better with physical therapy and go out there and face the business again"?

SS: If you really like what you are doing—which I do, I really love what I'm doing—it's like being a quarterback. How did Joe Namath play with his knee? I don't know.

AK: What are some of the satisfactions you have gained from your work?

SS: Back during the time when I was doing political documentaries, the work that I was doing was not only what I consider to be good work technically, but things that actually helped people. Working in the Third World a lot, I was able to show some of the problems in El Salvador and Guatemala and Haiti and the Philippines and India to my country, and actually be a part of changing people's perceptions of the problems of people overseas. And that's very rewarding, because you are a journalist as well as a cinematographer. I miss that, because everything I do now is drama, or re-creation of written words. So now, the most rewarding thing is doing really beautiful shots.

The thing is, however, the best documentary work I've ever done's probably been seen by a few million people. Whereas you can do one network miniseries and you can have twenty million people watch it in one night. The longer you stay in the business, the larger audience you want to see your work. That becomes a part of why you move up.

The other part is, now that I'm forty, I don't want to put myself through going through war zones carrying a heavy hand-held camera. I wanted to move into an area where DPs work until they're seventy-five, eighty years old. There are elderly cameramen still lighting major films.

AK: If you were pregnant, would you work, and under what conditions?

SS: It's always been something I've known from a very young age, that I could not bear children. I think that when that's an issue, it changes your perception of your work as a woman. And for better or for worse, the films I did became the children that I never had.

AK: What are your ultimate goals in camera work, and film and TV production in general?

SS: I'm doing exactly what I want to do. I just want to get better at it.

Geraldine Kudaka

At an early age, Geraldine Kudaka proved enormously successful as a camera assistant, making a comfortable living in the Bay Area on union and nonunion films. As a Japanese-American, she created a Third World and women's training program through NABET. She worked as a camera assistant on such films as *Death Be Not Proud*, *George Jackson Lives*, *Over Under*, and numerous commercials, as well as a staff stringer for the CBS Network.

In addition to her reputation as a consummate film technician, Geraldine Kudaka's poetry has also earned her high praise. When I first met Geraldine at a Behind the Lens meeting in 1985, shortly after her move from San Francisco to Los Angeles, I was immediately struck by her intellectual as well as creative and technical powers. Her article, "Union vs. Non-Union," the mainstay of the 1989 *Behind the Lens Annual Newsmagazine*,[1] was a large inspiration for my undertaking further studies of camerawomen and their needs. For Geraldine, the challenge and "dare" of camera work had long since been met, and she began to make plans to pursue independent filmmaking as a writer-producer-director.

Five years later, Geraldine has made substantial progress in her transition from below-the-line to above-the-line work. A video series that she produced and directed, *Massage for Friends and Lovers*, is in distribution, and she recently directed *Chinese Take-Out* for Showtime. She also edited the 1995 Anchor Books anthology *On a Bed of Rice: An Asian American Erotic Feast*. Currently, she is producing and directing *Random Selections*, a videotape series about cross-cultural views of issues that affect Americans: the first on race and gender, the second on aging, and the third on beauty. She is also developing her first feature, a film about Asian-American women.

AK: How did you first become involved with camera work?

GK: At UCLA, I had wanted to be a filmmaker in the most complete possible sense. At one point during school when we were all helping each other make student films, one of my friends said, "So, do you want to help me with my film?" "Sure," I said. "What do you wanna do?" "Oh, I don't know. I'd like to shoot." "Girls can't shoot." It was then that I realized that I wanted to shoot. Because of that challenge, that dare.

Also, during a break in school, I went up to the Bay Area to see a friend. There was a group called Film Workers Union that was being set up, and a top-notch camera assistant, Richard Paup, was teaching a camera assistant class. Through the class I learned the actual technology of working in the business. I got a job working as a cinematographer immediately afterwards, and then I started getting jobs in San Francisco working in camera. Because of that I decided not to go back to school.

When I left school, what I wanted to do was shoot. I wanted to master the language of film. I was so obsessed about films that I'd watch five to ten movies a week, every week. At the same time, I was learning my craft. I was so wrapped up in the technology, in understanding the craft of filmmaking, that I had forgot what movie making is really about—telling stories. I was very obsessive about clear vision, to the point of continually washing my car windows.

I started working as a camera assistant in 1970, and by 1975 had gotten into the union. By the simple fact that I was able to work, I realized I could become a DP. This was an important milestone in my life. I had spent so much time and energy fighting, breaking through doors, that I had lost sight of my original goal, which was to make films. I had wanted to shoot as a means to making films.

When I realized I could become a DP, my eyes opened. It hit me that I did not want my obituary to simply read, "DP"; I wanted to make films. I was wasting time.

I started making a political documentary, and ended up in debt. I had no financing. Everything I had went into this film, and still it wasn't enough. I worked three features, back to back, in an effort to raise money.

Well, I was crazy. I ended up with an ulcer. That's when I decided making movies wasn't worth my life. I left the country and when I came back, I got out of production. I started a film program at the San Jose Museum of Art.

Working at the museum brought me back to the aesthetics of film. I love films. At the same time, I helped a friend, Wayne Wang, make *Chan Is Missing*, which catapulted him to success. His success gave me the courage to put together another project, this time a theatrical venture. At the last minute, the financing fell apart.

Three years ago, when I first joined Behind the Lens, I discovered an exhilarating vision and creativity. There was a creative energy which included long-range projects. I was excited about the other members.

Since then, the vision has shrunk. We focus on getting jobs and advancing our careers through concentrating on things like the directory and networking. All of this is important, but at what price? Networking, promoting oneself, is part of having a career. It's something one does regardless of a group.

I'd like to see BTL develop projects which would help not only camera-women, but also contribute to the further evolution of our whole industry. By this, I mean creative projects such as instituting a dialogue regarding feminist visual aesthetic. Is there one? Is there a particular vision I have because I am a woman? Or creating a record of our history, an archive depicting the achievements of camerawomen.

AK: Can you describe the resistance and/or support that you've gotten as a camerawoman?

GK: My family did not view working in the film business, or my whole creative, artistic endeavor as a "career." Finally, in my thirties, they recognized that I was actually making a living. I was on a TV program about filmmakers, and my mother's friends saw it, and they called her up and told her. I think it was the first time it became concrete to her.

To her, the life-style I lead is incomprehensible. She comes from a poor, working-class ethic. The whole creative filmmaking idea that one would have the audacity to want to say something is beyond her comprehension. She believes that in order to survive in this world, you have to bow down to stronger powers and acquiesce to them—even though she, herself, is a very strong woman.

I got into film partly because I was political—I had been in the Asian movement. That's actually how I got into UCLA film school, through

Asian-American community politics, and through a Third World program at UCLA that had gotten special funding from the U.S. Department of Education. I think if it weren't for Ethnocommunications, I wouldn't have gone to film school.

And in the San Francisco Bay Area Film Workers Union, there were politically conscious people who believed women and Third World people should be represented in the film industry. I also feel that, at a later point, there was a certain amount of patriarchal tokenism—that I was the heavy political from the Third World community that people took under their wing.

I don't want to sound ungrateful when I talk about patriarchal tokenism. One guy, because of his own beliefs, went so far as to fight the union, and to a certain degree, he got blacklisted because he believed that I should be in the union.

AK: And you did get into the union partly as a result of his efforts?

GK: Yes. Definitely. I think I got into film to make films, to be a director, because I had something I wanted to say. But I became so intimidated by the technology and becoming a professional, learning the trade, that at one point I was heavily involved in union organizing and labor politics.

AK: So it wasn't just a matter of feeling intimidated by technology. Perhaps you were also intimidated by the power structure using the technology. And that was what you were fighting with your union involvement?

GK: Yes. But it was beyond that. I was very young and very rebellious, fighting everything. I did not know how to relate to white people. I was very much involved in setting up a Third World and women's training program in NABET. I wanted to see more Third World people actually having the skills and the technology to make films.

AK: So you identified very strongly with other minorities struggling to achieve these aims. You had a definite sense of community.

GK: But I also felt alienated and isolated from that community. That's why I was trying so hard to incorporate them, because I felt very split between the white film world that I worked in, which was basically middle-class alienated people, and these lower-class Third World people that I hung out with.

An example would be this one picture I was working on. The guys I was working with did not know how to deal with me, and actually resented my being there. When I'd walk by the truck, they'd whistle and call me Yokohama Mamma [*laughs*].

On the other hand, there was a certain amount of resentment that my artist friends had, seeing me working in the film business and making money.

AK: Are you in the union now?

GK: Yes. I think people put a tremendous amount of weight on the union. It gives them legitimacy. I think that's bullshit. It's a status thing. I don't think that you are a camera assistant by having a card, or by having somebody else tell you this is what you are.

The deception lies in where one places the power. The whole industry is set up in such a way that, individually, we all lack personal power. We don't take responsibility for our lack of power. We sit at home waiting for the phone to ring; we're always at the beck and call of somebody else. And along the same line, the union fosters the attitude, "The union prevents me from doing . . . " something.

You know there are a lot of ways of making films, there a lot of ways of shooting. I think it really comes down to, individually, how one perceives and feels about oneself.

I think that I was more naïve then than now. I had actually surrendered more of my self-esteem to the outside world. Whether I was working or not determined how I felt about myself. That means that you don't have the ability to feel good about yourself unless somebody else validates you. That produces stress.

I turned down a very big union picture when I was beginning, because the political group that I had worked with, and that I owed something to, was making a feature. I was told, "We're going to have B camera stuff, and you can be operator." I was assisting then, and I thought, "Oh, great! This will be a chance for me to move up."

When they started shooting, and the moments for B camera came up, it was like all of these "brothers" were breathing down my neck. There was this tremendous amount of pressure, because I knew they all felt they could do the job—shoot B camera—better than I could, even if I was the camera assistant that was supposed to be the B camera operator. It intimidated the shit out of me. I resented them because I felt inadequate.

I look back, and, of course, if I were in their position, I would feel the same way. It was my problem that I felt inadequate, and that I felt they should have been supportive by saying, "Gee, it's great to see you operating. It's wonderful," instead of having the human reaction of, "Fuck, *I'd* rather be shooting."

AK: How has the industry changed in its perception of women?

GK: Fifteen years ago, I was hired on *Streets of San Francisco*. The day before the show started, I was fired because the DP found out I was a woman. He was an old Marine who refused to work with women. I was very angry about it. Losing that job made me feel so futile.

Well, it's such a funny world. I recently assisted this guy, and we started talking, and lo and behold, this guy was the very same assistant who replaced me on that show. And today, he was operating, and I was his assistant. Needless to say, the irony hit me. If I had been a man, I would have been in another position. Yet I can't say I regret being a woman.

One thing that has changed is that people don't automatically assume you're sleeping with somebody and that's why and how you got there. I'm glad that women don't have to fight such battles anymore. Maybe it's because a whole new generation is making films. I don't know. Maybe it's because I'm older and I'm not so cute and delectable anymore.

If I'm physically worn and burning myself out, I can't concentrate or focus. Focus is a very mental job. You can't connect without having your own vitality, your base level of energy. When producers abuse you so much that you're so tired you don't care, it's criminal abuse. And in the end, at dailies, there's only one person accountable, and that's you. Your work shows, and no amount of justification is going to make it better.

AK: What do you think it will take for camerawomen to be treated equally in the industry?

GK: Time. A lot of time.

The majority of people in this industry are basically blue-collar workers. Like any other industry, most of our jobs are trades, and most of the workers hold pretty conventional work values. Paradoxically, women who have the balls to get into crewing don't have a blue-collar mentality of "doing a job just because it's a job and they need a job." Women with that kind of mentality are happy remaining secretaries.

Job discrimination will change when our coworkers, our crew brothers, accept us as a natural course of events, when we're more than a rarity. This is slowly happening, but at the same time, our country is reverting back to some pretty conservative values. The new wave represents our hope. Because of them, I think we'll see more women lighting sets. We'll see more women making films. The infusion of new blood has revitalized our industry.

AK: Does the same answer apply in terms of minorities?

GK: Yes. As a result of the turmoil of the '60s, the doors were opened to a few black men. Some of these men are top assistants.

AK: Have you yourself experienced solidarity or seen positive communication between minority men and camerawomen in terms of parallel goals in the industry?

GK: You mean as an overall trend? Yes, I have. But I also think the work environment demands special kinds of interactions. Due to the long hours we work and the pressures involved, we choose to work with people we get along with the best and with the least amount of hassle. There are some women that I would prefer not to work with just because I don't want to spend time with them. And of course, there are some men that I'd prefer avoiding. This is not a question of sex or race. It's a matter of personal fit.

AK: What kind of men do you avoid working with?

GK: Men who dislike women. Of course, there's a more subtle form of misogyny. Some men don't know how to deal with women as an equal working partner, or, heaven forbid, as their boss. It's accepted that women in front of the camera have power. Star power. But behind the camera, the common euphemism for DP is "leader of men." A woman calling the shots is naturally emasculating in an industry based on insecurity. By this, I refer to our freelance status. We have no job security. We are only as good as our last job. Our self-esteem is based on our earning power, which is the only tangible proof of our worth.

You have to understand what you're dealing with and why you're dealing with it. If you're trying to raise someone else's consciousness, they will not want to deal with you. Whereas if you understand where they are coming from and why they are coming from that place, it can create a certain rapport. Then you can strike a harmonious chord. You can have a relationship which is beneficial for you and them. But to approach it assuming they have to understand where you are coming from is wrong.

If even the most hostile man worked with women where, instead of the feeling, "This woman's out to cut my balls off," or "She's out to get my job," or "I can't trust her," there was a set camaraderie that developed, this man would have a better attitude towards working with women. It works. It's something he'd have actually experienced which you can't create through simply consciousness-raising.

At the same time, assisting is a technical service job. It's something that's easy for women to fit into. It's like being the perfect wife on the film set. A wife traditionally creates a home by building the nest and supplying the food and nurturing; on a set, an assistant provides all the tools for the cameraman. An assistant plays the support role. We build the camera and supply the film and support for the cameraman.

In Eastern philosophy, this is a balance called yin and yang. The feminine, the yin, is the receptive, passive, dark, and cool side. The yang is aggressive, male, sunny, and warm.

A man I assisted recently moved me up. I started shooting, and in shooting, I discovered that the key to my shooting was using the camera as a vessel, a receptacle. By this, the act of shooting becomes yin. My whole consciousness becomes focused on the relationship between what happens in the eyepiece. What is in front of the camera. I and my camera become the passive recipient of images created by what is in front of the camera. I respond. My lens size changes. My position changes. It's like a love affair, a mating dance or ritual.

Yin and yang are in a constant state of flux. The yang takes over when I light, when I become the dominant, aggressive force. I make the light happen. I change the balance, yet the essence is still there. What is in front of the camera, the actors or talent, still respond as they do. The shift of light is a subtle shift, an important shift, but in the end, the action in front of the camera is what counts. It maintains its whole, its integrity separate from the shifts of light. The yang recedes, the yin rises.

This taught me a lot. It made me understand on a very deep, primary level the necessity for women to keep and nurture this thing we call femininity. This femininity isn't pink froufrou. It's something deeper. It has to do with the ability to completely tune in to something else, to have your whole psyche keyed up and aware of another wavelength. It's not women games. It's the receptive—the focused ability to tune in to something else. It's a quality that men have, though men aren't generally encouraged to develop the feminine. And in this business, we women are taught we have to be yang. We have to be aggressive. We have to push, to make things happen. That's true, but this other quality, this focused receptivity, is necessary to shoot.

AK: What are some of the satisfactions you've obtained from your work?

GK: Working in films has broadened and opened my perspective on life. If I hadn't had the opportunity to be in films, my life would have been much poorer. Through film I have seen things I would never have seen otherwise. This was especially true in the beginning, when I did a lot of news and documentaries. I traveled to Mexico. I worked in Asia. Through work, I have seen parts of America I would have not seen. I saw Middle America. I met with the Archbishop of the Mormon Church, met with Ronald Reagan. I hung out in Palm Springs with the idle rich—something I would not ordinarily do.

AK: What are your ultimate goals in camera work?

GK: My ultimate goal is to produce and direct my own films. Historically, the first camerawomen in this industry were women who also produced and directed. If you want to shoot a movie, start a company and hire yourself as the DP. Wait around for someone to give you a chance? Hey, we all want to get married to Prince Charming? Right.

NOTE

1. Geraldine Kudaka, "Union vs. Non-Union," *Behind the Lens Annual Newsmagazine* 4, no. 1 (December 1986): 1–5, 25–44.

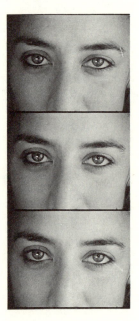

Amy Halpern

Born and raised in New York City, Amy Halpern was a modern dancer before applying her fascination with visual movement and light to filmmaking. After briefly studying film at the State University of New York in Binghamton, she began making her own films in 1971. She was one of four founders of The Collective for Living Cinema (1972–1990), an organization dedicated to showing experimental film work, and, after moving to Los Angeles in 1974, cofounded the Los Angeles Independent Film Oasis (1980–1985). In 1995 she completed *Falling Lessons*, a one-hour film about eye contact, described by Kevin Thomas of the *Los Angeles Times* as "a stunningly sensual, life-affirming experience from a major experimental film artist."[1]

Amy holds a BA and MFA from UCLA's film school, and has taught film production, history, and theory at UCLA, California State University, Northridge, and Otis-Parsons Art Institute, as well as giving numerous seminars on lighting for film and video. She is currently teaching in the School of Cinema-Television at the University of Southern California.

Her main employment, however, has been working in the motion picture industry as a gaffer, cinematographer, and lighting technician. Her numerous credits include *Stand and Deliver*, *Tremors*, *I'm Gonna Get You*,

Sucka, My Brother's Wedding, Godzilla '85, Guests of the Astoria Hotel, and *Ambassador Hotel.*

AK: How did you first get interested in camera work?

AH: It's always seemed a logical necessity that I would shoot film, because as early as I can remember, I mean little—when I was four and three—I remember existing mostly through my eyes.

The first physical training that I had in terms of visual expression was dancing. It was very useful training in terms of cadence, movement, formal structure of any art form in general, work with music, presentation of objects in space, and movement through space.

I knew that dance wasn't my form. I think it's a limited medium, specifically because (a) it has no close-ups; and (b) the person who's doing it, feeling those movements, is in the best spectator position. That's the tragedy of it, that a fixed location in a proscenium arrangement is not the best position for the spectator. Also, (c) it's thoroughly entrenched in the human form.

We human beings spend so much time looking at human bodies anyway, and evaluating them, that dance overlaps too smoothly into looking at the bodies move. We read bodies in our usual perception of the environment. Furthermore, everybody's body is different, and the one we are born into is not necessarily the ideal form that we would choose as instrument.

AK: As a female artist, I would think that would be an even more weighty consideration.

AH: I guess, because you're already being read so much of the day via your body, that you have to carry it on into your main form of expression is infuriating, maddening. So I knew dance wasn't my form, although I didn't know what my form was.

The other important training I had as a dancer is that I learned very early that to make art is a privilege, and that naturally one does something else to support it. It's best to avoid ever putting oneself into a position of having to be paid to make art, because then you're being paid to produce a product as per the specs of your client or boss, which is a different activity from expression motivated by the impulse of the information itself. Of course, you do something *else* to afford the privilege.

So from the age of sixteen, I was typing for a living. If you have a complete distance between how you pay your rent and keep yourself solvent, and what you actually do as a human being, then there's no interference, or pollution from other motives. You learn how to preserve your own brain space.

My other real occupation was founding The Collective for Living Cinema, an organization started in 1972, dedicated entirely to showing experimental and unusual film work. It was founded by Ken Ross, Phil Wiseman, Mark Graff, and myself. We programmed all the films, projected all the films, set up all the chairs, the whole thing. Bit by bit it grew, and people joined us. The Collective ran successfully on grants, in its own building, until its 1990 demise.

I wasn't sleeping with any of the other three—I was the fourth comrade. When Kenny and Phil had the first screening of their own films, we were all on the same program, premiering together. But when I left NYC, I was perhaps forgotten. I hadn't been a signatory on the grant applications (though co-author)—perhaps that was a serious mistake in modesty. When the ten-year retrospective of the Collective was put together, screenings held, a publication released, my work was excluded. This is actually a pretty significant pain in my life, because I was written out of that history.

In L.A. that kind of success for an experimental filmmaking theatre seems impossible. A group of filmmakers here founded the Independent Film Oasis of Los Angeles, but we only managed to survive for five years on grants. To whip up an audience for experimental film in this town is very difficult.

AK: How did you get to make your first experimental film?

AH: Having been sad and frustrated about the dance medium, I knew there was something else I had to do, but wasn't sure what that was, because I figured that, like the literature I was fond of, the painting I related most to, and the music that I liked, it had been done already. I am opposed to doing what is redundant.

Then I went to the State University of New York at Binghamton, where I thought I would study architecture. I happened to join a film club to see lots of films not otherwise available, and also took a film class. It turned out that Binghamton at that time was a hot spot for experimental film work in the United States. In the period of time I was at Binghamton, I got to see the vast bulk of what had been made in experimental film.

Ken Jacobs and Larry Gottheim were teaching experimental film. And everybody else in new filmmaking passed through: Hollis Frampton, Peter Kubelka, Michael Snow, Ernie Gehr, Stan Brakhage—everybody important came through there and some of them were people I spent a lot of time with.

I realized the full scope of the filmmaking medium as being as extraordinarily young as it is—less than a hundred years old—and the fact that some of it actually hadn't been done yet. And I discovered to my complete astonishment that the films dearest to me had not yet been made. This apparently was my task. And I'd better get down to work.

AK: You began filmmaking pretty much at the same time that the women's movement was taking off. All the examples you've mentioned have been male. But in forging your way as an experimental filmmaker, seeing films mainly by men, did you also feel that a woman's consciousness entered into that, or was that a separate issue?

AH: No, because some of those men that I've mentioned, their sensibility is perhaps of the sensitive, responsive nature that women are spoken of having.

AK: The androgyny of art.

AH: Exactly. I went to Binghamton in 1970 and I dropped out in 1971, after six months. I stayed there working with Ken Jacobs, but wasn't in his classes. I was working with Ken's 3-D shadow-play company, the New York Apparition Theater. We were doing visual experiments with shadows and colored light, and performing for children and adults. By 1972, I was living in New York, working full-time as a typist, founding the Collective For Living Cinema at night, and beginning to make films, initially in eight-millimeter, alone in my apartment on West 101st Street. I had an extremely minimal social life. I'd get together with the other Collective people to work, at other times wander around and talk with strangers, but essentially, I was in my apartment messing with the camera.

AK: Eight or Super 8?

AH: Regular eight. The reason I was attracted to regular eight is its beautiful symmetrical relationship to the other film formats, in that it is precisely half of 16mm. In fact, I bought my Rivas 16mm splicer, because I could cut eight on it, and also knew that I was going to shoot 16mm shortly.

AK: Can you discuss the transition from making your own films to doing camera work?

AH: It was natural to do camera work, because all of the preoccupations in my life had been visual. It was natural to move the camera, because I moved, and I lived completely in my eyes.

Since I was not a dancer at that point, but knew the pieces that the company did, I was made their lighting technician. I didn't design the lighting—I *performed* it. I ran all the light cues in the concert season.

I had always thought "technician" was a dirty word, because the guys who'd come in and run the cues were so insensitive to the music and to the imperative of a certain gesture, a certain movement and its necessary light. Dance is so vulnerable to variables beyond the performance. For example, you have ten people on the stage and they all lift and lean back. Perhaps the most significant thing in the composition is a space of six inches between their thoraxes and chins. If you're in an audience in proscenium arrangement, you only have a clue of this; and if there's a mistake in a lighting change, or loud accidental noise, even that clue may be lost.

I was suddenly thrust into the position of being a technician. So I said to myself, "No mistakes." The glory of running lighting changes on a dimmer gave outlet to something I had been playing with for years. That was my first official lighting kick.

AK: How did that move into camera work?

AH: Camera and lighting are parts of a whole. In this town, this is divided into two professions. So my time is split between being a gaffer and a cameraman.

Ever since I was little, I would turn off the overhead lights in a room, because I would be more interested in the light coming into the window, and I hated the way the overhead light blended with the color of the light coming in from outside. I didn't know anything about color temperature, I didn't know about film stock, or about the photoreactive qualities of chemicals. I just knew it aggravated me the way the different lights mixed. I'd turn off the overhead lights, and if there were Venetian blinds or curtains, I would sit and play with them. The adults were always asking, "Why are you sitting here in the dark?" I was regarded as a weird little girl for playing with light. It came as an immense surprise to me, years later, moving out to California, that I could actually make a living doing something that was my natural proclivity in the first place.

It was by necessity I had to pick up a camera, but I felt that it was an exclusive and occult sect of people who knew how to use them, and I didn't find anybody forthcoming with the knowledge. So I borrowed cameras and practiced shooting.

The first elaborate production I pursued was prompted by seeing Mikis Theodorakis in New York in 1972. I went to see him at Lincoln Center. His hands, when he conducts, seem animate objects unto themselves. I went to see him perform again, in Bridgeport, Connecticut, and afterwards spent time talking with some of the musicians. They said, "Why don't you come and film us in Philadelphia tomorrow?" It was Sunday, and I had to work at my typing job the next day. I thought, "My God, Theodorakis's hands. I've got to film his hands if he'll let me."

So at midnight I called Kenny Ross, one of my colleagues at the Collective. He had just bought a brand-new 16mm Beaulieu, and I had hardly even handled it. I said, "I need to borrow your camera. I realize it's a ridiculous request, but, on the other hand, all of the premises under which we established our organization and our friendship make it an unquestionable thing that you lend it to me." I'm not normally this forceful, but when you're on the crest of a wave, you do different things. I ran home and got the film stock together. I didn't sleep. I went to Theodorakis's hotel in the morning and called in sick from the lobby. While I was on the phone with my sympathetic supervisor, the dime dropped in the payphone. "Boy, what phone service!" she and I agreed. Then I went to Philadelphia on Theodorakis's bus.

What concerned me in *Filament* was the live, rebellious aspect of each of Theodorakis's hands. I had two film stocks: Plus-X and Tri-X. I went for progressively grainier stock, and I went with the stage lighting, facilitated, as I knew would be the case, by the fact that he wears dark clothes.

Needless to say, it was very charged at the shoot. And I was backstage. Being in the wings while he played this powerful political music, and hand-holding the camera the whole time was so electric, that static electricity passed through my hands into the camera. At certain gestures that he makes in his conducting—forceful and emphatic—there's a light streak, from the same side of the frame that he's facing, that looks like lightning bolts. Two or three times in the course of shooting, these sparks exposed on the film.

AK: I've never heard of anything like that.

AH: It is quite possible for static electricity in a camera to make an exposure on film. But at that time, I couldn't explain it except in mystical terms.

Entering the occult realm of technical knowledge seemed necessary to me, especially as an experimental filmmaker who might make a deliberate choice to do something that is not usual, or a choice to do something that looks more raw or less raw. It was never sufficient to me that someone would say, "You were lucky you got that effect." I decided I needed to get technically adept so I could be answerable for anything that I did—and be able to explain how I got it.

AK: Did the quest for technical knowledge prompt you to move to California?

AH: My parents had moved to California because of my father's work. I had decided to go back to school, to someplace where I would have an unquestionable right to handle film equipment. NYU had accepted me, but did not offer any financial assistance. My parents said, "UCLA is a state university. It only costs about $1,000 a year for residents." At that time, NYU was about $4,500, and there was no way I could afford that.

So I came to Los Angeles with the intent to get into UCLA, and did my undergraduate and graduate work there. What this meant was working on films. Because the only cinematography classes at the time were taught by a very charming Czechoslovakian gentleman, Frank Valert. He asserted in front of large groups of people that women could not do cinematography. I liked his manner of presentation in discussing technical aspects of how film is exposed, but I got virtually nothing from him except explicit discouragement.

I shot a little film test that I thought was hysterically funny, called *Plausible Light Source*. It's a garbage can seen through a doorway, and it's got a bright strip down the right side as if it is being hit by light from the side. Someone walks through the door and turns the can, revealing the fact that this stripe of light is actually a spray-painted line. It was a one-liner, but Valert didn't get it, though others did. I don't think he was that astute about light. Not only that, he was also a very negative force, since he was the only cinematography teacher at UCLA for years and years, and UCLA was an important doorway.

One day this girl came up to me, practically weeping. She'd gone to apply for the class, and after the first class, she went up to have Valert sign her paperwork. He declined to do so. He said, "There are already too many women in the class." She said, "But, there aren't even fifty percent." He said, "That's enough—a woman can't do it anyway."

So I basically learned by working on shoots, initially on student films, and then on professional ones. My family thought it was a joke—and a big problem, that I would work for free to learn something.

There are artists like Shirley Clarke who felt they had to do a crazy-lady act in order to be taken seriously as an artist. Shirley's one of the least crazy people I ever met in my life. She's totally brilliant and clear-thinking.[2] Yet it is easy for either of us to fall for an image of ourselves as nuts, when friends say, "How come you're spending your time doing art and not making a living doing something more secure? You're crazy!" It's really a hoax.

I'd literally be setting a light and have a DP look at me and just shake his head and walk away and ask someone else to set that light. It was nothing personal; it's just that he didn't like seeing a woman with equipment. And that was very depressing.

Later, I was surprised to learn that I could actually make a living doing lighting and camera work, honing my technical abilities, and getting my hands on the tools.

I have developed a certain sense of machisma in order to do this job, because I am frequently the only woman in the light/camera crew. Machisma is bravado—it's a stance. You put your boots on; you put your gloves on.

I've been on sets where people have said, "My God, I've never seen a woman work this hard," because I'm carrying two HMI ballasts or moving 10-Ks around, and I say, "Don't be silly. Haven't you ever seen a mother with a two-year-old?"

I feel that I'm paying financially for the fact that people aren't used to seeing a woman with a camera. On the other hand, I think it's sexy to see a woman carrying a piece of camera equipment, especially if she's not nervous about how she looks.

People, in particular grips, rent-a-cops, and firemen, tend to make remarks. A lewd remark could put me out of commission conversationally for half an hour. I was verbally a prude. I found that this was quite a liability in a business where, especially the later it gets in the course of a day's work, the more the jokes turn to sex. So I've developed the ability not to blush. I've also learned the art of making a grip blush.

Once a sound man who is a rather racy individual actually put his hands on me as we passed in a doorway when the whole crew was leaving for lunch. My impulse, as an older sister and as a New Yorker is, if you put your hands on me when you're not invited, you'll get slugged. But I was carrying a 2-K [a 2,000 watt light] and my hands were both engaged, when he put his arms around me in a full-bodied hug. I didn't want to insult his apparently fragile self, nor ruin the good feeling of the crew as a whole, so I said, "Don't turn on equipment you don't know how to operate." He was dismantled, and dropped me like a hot potato, and everyone laughed. He understood me—after all, he owns his own Nagra, and wouldn't want anyone touching it.

AK: What do you think it will take to get the camerawomen to be treated equally to cameramen?

AH: Discrimination against women in the industry is a monstrous but surmountable obstacle. I think the tendency to hire men and to have men in that position is such a strong precedent that it's been almost a vertical climb.

The sensitivity of women to camera and lighting is equal to or greater than that of men. It's proven time and time again by their work. It's just that the opportunities to do the work are rare. I think it's important that Behind the Lens exists, because there's no other old girls' club for cinematography in a town full of old boys' clubs.

AK: Could you describe the support that you've gotten from other people in pursuing camera work?

AH: Well, the specific support in camera work was from either other experimental filmmakers who knew that my work was good, or from strangers. People like Pat and Beverly O'Neill—cofounders of the Oasis in Los Angeles—Bill Moritz and Chick Strand gave support and trust, and occasionally loaned equipment. Baird Bryant, a wonderful cameraman who shot *The Cool World* for Shirley Clarke, hired me often to light and assist him.

Collaborating with brilliant people on their work has been very satisfying and supportive of my own—gaffing for Charles Burnett on his film *My Brother's Wedding*, for example.

I'm committed to making films about normalizing race relations. That's why I've worked at such financial disadvantage on certain films, in particular for Charles Burnett, Julie Dash, and Barbara McCullough. Although I work on all kinds of B material involving certain aspects of violence and drugs, for any film that is about race relations, no matter how small my technical role is on the crew, I will read the script first, because I will not in any way lend my energy to anything that is racist.

I'm also committed to films which normalize sexual relationships. The industry as it exists has barely scratched the surface of what an active female sexual appetite is. It's usually addressed, usually by men, as something frightening. Hopefully, understanding between men and women on this particular score will remove some of the bullshit that has been contrived as the so-called "war between the sexes."

AK: You've worked as an assistant cameraperson and gaffer as well as a cinematographer. How are these roles different?

AH: I'm more comfortable with myself as a gaffer/camera operator/ DP than I am as an assistant, because I don't think I am a good enough monk to be an impeccable camera assistant. Being a camera assistant takes a very particular talent and personality that's both unflappable and focused. It's the most responsible position on the set, really, and I admire it immensely. I can think of several people who are much better camera assistants than I am.

As a lighting cinematographer, however, the feeling of shooting something and framing everything is incomparable. I get as much satisfaction working as a gaffer to another cameraman with whom I have harmonious visual sense. I love that as much as I do shooting.

AK: You've been shooting your own film for the last several years.

AH: Yes. I'm about to get it printed, finally.[3] *Falling Lessons* is a film about eye contact and fear. And about longing and impermanence.

I've been very slow and nonaggressive in my manner of getting the film made. It will have taken me more than twelve years when I finally get a print of this film. On the one hand, I have remained responsive to the genuine impulse that fuels the film, and on the other hand, I haven't compromised anything that it demanded. So I've traded off in time. I'm much older now than I would have liked to have been when showing this film. But the payoff is the existence of a unique work. Mortality being what it is, I've been lucky that it's come to the point where I can have a print in a conceivable amount of time.

NOTES

1. Kevin Thomas, "Screening Room: 'Rhinoskin' Takes a Funny Look at an Actor's Life," *Los Angeles Times*, Calendar Section (Monday, March 27, 1995): F13.

2. "If your goal is a certain goal, you go right ahead getting it, and let them think whatever they want." Shirley Clarke, quoted in "A Conversation," by Storm De Hirsch and Shirley Clarke, in *Women and the Cinema: A Critical Anthology*, ed. Karyn Kay and Gerald Peary (New York: E. P. Dutton, 1977), 242 (abridged from *Film Culture*, no. 46 [autumn 1967] published October 1967).

3. *Falling Lessons* premiered in Los Angeles in 1995.

Nancy Schreiber, ASC

I met Nancy Schreiber on Karen Sperling's all-woman 35mm feature, *The Waiting Room*, in 1973, in New York—she was co-gaffer with Celeste Gainey, and I was the dolly grip. Shortly afterwards, she left for China to work on Shirley MacLaine's first documentary, and continued to work on all-women crews, in addition to gaffing and camera assisting on mixed crews, often as the one female member of the electric department.

In 1979, Nancy bought a 16mm Eclair. She started making her own film the following year, *Possum Living*, which won a Blue Ribbon in the American Film Festival. After several years successfully working as a New York-based director/cinematographer, she decided to focus her career on camera work, shooting a western in 1979 and other features since 1986. She joined IA 644 in the mid-1980s, after many years in NABET. Additionally, she shot numerous documentaries, television specials, music videos, and commercials, often hiring women as her camera assistants, and bought her own Aaton.

Some of the music specials she shot include long forms for Van Morrison and Billy Joel; the Amnesty International World Tour 1988 with Springsteen, Sting, Peter Gabriel, and Tracy Chapman; Sting's *One World*; and "Bruce Springsteen: The Conscience of America" for *Twenty/Twenty*. Her impressive list of documentary credits includes the Emmy Award–winning "Abortion Clinic" (shot for PBS's *Frontline*), *Through the Wire*, *Liberators*; and, most recently, *Visions of Light: The Art of Cinematography*, shot in high-definition video; *The Celluloid Closet*; and *The Good, the Bad and the Beautiful*.

Nancy has become increasingly involved in dramatic films, moving to Los Angeles to further her feature film career. She has worked as director of photography on such films as *The Obit Writer*, starring Mira Sorvino; *Scorpion Sting*; *Curse of Inferno*; and *Lush Life*, for Showtime. In 1994, she received an Independent Feature Project Spirit Award nomination for *Chain of Desire*. She was recently voted into the American Society of Cinematographers.

AK: How did you first get into camera work?

NS: I had been living in Ann Arbor, making underground films with a group called Ann Arbor Eye. As a kid, I did a lot of drawing and painting, and I was going to art school on weekends. My mother was an art dealer, and she worked at a museum, so there was always art around. Then in college I did a lot of still photography. I've always expressed my feelings by painting with light and color.

In 1972, I came to New York and took a six-week crash course in filmmaking at New York Institute of Photography. Then I answered an ad in the *Village Voice* to be a production assistant on a 35mm feature, *Werewolf of Washington*, starring Dean Stockwell, with Milton Moses Ginsberg directing. He had directed *Coming Apart* with Rip Torn, and he had an underground following. This film was very low-budget and undercrewed, so during preproduction I did everything from props to getting wardrobe to being the Best Boy.

Growing up in a middle-class Jewish home, I knew nothing about electricity and tools. I remember the first time I fixed a telephone, I thought that magic had happened [*laughs*]. It was a miracle. It was very exciting to have hands-on experience in what was considered a male domain.

My career as a gaffer just took off. By the second year, I was already gaffing a 35mm feature. I had really very little problem getting hired by men. Maybe because they heard I was good and fast. I was generally the only woman.

When I went to China with Shirley MacLaine on an all-women documentary, there were four of us. We all became really friendly, and that was terrific. Joan Weidman, the cinematographer, must have found it really rough to sustain being a woman DP at that time. (She later became a successful production manager and producer, and currently works for a completion bond company.) Claudia Weill was the director and main cameraperson. I was hired as the AC/Gaffer, so I had to load two cameras and gaff. And Cabel Smith was the sound recordist.

I never really wanted to be an AC, because I have this visual background, and I mostly was interested in light. Only on these low-budget documentaries—like Shirley MacLaine's and Joyce Chopra's film for the Ford Foundation in Africa—was I doing two jobs. The camera equipment, I just figured I would pick up along the way, or have a great AC, you know, when I was shooting.

Numerous commercials were happening in New York in the early seventies, and it was wonderful working as a gaffer. But I realized that certain people I was working for didn't know how to light, and they were getting all the credit for the lighting. I thought, "Wait a second, something is wrong here—this is the time to make my move." So in '79 I bought a 16mm camera, an old Eclair, and I started trying to get shooting work.

I decided in '79 to make my own film. Part of why I did it was to show those people that, yeah, I could do documentaries if that was where the work was. I could compete with the guys. Documentaries were the most open arena for accepting women as directors, producers, and DPs. So I raised the money, and produced, directed, and photographed this documentary called *Possum Living*, and it became very successful. It got a lot of awards, and was featured at New Directors/New Films at the Museum of Modern Art, but I didn't want to go on being a director.

I went on to make a couple more films as a director-cameraperson. I realized that people were having a hard time categorizing what I did, in that, if you wanted to shoot, you just couldn't direct and shoot, although I worked with Marlo Thomas on a children's special in that capacity. If people thought of me as a director, they really didn't think I was serious about being a DP.

In 1982, I said, "Wait, something's going on here—I really want to be shooting features." So I started shooting low-budget dramatic films, while shooting a lot of documentaries. I always operated myself, as a DP. I worked on *Middletown, USA* for Peter Davis, and two *Frontlines*, including "Abortion Clinic," which was very successful. I was content that I had made the right decision to just follow one path, so people wouldn't get confused, and directors wouldn't get threatened that I knew more than they did as a director.

Being a DP is a lot about taking risks, pushing oneself beyond what's comfortable, whether it be in composition, choice of lenses, lighting, or the kind of movement or nonmovement. The scene usually dictates the normal choices, but I like to work with the director to go beyond "normal" and yet still have "the look" remain unobtrusive and organic to the story the director is telling.

My job is also very much about "process." That's why I love prelighting. I'll have a blueprint before a shoot (i.e., a lighting diagram or a concept), and work from that with an open mind and open eye and heart. That's where the true creativity comes in—being spontaneous as I build the light in a room, layer upon layer, until it's somewhat polished. At some point I know it's time to stop. (Often it's the nature of the schedule or the A.D. [Assistant Director] which dictates the end of my prelight.)

I also work very closely with the production designer, and feel the exchange of ideas *early on* in preproduction is crucial. Too often DPs aren't given enough prep time, so that preproduction becomes a bit hassled.

In the last few years I've really turned things around in terms of the amount of dramatic work I've done.

AK: What kinds of support have you found in your work?

NS: None [*laughs*]. I remember once showing up at my mother's in Florida—I was a gaffer then—with the AC and cameraman and all this equipment. My mother was just horrified. She had no idea what I did. It's hard. In fact, my mother kept asking why I didn't get a full-time job—you know, "Isn't it time you settled down?" I'd say, "Mother, what I do, there are no full-time jobs." So she'd say, "Maybe you should look into another line of work." [*laughs*] She's more accepting now.

I think they felt bad for me that I was still alone in my life. That relationships hadn't worked out because I was on the road for two months at a time on a feature. Guys seemed a bit miffed when they perceived I put my career first. And it is true, that the camerawomen I know didn't have relationships, and sound women I know all did. I took my own little survey.

This has changed. I do have love in my life today, and other women DPs likewise are in relationships. Maybe we all had to get successful before we felt comfortable enough to turn down work and be with our significant others.

AK: What about support from other crew members?

NS: Oh sure, absolutely. Mark Obenhaus was very supportive. He would loan me his camera, before I had my own. If I ever had a mentor, he would probably be it.

Occasionally I used to work with crews that had attitudes. Like I went to Florida for a big shoot down there, and I had to use a local crew. When I arrived to go scouting with the director, the gaffer, and the grip, these guys were 300-pound, typical teamster types. My first reaction was to be totally scared, but I just got over it and showed them that I knew what I was doing, equipment-wise. By the end of that shooting day, I knew I had their respect. By the end of the shoot, we were like old buddies. And it was a wonderful feeling.

You have to push through that fear. You really do. I remember being kidded a lot as a gaffer, because I was always shooting in midtown high-rise buildings, and they would say, "We're not going to let a woman tie into the power." It was very difficult. I had to stand my ground. I would put this hard front on, and show that I knew what I was talking about by rattling off a lot of electrical knowledge. I just had to really, really believe in myself.

I remember when I first got into NABET in 1974, somebody on the board asked me how much I weighed, because in those days, people were still using Arcs, and they worried that I wouldn't be able to pick one up. I said, "I don't think any man picks one up by himself anyway."

Then I moved up as a cinematographer, and a couple of years later, I got classified as a DP. I was the only woman DP in NABET for a while. There were lots of women in IA. It's probably one of the reasons why I wanted to join IA, so I wouldn't be all alone.

AK: You've talked mainly about the fact that you know a lot of supportive crew members. But what about the situations where you encountered discrimination?

NS: Usually, once I'm hired, I'm able to turn things around. But I've had a lot of problems getting hired as a shooter, because it's the power position on the crew. I run a crew and men have to listen to me and what I want to do. I have to be a diplomat. I have to know how to deal with the production people and stay on time and on budget. Once I get hired it's fine, because I've learned how to be assertive without being aggressive, because they hate aggressive women. If men are ornery, they can get away with it more than a woman—they're considered artistic [*chuckles*].

AK: Do you get paid as much for your work as a man?

NS: I think I do. I've heard sometimes people say I'm expensive, but it's just what men are getting. It varies. I don't do much documentary work anymore, but on low-budget documentary films, it's $750 to $1,500 a day with gear. One week recently, I worked for a woman director who had no money. I was working for free, because I really liked her, and I liked the project, and there were a lot of women on it. Now I'm trying to be more careful, because I have an agent who gets her ten percent, so I can't always afford to shoot low-budget films.

AK: What does it mean to you to work with other women on the set?

NS: Well, I remember once when I hadn't been shooting all that long, I preferred hiring a woman assistant. I never really realized until later what a political statement that was. Hiring me as a DP was probably a big thing for the company, anyway. And once getting over that barrier, my showing up with a woman assistant must have blown a lot of people away.

AK: What was the political message, to them?

NS: That I was a feminist, and I didn't care how it "looked." I've heard of a case of a film with a woman director, and the company didn't want another woman on the set. They thought that that wouldn't look good for the producer or the company. So there is definitely discrimination. But you can't dwell on that.

There was that time in the early '70s and '80s when we all worked on lots of underfunded, all-women films. Then I made it in the man's world, and got fair pay. And that was very gratifying. Now, there is more integration of women into the mainstream. I still work on a few all-women things. You know, it's not seen as a political statement as much, although obviously it is.

I remember that on this Pink Floyd job, out of fourteen camera operators, I was the only woman. I noticed that the women ACs were very nurturing. Even though they were technicians, they were in that role again, of helping the men.

Everything that we do as women is judged when the next woman comes around. For example, there's a woman who shot a film who didn't do a very good job, and it was very hard for any other woman after that to go into this production house. And you know it wouldn't happen for men. On the other hand, there seems to be a lot more camaraderie among women than among men. Men seem so much more competitive about making it.

I think the most frustrating experience in trying to make it as a DP in features has been watching the men who were former assistants or gaffers start shooting and have their careers take off, when they have a lot less experience and I know my eye is as good or better. I'm not the only woman that's seen this. I mean, you hear about these twenty-five-year-old wonders, but you can't have the anger, because it doesn't get you anywhere.

AK: Your resumé is a testament to focusing on the progress instead of things that don't come your way.

NS: Right. But believe me, I beat myself up a lot about why I didn't get this job or that job. It solves nothing; it's nonproductive. Men go through that, too, but I really believe that it's easier for them. It's still a male profession.

Jo Carson

After studying film at UCLA, Jo Carson's technical excellence drew her from freelance cinematography and producing to full-time special effects work. Some of her experience in special effects has included working as a lighting camera operator on Tim Burton's *The Nightmare Before Christmas*, assisting Harry Walton for Phil Tippet on the two-headed monster sequence of *Willow*, shooting DNA models for *The Infinite Voyage*, and lighting and shooting the bumblebee sequence for *Honey, I Shrunk the Kids*. As Camera Operator and Head of Matte Photography at Industrial Light and Magic's (ILM) Matte Department, she worked on *Kurosawa's "Dreams"* and other films.

In addition to special effects camera work, Jo Carson has also shot numerous live action films, beginning with her own prizewinning documentary about Nepal—*Himalayan Pilgrimage*—and *Private Spy*. She has also worked as Director/Cinematographer on *Dancing with Gaia*, a documentary on the reemergent goddess, filmed in the prehistoric sacred sites of North America, Western Europe, and the Mediterranean. Most recently she worked as a lighting camera operator on *James and the Giant Peach*, under Director of Photography Pete Kozachik.

As President of Behind the Lens, Jo Carson encouraged IA 659 to open the Camera Assistant Training Program and a Loader Training Program to more women, and helped many camerawomen find work. Throughout her efforts ran a special brand of understated, cordial feminism, the effectiveness of which would have made her great-great-grandmother, Mary Wollstonecraft, proud.

AK: It's interesting that you are a descendant of Mary Wollstonecraft. When you were a young woman, society was again promoting the concept of women doing whatever they wanted to do, and people like Mary Wollstonecraft were being taken very seriously. I was reading in Wollstonecraft's A *Vindication of the Rights of Woman*,[1] first published in 1790, how many women waste their lives away, who couldn't practice as doctors, or farm managers, or whatever. Instead, they "hang their heads, surcharged with the dew of sensibility that consumes the beauty to which at first gave luster." First of all, she's talking about women whose lives are spent as beautiful objects for male consumption instead of in careers. Second, the "surcharge of sensibility" traditionally could not be used by women in their work. Third, she's talking about being an object of beauty instead of creating something of beauty. Camerawomen are, in fact, concerned with creating images of beauty, using a highly developed "sensibility," in order to do technical, creative work. Do you ever put your own career into the context of feminist history?

JC: As one of the pioneering feminists, Mary Wollstonecraft began to unlock certain doors. I suppose that I wouldn't have the opportunities that I have today if people like Mary Wollstonecraft hadn't spoken out as they did.

I seem to have, on my mother's side, an interesting lineage of women who are strong, artistically inclined, or artistically capable. My grandmother was a landscape painter, and she worked in a photographic studio, which was very unusual in her time.

My mother was the editor of the college newspaper at San Francisco State, and then she traveled as a journalist and reporter. My mother raised me with the encouragement to pursue whatever was in me to do. I think I got lucky, because there aren't that many children raised that way.

AK: What attracted you to shooting film to begin with?

JC: As a little girl, I could draw and sculpt things that adults gave me a lot of pats on the back for. I assumed for a long time that I would grow up to be an artist. But when I was in my first year of college, I realized that the art scene was very static.

I was very impressed with Jim Morrison's poetry, as well as his music. *He* was going to UCLA Film School, and so I thought, if it's good enough for him, it's good enough for me. I applied and was accepted to UCLA Film School starting my sophomore year of college.

When I was going to UCLA, I went to Nepal for three months and shot a documentary—actually, to be accurate, I should say I did *half* the camera work. Then I came back and edited it into a film.

I didn't actually do the opticals on that film, but I ordered all the opticals and hung out with the fellow who was doing them. It was a tiny company called Universal Space-Time Sea Pig Optical Printing Company. I liked the people that were running it, so I got involved in learning how to do optical printing. I bought a J.K. optical printer, and I did a lot of opticals for other students and for local educational documentary and 16mm type of customers. I guess that's really how I first got involved with special effects.

I didn't feel any restrictions at that time—we're talking about the early '70s—because of my gender. It wasn't until I was out in the professional world, trying to get involved in camera work, that I started realizing that I was trying to enter an extremely male-dominated profession, and that if I wanted to do it, it wasn't going to be easy.

When I first started thinking seriously about doing camera work professionally, there were just no women that I'd heard of, except Leslie Hill, who had gotten in on the Camera Assistants' Training Program. I was working in the mail room at Universal Studios. I would go and hang around the camera department and offer to load magazines for free, and the guys would say, "Sure, sure, sure—and by the way, what are you doing for dinner tonight?" That was depressing, and I began to think of it as knocking my head on a stone wall. So after an initial foray into trying to get involved in camera work, I backed off for several years.

What happened was, I was able to show one of the student films that I had made at UCLA to Joe Hiatt, the head of the studio facility at Universal Studios at that time. I was able to meet him through becoming friendly with his secretary. He looked at my student film, and loved it.

They opened up a new company in the summer of '78, doing *Buck Rogers* and *Galactica*. They didn't know me from anybody, but they needed a production assistant. Joe Hiatt said, "This is the person that you're going to have as your production assistant." I don't think that they were that thrilled, but they went along with it. Soon I was trained to be a production coordinator there.

Once I got on the effects stages, it was a whole other story. I mean, there were those blue screens—that magical blue! I just loved it! I started hanging around the stages after work. I would ask questions like, "Hey, what's that? How does it work?" The guys took to having me there, and as time went by, I would get so I was punching the buttons on the computers and learning how to do basic elements of camera work.

Somewhere around that time, good ol' Estelle [Kirsh] got me on this low bucks or no bucks feature as a second assistant trainee. Most of the time I was loading and unloading magazines—she really taught me how to do it. Estelle had been in the Camera Assistants' Training Program herself, and she really knew her stuff.

Then I got work in special effects. I produced several commercials that were special effects commercials, one of which was an International Clio Award–winner for Lego Toys. That was the first time—1980 or so—that anybody had ever put stepper motors and a motion-control computer onto a pitching lens with a snorkel type of arrangement. The people who came to me had looked all over the world trying to find somebody who could put this together for them. I was working with some very good people—Richard Bennett at Cinema Engineering, and David Stipes, who had many years in special effects' camera work, and Continental Camera's pitching lens, which is Bob Nettman's invention—and we all worked together to set it up. It was kind of a coup.

And then there were these motion-control images of the space shuttle, and what it was going to do on its voyage. I produced that show for Metavision, and got very involved in assisting on the camera work. And later on, I actually shot quite a bit of footage for that same space shuttle—lighting and shooting the model.

I was very proud of the space shuttle. All that work was wonderful stuff, and very significant historically. And it got played all around the world. When the space shuttle first went up, and it went out of camera range, all these different TV stations cut to our footage. There were millions of people watching this very pretty footage that we shot. I felt really proud about that.

At David Stipes', we were doing a lot of special effect shows for Universal, Dino de Laurentiis, and other people. I got a couple of years' experience doing motion control, and lighting and shooting miniatures, high-speed shots and explosions, doing rear-screen projections involving adding live action elements to matte paintings and adding foreground miniature elements, and doing motion control moves on r.p. [rear projection] set-ups.

I also did some live action gigs. Then I got in at Introvision as a camera assistant for two years. I used their big dual matting front screen projection system, which allows people to appear to walk around in environments that literally never existed except as miniatures or photographs.

Later, I got this offer to go up to Industrial Light and Magic, and I couldn't refuse it. I worked as an assistant on *Star Trek IV*, the movie, on *Willow*, and on *Innerspace*. My cameraman on *Innerspace* was Joe Fante. We shot the artery raceway sequence, which was like you're inside the guy's blood vessels, and you see all the blood going past you at a horrendous rate. I also worked as effects operator on *Honey, I Shrunk the Kids*, and as operator on *The Infinite Voyage* for WQED-TV.

It's a great feeling when you've spent a long time—as on *The Infinite Voyage*—working on an 84-pass shot on 360 frames of film.

Basically, a special effects assistant does very similar things that they do in live action. You keep more elaborate camera reports and very extensive camera logs, however, so you can go back and repeat situations. You are also in charge of changing lenses and filters and setting up the magazines, loading the magazines and lacing the film into the camera, and all the kinds of things that an assistant normally does. And then you wind up getting involved in moving the C-stands or sandbags or whatever, rolling whole model movers from one stage to another, setting up shots, and rigging them. (A model mover, in this case, is a computerized mechanical rig that can move a model in three-dimensional space—east-west, north-south, pan, yaw, or roll.)

They do have stagehands there, who are called stage technicians, who do lighting and grip work. But sometimes they're not there, like on the night crew, and I worked on the night crew for a long time on *Star Trek*. So then you just do it yourself, from four or five in the evening until you're finished—hopefully one, maybe three, once in a blue moon seven in the morning.

It's easy to remember the sequence of events dealing with all the effects houses that I've worked at, because each one is a long event—we're talking years. The live action things that I've done, although numerous, tend to get wedged in between all those effects gigs.

I think I'm at the point, and I have been for some time, that I'm not afraid of any camera. I mean, if someone wants me to shoot something, what camera it is is not a problem because I've learned the principles behind how cameras work. Beyond that, it's just a matter of picking up the particular camera and going, "Oh, OK, this is this camera and this is where *this* button is on this camera."

In terms of special effects equipment, I own a Mitchell motion picture camera. Those are very commonly used to shoot special effects with because the registration's the best. And then I've had a lot of experience with Vistavision cameras both at Introvision and at ILM.

Two other women worked at ILM in the past that I'm aware of—Mary Anne Evans and Bess Wiley. While I was working there, there were another two women, out of maybe twenty people in the camera department, depending on the show we're doing, but neither of them are working there right now.

There might be some other woman out there who is as involved in special effects camera work as I am, but if she exists, I don't know about her. I don't know of any who have made the kind of commitment I have over the years to this kind of work specifically.

Only occasionally have I felt that my being a woman is a problem in special effects. Like when they want to send a crew on location to shoot plates, they all usually overlook me. By "they," I just mean the generic "they"—I'm not referring to anyone specifically. People get used to seeing me on a stage. They think that I'm not really capable of going out on a remote location, which considering my experience in Nepal, is really not an appropriate thing to think about me. But people don't know.

AK: How have you handled stress as a camerawoman?

JC: Badly! I internalize it. And I think that's true of most people when they're under stress. You can't have a tantrum on the set—no way. You have to figure out some way of maintaining a professional attitude, get the job done, and try to make it easy for people to work with you, because that's the most important thing. You want people to like you because you want to have a good on-set camaraderie—just like everybody else does. But sometimes I give away my authority. It takes me a little while to even recognize that I've done that, because I have very much of a "going along" attitude. So sometimes I will go along with something as if it's a reasonable suggestion, when in fact it's not an appropriate suggestion, given that I am in charge.

I've never actually fired anybody for being "insubordinate." "Insubordinate" is an extreme word. We have occasionally come to a parting of the ways.

I really like camera work. It's so technical and specific and hands-on. You get a sense of satisfaction from physically doing the work. And the people in the field are great. The awards that I've gotten are a source of satisfaction. I got an Emmy for camera operating at Introvision on *Huggabunch*, and these things make you feel like your work is appreciated. That's important to all of us.

In live action, I think camera operating, lighting, and shooting are just wonderful. You have this opportunity to use your eyes, and to work with people who are there to help, that want to do the job. A couple of weeks go by on a set, and you get real close with each other, and you know what people can do, and you know what you can ask of them, and it gets to be this functioning unit—this machine, almost. That's a real nice feeling—the camaraderie.

As a camera operator on Tim Burton's *The Nightmare Before Christmas*, I was usually responsible for three sets at a time. Like most large special effects shows, the daily work of lighting was pretty much up to the camera operators. It was my job to light the shot, set up and program any motion control moves, and work with the animator to compose the framing in a way that would work with the moving puppets. Pete Kozachik, the Director of Photography, worked closely with all the camera operators to maintain the look and visual continuity of the whole show. Pete was in close communication with the director, Henry Selick, and often served as our liaison to him. I enjoyed helping create the look of *Nightmare*. I always want to be as unbiased as possible when it comes to interpreting a director's vision. The fun and challenge of my job is to be flexible and open to seeing, and creating, a wide variety of "looks."

I've been supporting myself with this for a long time. I think that if, in fact, I were a man and had the exact same experience and commitment level, I might very well be getting more money for doing the same thing, or very similar things but with a different title. But it's not something I think about often.

NOTE

1. Mary Wollstonecraft, *A Vindication of the Rights of Woman* (Buffalo, New York: Prometheus Books, 1989).

IV

EMERGING CAMERAWOMEN

I think 1,800 people actually took the test. They only took seven people, that time. . . . In the live action category, I was the only woman they took.

Sabrina Simmons

At some point you have to decide as a parent, what's more important, my kid or my career. I always opted for my kid. Now that she is old enough to go off and do her own thing, I get to opt for my career.

Sandy Butler

I set myself a goal that I was going to be in the International Photographers Guild by the time I was twenty-six. I got in a week before I turned twenty-seven.

Alicia Sehring

Sabrina Simmons

Sabrina Simmons studied filmmaking at the University of Southern California. Upon graduation, she found herself one of 1,800 people taking the Camera Assistant Training Program test. She was one of seven people to be accepted into the program in the live action category, and the only woman. After successfully completing her training, she joined IA 659 and began to work at Paramount Studios on *Mork and Mindy*. Since then she has assisted on numerous television shows, including *Air Wolf* and *Dukes of Hazzard*; movies of the week, including *Polly*, *One More Time* and *Leave Her to Heaven*; and feature films including *Bird*, *Impulse*, *Miracle in the Wilderness*, and *White Men Can't Jump*.

One of the only African American women who have had a successful career as a camera assistant on union films,[1] Sabrina has been working as a second camera assistant for six years, and as a first camera assistant for over ten years. She has also been producing and directing independent projects, including a commercial for the Hispanic Language AIDS Hotline Project. She has most recently directed the documentary *Sistuhs: Mothers, Daughters, Wives.*

AK: How did you get interested in camera work?

SS: I was at USC, and started taking film classes. Everybody wanted to be a director. Common sense said you can only have so many directing this project. So I started doing camera stuff in school. One of the camerapeople came to a lecture/seminar class one day and invited me to watch them shoot a two-day commercial. I then started talking to a PA who wanted to get into camera in the worst way. He asked if I had heard about the "Lucky Ten." This is a program for camera assistants offered by Contract Services where they take ten people—thereby the Lucky Ten.

So I turned the paperwork in and took the test. I think 1,800 people actually took the test. They only took seven people, that time. In the live action category, they took seven people. I was the only woman they took.

We did the program for a year. They had strikes galore during our testing and our training program. We got out and there was no work anywhere.

I ran around a lot trying to get work at Universal and CBS. I had done a lot of television during my training, and it seemed clear to me that the only way you could get a shot was if somebody died. Because these people just did not leave their jobs, as far as I could tell.

I didn't feel like I could schmooze with the boys because I wasn't into football and they weren't going to invite a girl over to the family barbecue unless I had a husband to bring with me. I felt like an outsider a little bit.

One day I just happened into Dick Barlow [in charge of hiring at CBS]. He had this way of making you feel like you were nothing. Instead, I acted very cheerful and said, "Oh, no, everything is great. I'm working on this other show over here, you know." I was very up, and two days later my phone rings. "Can you come in for some day calls on this stuff?" I couldn't believe it. Success attracts more success, I guess. Anyway, that's how I got started. I started meeting people through day calls.

AK: Describe the resistance and support that you've gotten from various people.

SS: I don't like to sort it out and say these people were supportive and these people were a hindrance. I'm not consciously aware of these things. I just kind of float through and if nothing really sort of comes by and beats me on the head—something horrible—I don't really pay it a lot of attention.

Now that I think about it, I did have a couple of people do some bizarre things to me. I ended up leaving the show. I just thought these people are crazy, and it's better not to be around them. That was the first experience.

The second experience was more like, "I don't need this. This is ridiculous. You find yourself someone else to beat on tomorrow, because I won't be here." I took all my stuff out of the dark room and said, "You go find yourself somebody else."

From that day on, I haven't dealt with any more hideous people. That really colors how I feel about my work situation overall. You meet a lot of people with mental problems who take them out on their camera assistants, and you feel like you can't say anything because they'll take the job away. If you think like that, then it'll make you crazy too.

The last three or four years, I've met really great, pleasant people. Some people I even consider my friends now. I didn't used to do that. I just considered them my coworkers. I'm getting more work with people who are great technicians and have wonderful personalities.

AK: What makes for a wonderful personality?

SS: Good sense of humor and even-tempered. Knowing when something is important and when it's not important. Allowing the other person to have space. To be able to have faith in the person you hired to work with you.

I had this one man who would send me out to the truck to get something that was already in his front box. Meanwhile, they're yelling, "Marks," and he stands right there next to the camera and he's not putting down marks. Dick Barlow would come on the stage and say, "Where's your second? Where's Sabrina? and he would say, "I don't know." I mean, he would do crazy stuff like that, and I'd let it roll off me. I had no idea this was happening when it was happening. I found all that out later, after I left.

I always got to work before him. One day I get there early, I take the equipment inside and put it on the cart. I'm putting the Panahead on the dolly. Here comes this guy walking towards me. I'm saying, "Hi. Good morning." You know, in very good spirits. He stomps up and yells to me in the most vehement voice. "I'm not the prick you think I am!" I was so taken aback.

I thought, he can't be talking to me. I look behind me and there's nobody there. I couldn't believe this man. I didn't know what to say. It was so crazy. So I said, "I haven't said anything about you. Why are you acting like this?"

I was generally always around the camera. This guy wasn't. So the operator started saying, "She's really good. She's better than the First." I think what was really happening is that the operator was saying bad things about this guy and somehow it was getting back to him. In the translation it was turning out that I was saying something. I don't know. Maybe he was afraid of losing his job. That's me trying to make some intelligent reasoning to his insane behavior. Because all I saw was the insane behavior.

I don't remember what I did after that. I guess I did a movie of the week or something, and got in with these other people who were pleasant and nice to work with.

I think what people have said about "Never leave a show. It's better to be fired than to quit," that's just a crock. If people are really abusing you and you're absolutely miserable, you're not doing a good job anyway. So why should you stay and brutalize yourself? It's not worth it.

My support comes from my peers encouraging me to go do shots and telling me that I'm ready. They'll say, "Come out of that darkroom and go do this shot." They will ask me if I want to do a shot instead of making me beg them to do it. It's more that they are offering me the chance to do it.

The guy I'm with now, Tony Rivetti, is an amazing assistant. His camera abilities are breathtaking. The most complicated, difficult shots, he can literally walk in, sight unseen, and do a perfect job. His confidence results in his telling me, "I have to go do something else. Cover the rehearsal for me." If I did a rehearsal for him, he could come back and I could tell him, "That person is 5'4. Over here we're 8'6. Over there it's 7'9." He would go, "Okay, fine. We're ready to do the shot." It's those little, tiny things that add up and make you feel like you're capable of doing the job and that you're good.

Being an assistant doesn't call for any real creativity or anything. Once you've got it down, you've got it down. Maybe people become restless a little too quickly because it's not that much of a challenge. But you can see the difference in an operator, cameraman, or first assistant who's never done the job alone. They're so much more difficult to work with. I didn't want to be one of those people who are made fun of behind their backs because they made mistakes. If they had just done the job alone a little while longer, they wouldn't even think of these stupid things they are doing.

You may get a show and have the director stand there and say, "Yeah. The top of that peak up there is where we want to stand and get the shot." A cameraman who has never been an assistant or an operator will say, "Yep, let's haul it up there." He gets in the jeep with the director and they go get the shot. Someone who's done those lower jobs before is more likely to say to the director, "Well, we could probably get the shot over here and it would look as good, if not better, and we wouldn't kill everybody." Or they'll know how long it takes to get up there.

AK: What do you think it would take for camerawomen to be treated equally to cameramen?

SS: Grips love having women on the camera crew, in my experience. I always point out to them, "See, you need a woman with little hands to get in here and tie down. Obviously you guys weren't thinking about men the way you structured them." They always chuckle and agree.

I just don't picture women schlepping equipment as much as guys do. Most guys don't want to schlepp it either. That's the thing, when people start jumping up and down yelling, "Equality, equality!" "Let me go out there and trudge through the swamps, get into the trenches and do this stuff." The men don't want to do it either. I can see you saying, "Well, you're at home, you're starving and you have to pay rent. If you want the job you should be entitled to have it." But do you really *want* it?

AK: Do you think that same question can be asked of minorities?

SS: I think minorities are another story. I don't think that you should say that you don't want to hire this person because of their color or that you do want to hire them because of their color.

Part of the problem (which nobody ever mentions) is that you get jobs because of who you know and how well you know them. If you just don't hang in those circles, if you go home to people who are not in that group, you never see those people who are giving out jobs. Then you probably will not get called because they don't know you. It's not that they are rejecting you. It's that they don't know that you're there to call.

AK: That's a good point. So then it becomes a social question, not just a work question.

SS: Yes. That's true.

AK: Do you also do independent work?

SS: Yes. I've done some nonunion jobs. The first nonunion job I did was right after the actors' strike. It was, in fact, with all the boys that I usually would be working with at the time: The entire camera crew was union.

Later, I got a call to work on a nonunion feature. The money was horrible, but I took it for a few days—unlimited hours, no overtime, or anything. I said I would do it because it would only be two or three days a week, B camera. I wanted the experience of being on the lens.

I couldn't believe it. They were all Indians. No chiefs. These people had absolutely no idea of what they were doing or how they were doing it. The key first was very bad at relaying information. That gets old when you're not making any money. You're carting all this equipment up hill and down dale for no purpose, just to turn around and take it back down the hill again.

These guys were so unorganized. We had seven cameras. I was asking what camera and lens was needed and where I should set them. They were stuck. I kept repeating the question. I would get a decision out of them. I'd go back to the camera truck in a light jog, brisk walk, put the thing together. I would then stand there with the camera, going, "Okay, now where do you want it?" It was like they had sent me to prepare the camera as busywork, because they weren't ready for it and couldn't believe that it could be back in less than ten minutes and ready to go.

AK: How do you handle stress as a camerawoman?

SS: In that case, they said one day, "We're not having B camera tomorrow and you don't have to come in." The next time they called, two days later and asked, "Can you come in?" I said, "No. I took this other job and I can't make it." That was how I handled that stress. I really wanted to miss the last week of the show because I knew that was when they weren't going to pay people. Sure enough, checks bounced.

They said, "You don't need to worry about your paycheck as long as it's coming from the payroll company. Because the money has to be put up front." I knew the minute it's coming from the production company, you worry. When we got the last check I said to myself, "You do not pass go. Go directly to the bank. Do not deposit it into your account. Go to the bank and cash the check." They were unscrupulous. I got the last of the payroll money. There was a guy from the crew behind me. They could not cash his check.

AK: How do producers get away with being unscrupulous?

SS: They can promise the crew normal wages, work them like dogs and after all this not pay them. The reason being, people on a nonunion crew are usually under thirty-five—kids who really want to get into the business. People come to Hollywood from other states, other countries with the attitude of, "I don't know. I need to learn. I have to pay dues." They expect to be abused in exchange for learning. There is always somebody new to put up with that.

AK: Are you the first African American woman to be working union camera?

SS: No, I'm not the first. Candy Foster was before me—she went to the training program first. I took the test twice. The first time, I got as far as an interview. I had nails—long nails. I had on a little knit dress—very fitted at the top and kind of flared out. I went out and bought new high-heeled sandals. I was dressed to kill. My roommate said, "Yes, you look like a secretary." Now that I think about it, I probably looked like I was for sale by the hour. I showed up at this little thing. I had studied—I got all the answers right. I was real quiet and shy, but I was smart. I didn't get in that time. Candy Foster was also black, and she got in.

Two years later, they offered the test again. I took it. When I went to the interview that time, I wore some painter's pants and I had this shirt that I frequently ended up wearing to work much later. I didn't do my hair up real nice. I had french braids crossed in the back. I had laryngitis and you could barely hear me talking. I answered everything right and this time I got in.

Candy had a lot of home problems. She had a bunch of kids, and I don't think her husband was very supportive. There is a period in there where nobody really knows who you are and it's hard to get work. If you already have financial problems and a lot of people to support, it really gets difficult. I just had to support my cat—I was still living with my parents. I could afford to sit around for the first year. But Candy kind of disappeared. My understanding is that I'm the only black woman.

AK: How do you handle this situation?

SS: I don't approach work or anything else saying, "I am a Black woman." When someone says, "We're going to shoot this film in the swamps. Do you want to come?" I don't think in terms of doing this in the name of women. I don't want to get wet and get bitten by alligators. I think in terms of doing a good job, because I want to have a good reputation. I want people to say working with Sabrina is working with someone who does a good job. Not because Sabrina is representing all black camerapeople.

AK: What are your ultimate goals?

SS: I want to run a studio. I'm not sure where I'm going or what I'm doing, but God forbid I get to be fifty years of age and I'm still schlepping camera equipment. However, I'm not miserable doing what I'm doing now. I'm a person who grumbles, curses, and rants when the clock goes off and it's dark outside. It's against human nature to get up so early. Consistently, once I'm in the car driving, I'm glad that I'm not stuck in some office with somebody thinking it's the end of the world if you don't get this letter typed. I'm glad that I don't look at the same people day in and day out—month after month—year after year. With features, on the other hand, you can see the light at the end of the tunnel. You know you'll be doing this three months, four months, or whatever. Then you know you'll do something else.

AK: What are some of the satisfactions that you gain from your work?

SS: The ideal situation would be the same camera crew, the same key grip and gaffer, but a new script and a different location each time. The people I'm working with now—Dean Semler, Paul Maibaum, and Tony Rivetti—are great, wonderful people.

I sort of take the money I make per hour for granted. I don't know how people get by on $7.00 per hour. Secretaries and department store workers have to come to work looking nice on that wage. As an assistant, you work in jeans and a tee shirt. If those jeans are neat, you're doing fine. I know this is petty, but I get a big charge out of this—in the summer when you're working—110 degrees, no shade in sight—you can go to work in shorts. How many jobs do people have where you go to work in shorts and nobody looks twice?

I'm not the person who looks around and thinks, "It's wonderful that new technical developments are out. Now let's tinker, we've got one more switch. Let's play with this piece of equipment." I'm not that kind of a girl. But I've done little repairs in the field.

I used to be real good with BL magazines [Arriflex BL]. Those things were eating up bits of films—you can have a foot of film stuck in this mag and you can't see it, wrapped up in the throat. I've taken those completely apart until they don't resemble mags anymore. It's time-consuming, but you go in the darkroom and take it apart, and then the thing works. I'm more likely to take a screwdriver to an Arri than a Panaflex. There's a kind of holier-than-thou feeling about the Panaflex. Also, it's electronic. It's less likely to have anything go wrong with it compared to the Arri that always seems to need some kind of adjustment.

AK: How has the industry changed in its perception of women who work behind the lens in the last several years, and how has this affected you?

SS: Well, when I first started, it was, "Let's see if she can move this equipment on her own." And then once you proved you could do that, then the guys would come over and try to help you, you know, almost to a fault. You'd have two cases, one in each hand, and people who were nowhere related to your department would run up and they would be taking equipment away from you.

What I usually said was, "I really appreciate it, but let's hold off, because there will probably come a day in the shoot that I will need some help, and I don't want to use up all my favors now. Let me do it now while I can, and when I need help, I'll ask you for it. Thank you." They were always very nice about it.

You can usually arrange things. That was the thing I noticed when I first started. I would get on somebody else's truck and they would put very heavy things up high. Men tend to do this rather stupid thing. Later, I would go out and set the truck up, saying, "Well, gee, I'm the one who has to come to get the stuff all the time, and I can't get it off there, so I'm putting it down here now." And they would say, "Oh, yeah, that makes more sense."

Years ago, the first shows I did, if I got the door for some guy because I was in front of him and he had his hands full it was like, "No, no, no, you have to go through first." Now it's more like you're a coworker. You're just kinda like one of the boys.

Before I was in the union, when I first started out, I used to hang out at the loading room at Universal, learning how to load magazines and stuff. It's called being a freeloader: I worked, but I didn't get paid for it. Bill Moore would grill me, intimidating me in a good-natured way. I remember sitting on some cases in the equipment room at ten or eleven at night, having this conversation. He had built this thing up about how awful it would be to have to pick up a BNCR on a stick and carry it, and how I wouldn't be able to do it because I was a woman. I didn't know that you didn't put this thing on sticks and carry it anywhere.

A couple of weeks later I ended up on the set of *Sheriff Lobo*. I'll never forget this. They had a BNCR on a Worrall head on a baby legs tripod on a mound on a hill. It was set up, they got the shot, and it was time to move the camera. Four stevedore-like men—big, burly, weight-lifting types— came over and put rods through the camera Worrall head and lifted this thing. They looked like they were having a hard time. It probably weighed 120 lbs. or more.

What really impressed me is that these guys were so big. I had never seen men like this before. They were straining. I almost fell off my perch laughing. Because Bill, two weeks before, had just said to me how I was supposed to carry this thing alone on sticks.

From that I learned a little lesson. You need to remember to use your own common judgment. To say, "Wait, I can't do this. I know I can't do this. Get over here and help me." You can't let yourself fall into these traps of who's the strongest, because you'll lose every time. What happens is some idiotic macho guy may, if he's stupid and if he thinks you'll fall into it, watch you move stuff and give you a bad time. My experience has been that they want to help you more than you need help.

Things that I move by myself, I've seen two guys moving. It's just that there's a buddy system and guys help each other.

You have to be wary of these guys that say to you that you can't move up too fast. It's different for each person. Some people need to be seconds for a long, long time, and they don't need to be first for very long, and then they can move up and be really good operators. Some people don't need to spend much time in the assistant mode at all, but they need to spend a lot of time as an operator so they can move up and be a good cameraman or camerawoman. You need to have some experience in each level. But how much you need depends on the individual.

Sometimes you have this guy standing there—he looks to be about thirty-nine or forty-two. He's telling you he was a freeloader for twelve years before anybody would ever pay attention to him and let him in the union. It was fifteen years he spent as a second assistant before anybody would let him be a first. He'll say he spent another fifteen to seventeen years as a first assistant before anybody would let him be an operator. And now he's so grateful to be an operator, and he knows what he's doing, because the first ten years as an operator he was an absolute embarrassment, and you don't want to make that mistake. So maybe you'd better stay an assistant for a while longer, and then move up.

Well, when you add up all this stuff this thirty-nine-year-old or forty-two-year-old man is telling you, you'd be like seventy-two years old. You sit there and do the arithmetic, this man is telling you that he's been working for at least twenty years longer than he's been alive. You know. So when did he start this? When he was a baby?

NOTE

1. Other African American camerawomen have included Jesse Maple, Candy Foster, and Michelle Crenshaw, who is currently an active member of IA Local 600.

Karen Williams Kane

Both daughter and granddaughter of successful union cameramen, Karen Williams Kane began her film career in April 1983, after passing IA 644's examination on her second attempt to join the union her grandfather had helped found. She had spent two years training without pay, going on shoots with her father and his assistants, and spending time in rental houses, mastering camera equipment. On her first job, she was promoted from second to first assistant. Since then, she has worked frequently with Patrick Morgan and David Norton on commercials for Diet Coke, Jaguar, Heineken, AT&T, and Pepsi, as well as assisting on other productions, including *Uptown Girl* and *Days of Thunder*.

In 1990, Karen moved to Los Angeles, transferring to IA 659 in April 1993. She specializes in the Image 300 high-speed camera, and is currently working as camera assistant with the Image 300 through Alan Gordon Enterprises in Hollywood. Some of her California credits include *Terminator 2*, *Twin Peaks*, *True Lies*, *Wiseguys*, and *WaterWorld*; First Assistant Camera—Blue Screen Unit, for *The Hudsucker Proxy*; and commercials for Nike and Bud Light.

AK: How did you get into camera work?

KWK: I've always been interested because my father, Lawrence Williams Jr., was a cameraman. He's still working today, as a matter of fact. He was not like regular fathers. Either he was here for a couple weeks or else he was away for a couple weeks, and it was always something different that he was doing. But when I was a kid, I thought being a cameraman was a job that everybody did.

My grandfather, Lawrence Williams Sr., was also a cameraman. He filmed Marilyn Monroe in *Gentlemen Prefer Blondes*. He worked for Twentieth Century Fox for at least twenty years. He was once president of 644, a long time ago. My grandfather died when I was only two. But even now, when I go to work in New York, people tell me that they remember him and what a gentleman he was. It makes me feel good.

I did a couple weeks on *Days of Thunder* down in Daytona, and my father was on that, too. He was one of the operators. I have a brother in Miami that's an assistant. We were all on it, so it was like a family thing. It was fun, but I like to do my own thing too. A lot of people don't realize that I'm my father's daughter.

AK: A lot of people think that one of the major problems with IA is its nepotism—that traditionally, people haven't been able to get into the union unless they are related to someone already in the union. Was your family helpful when you joined the union?

KWK: Actually, it wasn't helpful at all. I had a difficult time getting into the IA in New York. I had three brothers in 644, only one of them has stopped working now. Two of them are still in 644. The union played some games with them, too. We all had trouble scheduling our practical tests. We live two hours out of the city, and 644 called them up an hour before the test and said, "Well, we're having a test in an hour, can you get down here?"

When I finally got in for a scheduled test, I heard a lot of discriminatory remarks, which I would not care to repeat, because if the IA in New York reads this book, I'll be blacklisted for life . . . [*laughs*].

They failed me by two points. The camera rental house people who saw me in there for six months, training for the test, told me that if anybody should have passed it, it would have been me. I think, as a woman, they were harder on me. And the family being in it didn't hurt me, but it didn't help me; 644 expected me to give up, but I shook their hands and said, "I'll be back in six months." Three blocks away, I cried my eyes out—I cried my eyes out all the way home. But in six months, I went back and passed it. In April 1983, I got in. And now they like me because I work all the time, and I'm a paying member. They get a percentage of what I make, so now they're happy.

Once I got into the union, I was very lucky. One of my brothers had gotten a job, and he couldn't do it, so he put my name in. I showed up on the set of Fairbanks Films. There was a director from England named Patrick Morgan and a cameraman named David Norton, and we got along really well. I've been working for them ever since, on just about every job that they've ever done, starting out as a second assistant and moving up. David Norton had to be the biggest influence on me. Over the years, when I've gotten a little discouraged, he'd tell me, "You're good. You could be the best, if you just keep trying." He's taught me a lot. I called him the other day from out here in L.A. and he said, "Don't worry, you're going to do fine." And that made me feel good.

Being one of the boys—that's the best part about it! I get along with them well. When they say, "Lunch for one hour," it's like, "Come on, Karen. Come with us." The script lady will go off, and the makeup lady will do her own thing, or they'll go together, but with me it's always, "Come on. We've got an extra seat for you. Jump in the car and come with us." I mean, you get all the jokes and everything, but it doesn't bother me now. I tell them a couple of my own, and they love it. We go back and forth. I like it a lot.

The support in my family's always been good to me. I remember the first assistant's test that they failed me by two points—I had been beaten down so much, I was ready to give it up. It was the same week as my birthday. The next day, my mother sent me an assistant's case. I just couldn't believe it. It was her way of saying, "Don't give up."

Mom's been our business agent for the last twenty, thirty years. She's basically the secretary. People in New York say, "Say hello to your mother. I've only talked to her on the phone, but she's so nice." If it wasn't for her, we'd all be broke [*laughs*].

A lot of people when they come into the business, if they have family, they work for their family first. I haven't worked with my father too often, but I worked with him in Arizona on a car shoot, and I got to know him all over again. It was so much fun.

When we had the weekend off, we went to Tortilla Flats. We went into a store, and my father bought me an ice cream cone, and I almost cried. I said, "I don't think you've bought me an ice cream cone since I was ten years old." It brought back all these memories.

AK: Could you describe your training process? As a little girl, did you get to go on location, look at sets, or get to see how Daddy loads a magazine?

KWK: No, none of that. I never went on a set with him until I was in college. I went to the University of Miami for commercial art and film. I actually wanted to do still photography, but it was so competitive. I got interested in motion pictures in Miami, figuring that if I came up to New York to train for a while, I could possibly get in the union. I trained without pay for approximately two years, going on shoots with my father and other assistants. I went into the rental houses, asking if I could have an explanation of the cameras. Then I got lucky and got a job, and met a couple of wonderful people, who taught me a lot.

My first job experience was when we did Billy Joel's *Uptown Girl* with Mike Negrin, DP. My brother was the first assistant and I was hired as the second. Music videos always shoot for twenty-four hours. The second day, my brother had another job he had to go to, so I was bumped up to first, and it made me really nervous. But I got through it all right, and it actually worked out fine. They sent me a letter afterwards thanking me for giving an extra push afterwards.

AK: Promoted on your first job!

KWK: That was what made me nervous about it, but it worked out.

Another exciting job was a ten-day shoot in Miami for Pepsi with Don Johnson and Glen Frey—day and night shooting, with five hundred extras. Ridley Scott was the director. I was actually hired as a second assistant, but on the first day's shooting, the first assistant to Ridley Scott came down ill. Since the production company knew I had worked with English people before, they asked me if I would be on first camera with Ridley.

I spent the day with him on first camera and we got along really well. The next day I went back to my camera—second camera—and my producer came over and said, "We have a problem." And I said, "What, is there a problem with the film?" And they said, "No. Everything from yesterday is fine, but Ridley wants you to stay on first camera for the duration, since you started it." And I was "Wow!" I was on Cloud Nine.

I look back on it, and it was the best and the worst job [*laughs*] that I ever did. One night, I had gotten no sleep—we were working crazy hours. I found somebody to replace me, and took myself off camera. I didn't feel responsible enough, being as I had almost had three accidents on the way in. I think he respected that more than trying to do it and not being sure of myself. There are a lot of things to think about, being an assistant.

When I moved to L.A. in 1990 and called the union here, I said, "I'd like to speak to the business rep about joining 659." The secretary said, "Your name, please?" I said, "Karen Williams. (I wasn't married then.) She said, "Hold please." She came back on and said, "Your name?" I said, "Karen

Williams." She said, "No, the name of the *person* that wants to acquire a card." I said, "*Karen Williams.*" She said, "Hold on." She came back on and said, "No, I need the name of the *person* . . . " "Yes. Karen Williams. I am Karen Williams. I want a card. I am a member of 644." She was shocked! It was so funny to me, I said, "Oh boy, here we are, off to another fine start [*laughs*]."

I wound up getting the card, but that little resistance always gets me. It's like the battle's never over.

But I go in with a good attitude. Actually, people have been very nice. Once in a while I run into a person, whether it be a producer or an AD or a director, that's not warm to the idea of having a woman assistant. But I can tell, usually. I'll back off a little and I'll do my job, and usually by the time the job's over, they'll come up to me and shake my hand and say the job's well done or something. You know, it's their way of saying, "Well, I guess you really are OK." [*laughs*] If they don't, then that's fine, too, just as long as I do my job and everything looks fine [*shrugs*]. I took the time to learn my job well.

There was a camera out, called the Image 300, that Alan Gordon has in California. It's 300 frames a second. David started getting calls for it. Nobody knew how to run such a high-speed camera, so they had a NABET assistant come in on the job because he knew how to run it. I was still hired, because he had to have an IA assistant. I started saying, "Gee, I should learn how to run this camera." General Camera, which now has the Image 300, has this list that they give out: "This camera cannot be taken out unless with one of these assistants." To get on the so-called list, you had to be approved by Alan Gordon. I went down to learn the camera, and now I'm on the top of their list. So now when they call, they give my name out first. It's perseverence.

I would like to move up. There's a much better chance for me to move up to camera operator here than in New York. In New York, they have assistants, and they have DPs. And the DPs are usually cameramen, also. They light and they operate, or the directors operate. So I figure if I come out here there's a greater chance of me moving up to an operator, and then possibly one day to DP.

Personally, I like what I do. Part of it is being a woman and doing something different, and feeling good about myself. I don't know exactly what it is—it's not an ego trip. I know a lot of assistants, they love to talk how they work with the stars. But it's really not that. It's being involved in something big, and becoming a family with all those people. Then you don't see each other, and you do another film, and it's like another family. And then you run into them like three years later, they're still like your best friend. It's great. And the money's good, too [*laughs*].

AK: In New York, you said you were making more money than your brothers.

KWK: Yeah, that was tough. My brother had been working for Patrick Morgan and David Norton. When he got this call for a job, and he couldn't do it, and he replaced himself with me, they didn't call him again. He was really kind of upset about it. He was still working a lot, but he never really got over that. That's the reason I started making more money. If I hadn't worked for Fairbanks, and met that director and cameraman, I don't think I'd be where I am today.

I've worked with a lot of the same grips and electricians in the last ten years. They'll come up to me and say, "So, what's your goal? What would you like to do in the future? Would you like to be a DP?" I'm always lax about it. I say, "Well, I *would* like to move up to an operator, and *possibly* to a DP." I'm not going to say anything definite, because I'm still learning.

Everybody these days wants to be the director: this week PA, next week camera assistant, next week director. They don't want to take the time. But it's not something you learn in a year or two. Every time I work, I see different lighting, and I've been assisting for ten years. When I'm ready to move up, I'll know it.

Sandy Butler

When I interviewed Sandy Butler, I was pregnant. The steep hills of San Francisco, not to mention that first-trimester flight, made me apprehensive about my pilgrimage to a former Behind the Lens member who had left Los Angeles so full of anger about her experiences there. Being a single mother of a disabled child and establishing a career as a video camerawoman, with all of the irregularities of location work and long hours it entails, presented overwhelming challenges—especially to an ardent feminist like Sandy, sensitive to her often insensitive environment. But our talk was both warm and lengthy, ending long after my next scheduled interview should have begun. I was grateful to Sandy for bracing me to the realities of what combining motherhood and camera work might soon mean to me.

Soon afterwards, Sandy's daughter Ola won a scholarship to a prestigious boarding school, allowing Sandy the extra hours she needed to work in both San Francisco and Los Angeles. Her career has since blossomed, encompassing a full range of industrial, documentary, and television work. She joined IATSE Local 16, the San Francisco stagehands' local—which celebrated its centennial in 1992—and is the first woman ever to serve on its Executive Board. As a member of NABET 51, Sandy works as a video photographer and engineer. She has also joined IA Local 659 (now known as 600) as a photographer, through their merger with NABET. Ola is a student at Vassar College.

AK: How did you first become interested in camera work?

SB: To answer that I have to go back to my first career. I graduated high school in 1961. I was about to go to the Art Institute of Chicago, but at the last minute switched to architecture at the University of Illinois.

I was one of five women in a class of 300 men. I dropped out after a year and a half. The instructors said, "You don't belong here if you're a woman, so you'll never get more than a C in this class." A little sexism there.

After that, I worked as a civil engineering and architectural draftsman. I finally got to the point where I was very angry. Although I was advancing, I had to put up with so much shit. I had one man, a civil engineer, that I worked for on a freelance basis. He was great and I loved working for him. But he wouldn't let me go out in the field because he thought I would distract the men he worked with.

I ended up filing two civil rights cases against two employers. I won one, lost the other. By the time I got through the second one, I thought, "I can't do this anymore." It was a woman's issue for me.

In 1967 I had moved to California—East Palo Alto, across the freeway from Palo Alto, a predominately Black community. I got very involved in the community, but they couldn't understand when I said there is as much oppression directed towards women as there is towards people of color in the job force. At that time I was alone in my struggle. The women's movement that exists today was not what it was then.

I wanted to get into radio. In 1970 I started working as a news stringer and filling in as an announcer at KSAN and KMPX in San Francisco. One of the stations had a general strike and we all got locked out, and the other station went by the wayside for me.

But eight months later someone I knew from KMPX called and asked if I wanted to do a show at KPFA. I said sure. I became the only woman independent producer at KPFA at that time. Oddly enough, as women developed their consciousness and groups of women came around, I was the first one they competed against for air time.

Shortly after my daughter Ola was born—two months prematurely—I left KPFA. We had so many problems around her birth. She had open heart surgery the first time when she was two weeks old, and weighed two and a half pounds. There was a lot of politicking going on at KPFA, so I said, "Screw it." I lived off welfare for a couple of years, so that I could stay home to take care of my daughter, who needed me more than anybody else in the world.

When Ola was a little older, we lived down the street from the UC Extension. They sent out flyers advertising courses, some of which were involved with film. I got a scholarship to take a couple of filmmaking courses. One was a Super 8 workshop; the other was on sound recording. I lucked out with sound recording because the man who was teaching it was one of my former listeners, and even though I hadn't asked for a grade in the project, he felt I did well enough to give me an A. This really whetted my appetite. I saw a student-produced ad for City College's cinematography program, so I zipped over there, and started what ended up being full time studies. I received an A.A. in Cinematography from City College, and went on to San Francisco State as a special major in Film and Women's Studies. I was there for one year—took forty-five units in two semesters!—and graduated with departmental honors.

Then I went to UCLA for four years to get my master's degree. It was a devastating experience. But as a single parent with a disabled child, it worked out best for me to be in school. My daughter had lost a leg after a third operation, when she was two years old.

The first thing everybody does in graduate school at UCLA is a Super 8 piece that you do in one quarter. That sets you up for the rest of your time there. I did an autobiographical day in the life of me and my daughter. It seemed like four out of five of the other films that were shown at that time consisted of some kind of story line where a woman was being killed, raped, murdered, axed, or dismembered. I was really shocked. This was 1979. There was no sensitivity.

I went into partnership with two friends. We had a camera package—an Ikegami 79 DAL and a Sony BVU 1100. I used it to finish shooting my thesis, which won a couple of awards. Maybe because we had this camera package, I went in a technical direction when I got out of school in 1983.

I was forty years old by then. I wanted to be able to support myself as a technician while developing my own projects. One of the problems I faced was that the time I came out of school was also a time when there were many cutbacks in the industry. So I was not only dealing with the fact that I was female and forty. I was also dealing with the fact that everybody was getting laid off who had been there for years.

I finally landed a job as an assistant engineer in a postproduction house. It wasn't a camera job, but it was very relevant, teaching me a lot about video. When I started film school, I hadn't wanted to do video at all. Shirley

Clarke, with whom I studied at UCLA, said, "Switch to video. Work in video, because that's where it's all going."

By working in a postproduction house, I came to understand more of what I needed to know to shoot. Sometimes when I'm not working, I spend time with a friend, learning to tweak and repair cameras and gear. Video is the kind of thing where you have to understand the medium and technology that you're dealing with. It doesn't matter what end you're on.

A lot of what I learned, I learned on my own. I used to create projects for myself, shooting photographs. My favorite project was creating motion within a still frame since I didn't have the advantage of having the picture move. How do you create motion within a still frame? I would play with composition, exposure, and length. All of that builds your mind to do more later. The more you understand how to work the camera, the more you will be able to do certain things that others will never be able to do.

I had a certain amount of support from Behind the Lens, especially from Estelle Kirsh, who wound up being my roommate for awhile. There was a certain beauty in having Estelle as a friend in that she was always someone who was very dedicated to her work, and it was wonderful having someone who was really dedicated to her profession around me. I remember once she went out on a shoot and came back with a Worrall head. She set it up with a flashlight mounted on the head and practiced doing figure eight configurations and signing her name on the wall.

AK: What do you think it will take for camerawomen to be treated equally to cameramen in the industry?

SB: To me, what is necessary is to see women working on having a better attitude toward women. It's important and essential to fight for your own survival, but to be a feminist you must fight for all women. I would like to see, in all areas, women fighting for women. To see us join hands, reach out to other women, and stop back-stabbing.

Frankly, a lot of the protests staged by the DGA were very self-serving. It wasn't to increase the number of women in the Directors Guild, or to open up directing to women. Rather, it was to get the few women in the guild more and better jobs.

AK: How do you handle stress as a camerawoman?

SB: Not necessarily successfully. I freak out a lot. I work out a lot. I don't drink very much, because it really upsets my system. I smoke reefer. Depression is still a frequent guest at our house. Not a welcome one, but I have to deal with that a lot. I do what I can. When I'm really stressed out on a job I try to deal with it later. I try to not let these things show. There was a time when I wasn't that way. I have learned through the years to try and keep it to myself. You can't shoot and be stressed out simultaneously.

AK: How do you deal with problems of strength and how others perceive your ability to carry heavy equipment on the set or on location?

SB: I've gotten to the point where, if I can't lift it myself, two people should be lifting it anyway, number one. Number two, I went through a period where people would ask me before they even saw me, "Oh, you can run the camera, you can run the deck. How are you on Nautilus?" At that point in my life I was able to squat 200 pounds in the gym using free weights. I would tell them that and they would never speak to me again, they would be so threatened.

Frankly, you don't have to be Godzilla to carry most of the equipment you work with.

AK: Are there rules about lifting equipment?

SB: To tell you the truth, I really don't know. And anyway if there were, I probably wouldn't follow them. I would most likely just go ahead and do what I had to do on the job. As a freelancer, I can't be a prima donna.

AK: What are some of the dilemmas that face you personally as a camerawoman?

SB: I would like to share this incident because it's something you would face only as a woman. I went out on a live shoot for a large corporation's awards ceremony a few months ago. The first day of the shoot was in a large hotel. It was the first day of my period and I was having a real rough day. I was just bleeding like crazy. It was a long, boring rehearsal. I kept going to the bathroom every hour or two. Finally, after about the fourth or fifth time, the director started making comments about it. Well, if I had been in a real crisis situation where I couldn't leave the floor, I'd have stuck four tampons up there and it would have felt like walking around with a penis between my legs. It would have been handled. I wouldn't have been comfortable, but I wouldn't have had to leave. But since it was already so drawn out and there were so many stops, I just thought, "Why should I suffer discomfort?"

That's the kind of situation where I was in a real dilemma because I was a woman. Finally, at the end, I started making cracks about I wish that men had periods too so they could start understanding these things.

AK: Did they react positively to your humor?

SB: The next day I was in better shape and we kept going, but the director would say "Okay Sandy, if you need to go to the bathroom, you can go now."

AK: If you were to get pregnant, would the union help you?

SB: The union wouldn't do doodle squat.

Every woman has a different experience in her pregnancy. My idea when I was pregnant was that I would work up until the day I delivered. I was going to have a home birth with all my friends there. Some friends who were musicians were supposed to bring their instruments so that my daughter would come into the world among all this positive, creative energy. None of that ever happened. I had an emergency C-section at seven months, and Ola spent her first two months in intensive care, after open-heart surgery. I had to make some rapid adjustments to that situation.

People who don't have children don't necessarily understand the problems of people who do. I don't think anybody can understand what parenting is about until they're a parent. It's always been an uphill battle for me. Ola had open-heart surgery yet again, when she was twelve years old. I had times when I was so depressed I could barely get out of bed to see that my kid got to school. It's real hard just to be out there on your own, to be a single parent. I took any kind of job that would keep me working in video.

I have a wonderful child. It's taken a hell of a lot of hard work. People are beginning to realize that you cannot just bear children and throw them out the door, expecting that they will grow by themselves. Unfortunately we live in a state where the governor is vehemently antichild. He has vetoed every piece of legislation that would have had a positive effect on raising children.

AK: How would these legislative bills have helped camerawomen?

SB: One thing that is very difficult for me is when I get called out on a shoot for any length of time: Where does my daughter go? What do I do with my kid when I have to be out of town? I can't pull her out of school so I can go work. Frankly, if you are a camera operator or a grip or a gaffer, as long as you're in a business like this, where you are required to travel and go to different locations, ninety percent of the jobs that are available to you are going to have weird hours.

It's real hard to be a single parent and to do this kind of work. I also have to say that I don't think I could have done it without other financial means to rely on. I would have had to find some other work by now. You have to have strong bases. It's always difficult being a parent, but when you get so little support from your environment, when you've seen child abuse in public facilities cases, you cannot just say I'm going to put my kid in day care and it'll all be hunkey dorey.

At some point you have to decide as a parent, what's more important, my kid or my career? I always opted for my kid. Now that she is old enough to go off and do her own thing, I get to opt for my career.

AK: So would it be correct to say that being a camerawoman is a difficult career for a woman who happens to be raising kids at the same time?

SB: Yes. It's very hard to find a job with regular hours as a camera operator. I'm sure most of the women in 659 in L.A. go off for weeks and months at a time. What do you do with your baby? Do you bring your baby on that shoot? Even if you can bring the baby—suppose you're working with Lee Grant and you go off for six months and ask if I can bring the baby and she says, "Sure." That's swell for a one-, two-, or three-year-old. What happens when she's eight and has to be in school and do homework? Then there is all that separation. And somebody else is raising your child.

Even women with husbands are not in an easy position, because their husbands expect them to be the primary care givers in terms of the child. This is not to say that there aren't men who are the primary care givers.

AK: So your advice to women contemplating going into this career may be: If you think you may want to be a mother at some point, make sure you find a spouse who is also interested in care giving and flexible hours.

SB: Yes, I would say that. I would also say if you're thinking of going into this business, you better have a hell of a lot of dedication if you think that you can succeed.

I love going out on a shoot. Even when it's cruddy work, I love the work. Even when it's boring, uninteresting, yukky stuff, I love it. I love the feel of being behind the camera. Of having a camera on my shoulder. I love the technology. I love the excitement. I'm a real tomboy at heart. I like the craziness of ENG work. The insanity that goes along with crash-and-burn video. I would ultimately like to own my own camera package and offline editing system in order to do a lot more of my own projects, as well as shoot and edit for other people.

I like working a twelve- or fourteen-hour day and feeling good at the end of it. I like to get out there and troubleshoot. I love the work. I like working with a lot of men—sexist or otherwise. Frankly I'd rather be working with them than be married to them under any circumstances. I enjoy it. I like the thrill and the accomplishment. I like the aesthetics. I like being a part of the revolutionary technology. I feel like I'm part of a movement, in a sense.

I especially love traveling. I can't wait until the time when my daughter is safely and happily in boarding school and somebody beeps me on my pager and says, "We have to leave for El Salvador in an hour," and my bag is packed and in the trunk or two feet away and I say, "Okay. What gate at the airport?" Maybe someday I'll grow up, but I'm not that old yet.

Alicia Sehring

Alicia Craft Sehring visited the set of *Raggedy Man* while a student at the University of Austin, Texas, and fell in love with film. She pursued a film degree, specializing in cinematography, and worked on *Best Little Whorehouse in Texas* as a production assistant, hanging out on the set on Saturdays with the camera assistants.

After graduating in 1981, Alicia worked as a camera operator at CBS in Austin until she was accepted as a Cinematography Fellow at the American Film Institute. She traveled West, and worked as an Arriflex service technician at the camera rental house Otto Nemenz International while interning on *Scarface* with John Alonzo through the American Film Institute program.

Alicia Sehring has worked as first assistant camera on numerous features, including *First Kid*, *Born in East L.A.*, *Hollywood Shuffle*, and *Heartbreak Hotel*, as well as television shows such as *Star Trek: The Next Generation*, and *Beverly Hills, 90210*; and as a second assistant camera on *La Bamba*, *To Live and Die in L.A.*, and *Meteor Man*. She has also worked as director of photography on nonunion features, including *Dive Masters*, *Across the State Line*, and *Twilight of the Dogs*. She has also served as president of Behind the Lens.

Having joined IA 659 at the age of twenty-six, Alicia Sehring is at the forefront of a new generation of camerawomen whose attitude is clearly one of no-holds-barred enthusiasm towards the world of cinematography.

AK: How did you first get interested in camera work?

AS: I was nineteen when I started the film degree. I felt like a *very* late starter. There were people that I went to college with who had been making Super 8 films in junior high school. Our family had no cameras, except for Instamatic still cameras. There was one point where I looked in a motion picture camera and thought, "I'm never gonna learn what all those buttons are for." But now, it's second nature.

I remember friends and family saying, "Girls don't do camera work." And I said, "It's not a matter of what I should or shouldn't do. It just has to do with the way my heart goes." So I started taking film production classes and concentrating on camera.

The film teachers were great. My favorite one was Loren Bivens. Loren was always right there for his students.

His favorite thing was, *"Make movies!"* He was so gung ho, his voice was so deep and he was so charismatic, that you couldn't help but get wrapped up in movie making. You never felt ignorant, or that you didn't know enough.

When I was going to school, my parents paid for it. They had a Parents' Day in Communication, and they came up for that. Edward Dmytryk was my directing teacher. He gave this speech on movie making that left my father breathless.

I was hanging out in the editing room when someone asked me if I wanted to visit the set of *Raggedy Man*, which was a Sissy Spacek movie. So I said, "Sure!" And then on *Raggedy Man* I met the guy who invited me to Third Coast Studios. If I hadn't gone to the *Raggedy Man* set, you just don't know what might or might have not happened.

I know I got my internship through one guy at Third Coast Studios [in Austin]. He and I dated for two years after that. I worked at Third Coast Studios for two years, and that was great experience, learning production and postproduction. I just did everything for them.

But one of the producers said I smiled too much, and that it was unprofessional. Well, I had already seen the big boys working on *Raggedy Man* and I knew how silly professionals can get, and how fun-loving. I knew *Best Little Whorehouse in Texas* was in town. So when they brought in a film student to operate a camera on this Carole King show, even though

I'd been there two years—and they knew I wanted camera—I quit Third Coast.

That day, I wandered into the production office of *Best Little Whorehouse in Texas*. The woman there was frantic: "The other production assistant is not here yet, and I have a doctor's appointment. If you can stay here right now and answer the phones, you've got the internship." She left. I had the office to myself, thinking, "This is so lucky, I can't believe it!"

Then I said to her, "I'll work for free. The first five days, I work in the office, but on Saturdays, I hang out on the set with the camera assistants." Because, really, my goal wasn't cinematography then, it was just camera assisting. So I hung out with the camera assistants.

I was on *Best Little Whorehouse* for three months. People thought I was crazy, to quit one of the only production jobs in Austin, Texas, to work for free. But I knew it was the right decision.

When I got out of school in 1981, with a B.S. in Radio, TV, and Film, I got a job as a camera operator at CBS in Austin. But I had to quit when I got into the American Film Institute as a Cinematography Fellow. AFI was the only graduate school I wanted to go to. They send you a letter—actually, I think I've got it in my purse—saying, "We know you'd make a prominent member of the film society . . . "—this letter makes you weep inside.

Three weeks after I moved into L.A., I was looking for a place to develop some still film on Sunset Boulevard, and I couldn't find it. I wandered into the first door I saw to use the phone book. It was Otto Nemenz International. I didn't know what a rental house was—they didn't have rental houses in Austin, Texas—and I had never seen so many cameras in one place. I said, "Wow, look at all these cameras!" And they're like, "Cute little girl, here's the phone book. Get out of our face, we're busy." They were just getting ready to move.

About two months later, Keith Peterman, one of the camera assistants from *Best Little Whorehouse*, invited me to watch him prep cameras for *Flashdance*. We went to the rental house—it was the new one. They said, "Didn't you wander into our store a few months ago to use the phone book?" Well, they thought I was so gung ho, that they said, "If you'll clean filters and cases for free, we'll teach you the cameras." So I started working there part-time, 'cause I was at AFI at the time. They'd get mad when I'd leave, but I said, "Hey, I'm working for free. I've got other things to do, and people to see." So they started paying me part-time while I was still in school. And the day school was out, I was full-time.

I don't know how I found the time for all this, but while I was a first-year student at AFI, I was working on a second-year film, I had a part-time job at Otto Nemenz, and I had a four-month internship on *Scarface* with John Alonzo. That was my training.

When I was at Otto Nemenz, he had recommended me for a job. The cameraman said, "Oh, it's a tough show—it's in Arizona. We need to hire a guy." If I had been there, I would have said, "OK, why don't you and I run around the block and see who wins? Let's climb that tree and see who can get to the top fastest." If you want something bad enough, whatever handicap people think you have, that's all bogus. If you want it bad enough, you can get it, as far as I'm concerned.

The Cinematography Fellows at AFI were all so incredibly supportive. There were only two women accepted that year: Beth-Jana Friedberg and I. I've never been made to feel so comfortable in a strange surrounding in my life. We all worked on each other's projects. If somebody dropped the ball, there'd be somebody there to pick it up. One person would lead and the others would follow; then that person would be a follower and the other ones would lead. We would teach each other everything we knew. AFI was a great experience.

AK: What about resistance?

AS: I get resistance every now and then, but it's usually just a line here or a line there. One guy, in the middle of my talking about underwater photography, picked up his tray and said, "One day you'll make somebody a great wife," and just walked away.

And then this whole thing with *To Live and Die in L.A.* I was replacing an assistant who had gotten fired. That day, they got a negative report of scratched film. Well, the director, William Friedkin, saw the report, found out they had to reshoot, and then saw me, a newcomer, loading mags. You'd think this guy's made films long enough to know that the report you get today is from mags loaded yesterday. I wasn't even on the set yesterday—I'm the new girl on the block. And another thing, because I used to be a technician, I can find problems even before they happen, so I'm an asset to any film group. I even found a mag that was jammed, and I took the thing apart.

He ended up pulling the DP, Robbie Müller, to the side. Friedkin said, "Who was the little girl on my camera truck? Does she know how to load a magazine?" Robbie Müller said, "Well, of course she does. She's a competent assistant. Don't talk bad about my crew!" You know, stick to your own job.

The second unit DP went up to Friedkin and said, "Look, just last week she firsted for me, she's a good AC." But that was the straw that broke the camel's back. I think Robbie Müller had had enough of this director, and quit. The next day, the whole camera crew—except for Beth-Jana, because she was working with the Terra Flight of Bill Bennett, the only one left of the original crew—we were all fired. I was only going to be on it for a few more days anyway, because I had a prior commitment. And that weekend we were going to interview William Friedkin! [*laughs*] Here I was going to be firsting, keeping him in focus, and he was worried that I knew how to load a magazine? I mean, get real.

AK: How do you handle stress as a camerawoman?

AS: I remember reading about some girl in an article who said, "Never let 'em see you cry." And I say, "So what? Big deal." I mean, you watch directors kick script supervisors' chairs halfway across the set when they're upset. I think shedding a couple of tears behind a lens is not as bad as screaming your head off, punching out other people. I try not to cry right there in the middle of everybody, but more than once I've walked behind the stage or a set and cried by myself, wiped it off, and walked right back onto the set like nothing's happened.

Every now and then a guy will say something rude to you. I had one key grip tell me to get my own apple box. But those kind of people, I just don't work with. I told the producers of the first feature I was ever hired on that they were the biggest, rudest guys I'd ever met in my life.

AK: What was rude about them?

AS: They used to do pornos. This was their first nonporno film, and they were sleazy. Like, they had this van where the transmission was held on by seatbelts. I just got bad vibes. Usually if you can smell a rat, there's one around you [*laughs*].

The director and the cinematographer said, "Alicia, don't quit, we love you, we want you to stay. You don't work for them, you work for us." By the end of the show, I was the only one left. Everyone else in the grip, camera, and electrical departments had either gotten fired or quit.

I think just being a stubborn-ass Texan really helps me. I just bought a T-shirt that says, "It's never rude to talk crude when you're from Texas." I'm a lot different when I put on a dress and makeup and go out. I have no problem being an ornament, no problem at all. And I have no problem talkin' filth with the guys on the set. I mean you tell me a dirty joke and I've probably got one three times as good as that one.

Strength? There's a lot of it in my head. I like to act tough, therefore I feel tough, therefore I can lift things with mind power. In interviews they say, "How can you carry the camera?" and I go, "You wanna feel my muscle? [*slams table*] Feel this!" I literally have the producer or production manager feel my muscle, which is really ridiculous when you're trying to be professional at a job interview. But I mean how else are you going to get them to understand? And they go, "Oh, you lift weights." And I go, "Yeah. The world's most expensive weights: motion picture cameras. I do it every day in my job."

It's like show business. I don't really believe in throwing the camera over your shoulder unless you're just going a little ways, because there's too much stress on the head and on the quick-release plate on the Sachtler head or on the pin that holds it in. It's just as easy to break it down, and it's safer, and it doesn't look so wacko. But the first day of any film, I'll throw it over my shoulder, just to prove I can do it. And that's all they really want to see. It's like, "Can she carry that camera? OK, she can do it," and they move on to their next problem in life [*laughs*].

Sometimes big old guys think that they're just born strong. [*laughs*] But I have never thrown my back out, like you hear men do all the time, and I'm 5'4". Just because they're 6'6", people think they're better for the job.

I love carrying the cameras. For one thing, the physical part of the job allows me to eat more. If I didn't have this way of burning off calories, I wouldn't be able to eat so much, and I'd have to jog, or something that I hate [*laughs*].

AK: Could you describe the process by which you got into the union?

AS: Somebody said it was really hard to get in. Therefore I wanted to conquer it. I set myself a goal that I was going to be in the International Photographers Guild by the time I was twenty-six. I got in a week before I turned twenty-seven. I was really pleased with myself. I was, once again, at the right place at the right time—I was on *La Bamba* and it organized. If you had worked thirty days on it, then you got in the union. I had also joined NABET, long before that.

AK: Could you talk about what kinds of accomplishments Behind the Lens has made while you've been its president?

AS: Behind the Lens is the biggest support group I ever had. BTL enables women to learn new skills and keeps its members technically-up-to date. In a BTL seminar at Panavision, you take the camera apart and put it back together in a comfortable environment.

A lot of guys want to be technically up-to-date, too. They like the seminars, they like the screenings, they like the networking, and we're getting a lot more male members, which I think is great. I never believed in keeping men out of the organization anyway. My vote on that carried.

I never believed in men wanting to work with all men; or me, as a woman, I wouldn't want to work with just a bunch of women, I mean, how boring. Fifty-fifty, to me, is the way it goes.

AK: How often does it go like that?

AC: Not very often, but it's getting there. On second unit *Star Trek,* I'm one of the only women there, but the first two out of three features I ever did in Hollywood, I worked with women camera assistants: Beth-Jana Friedberg and Laurie Towers. It seemed normal to me.

AK: What do you think it will take for camerawomen to be treated equally to cameramen in the industry?

AS: Just seeing a woman's work and knowing a woman shot that is really all it's gonna take. When I first started assisting, there weren't many assistants. Behind the Lens has *a lot* to do with the fact that there are so many camera assistants out there. And now, people are so used to us, that having a woman camera assistant is no big deal. I hardly ever see any discrimination anymore against women camera assistants.

Camera operators and cinematographers, now, that is a different story— where male camera assistants got in the union at the same time as female camera assistants, and they're moving up and we aren't.

I got to shoot the first movie International Film Group did—*Crazy Al.* In the swamps of Orange, Texas, twenty minutes from the Louisiana border, we shot a 75-minute movie in nine days. It was almost all exterior, but I still lit a bar, a hotel room, a hotel lobby, a butcher shop, and a grocery store. I did some aerial work for them: I shot a boat chase sequence through the swamps which looks gorgeous—all those boat wakes from the air. And then we shot a boat chase sequence on the boats. We shot a lot of hand-held through the reeds in the swamps, running with the camera and falling down, following the guy. That was an incredible opportunity. I was nervous, but I knew that I had been on enough sets that I could conquer it without any problem. And I did a great job. My operating was great, and I was really pleased. I felt like a total asset to their crew, 'cause I was this moviemaker from L.A. I knew how to run a set and how to keep things moving. I think that's how we shot so quickly.

The second one we did, *Dive Masters,* was through the same company. I got to do some aerials from a Lear jet, filming the pilot and looking down as he was coming in from a landing and up from the landing to takeoff. That was pretty thrilling stuff, as well as filming on sailboats and yachts and cruisers and little boats and water galore. It's so much fun working for this company. It's like a little family.

Being the cinematographer on these nonunion films is a great experience, but to be a camera assistant on something as great as *Star Trek, The Next Generation* is a thrill. When I was in film school in Texas, the thought of going to work on a major lot in the camera department was such an incredible goal. The fact that I've reached it is a dream come true.

I love it when life makes a complete circle. One of my goals would be to go into Otto Nemenz—he's so proud of me now—to rent a camera for a film that I'm shooting. They're the ones that gave me my start cleaning filters for them. To me, that would just be a dream.

I had to keep changing my goals once I achieved all the goals I set out to achieve when I moved out to L.A. A few years ago, I got a little confused. Did I want to shoot? Because I had achieved my camera-assisting goals. Did I want a family? And I decided to go after cinematography, to keep working. I wasn't ready for settling down yet.

The film I met my husband on was *Twilight of the Dogs*. He drove a tank in the movie and I was director of photography. I kept having to photograph this cute tank driver!

I definitely see myself working and having kids. I see myself working as a union DP by the time I have kids, or maybe on a show like *Star Trek* or any major lot TV show. By *then*, they're bound to have child care. I mean Paramount's got child care. I mean, child care is such a measly little pittance. It costs pennies to run a child care center, compared to other costs of studios. A little room with some toys and some people, big deal. I definitely want a family, but I also want to be a world-famous cinematographer.

There is nothing like the feeling of going onto a great set and doing a great job. Standing there on a mountaintop with your camera, getting ready to shoot this great scene with horses and cowboys or something. I mean it is an awesome feeling to stand there and go, "I'm at work? You call this work?"

When I read the script, I begin lighting in my mind. I light for the mood, the characters, the tension of the story, the dramatic impact. Each shot, each set-up, I treat as a separate "masterpiece." There is, in my mind, no such thing as a "pop shot." I care about what each shot looks like, whether it takes five minutes or five hours to light. I concentrate on the background as well as the characters in the foreground. What falls off in the background, what goes out of focus, what the set shows, including how the patterns of lines and curves form, are all part of that "masterpiece." I love to see a shot that has the entire frame, the background, the foreground, what's in focus, what's out of focus, what's lit, what's not lit, etc., working together for a magnificent shot.

My goal, as the director of photography, is to make the director look good. If someone compliments the photography, I want this to reflect the director's work. Communication is extremely important between the two, especially understanding his or her vision for the film. I give directors what they want, but I'm always making certain suggestions to better the look. Whether or not they choose to go with them is their prerogative, because it is their film.

I love walking onto a set. It cracks me up to be this blonde, blue-eyed little girl that's a hard worker, who's strong and knows her stuff to boot. I can go on any set and feel proud, knowing that I work hard, I do a good job, and that I'm going to be meeting new people and having new experiences.

Selected Bibliography

ARTICLES

Abbe, Elfrieda. "Michelle Crenshaw." *Angles: Women Working in Film & Video*, 2, no. 4 (1995): 12–16.

Allen, Stuart. "Redefining Cinematography: The Modern Generation of Feature Film and Television Cinematographers Continues to Reshape the Art of Filmmaking." *Film and Video* (February 1995): 48–58, 68.

Bailey, Liz. "Mothering & Careers: Don't Deny Yourself the Joy of Mothering or Photography." *Behind the Lens Annual Newsmagazine* (winter 1989–90): 8.

"Behind the Lens Honors Paramount Childcare Mentors." *Behind the Lens Annual Newsmagazine* (winter 1989–90): 1.

Brenner, Jane. "The Eye Behind the Still Camera." *International Photographer* 55, no. 10 (October 1983): 16–19.

Bushnell, Victoria. "Walking on the Edge: Cinematographer Judy Irola Brings an Experimental, Documentary-Based Approach to Her Diverse Projects." *Film and Video* 9, no. 10 (October 1992): 76, 78–80.

Butler, Kate. "Foreign Exposure: On the Set of *Mississippi Masala*." *Behind the Lens Annual Newsmagazine* (1992): 14, 16, 19.

Butler, Rachel. "Focusing On Breaking Down Barriers For Camerawomen." *The West Side Spirit*. 6, no. 38 (18 September 1990): 1–2, 18.

Cansino, Lorna. "Babes, Cameras, & Life!" *Behind the Lens Newsletter*, Special Annual Issue, 4, no. 1, (December 1986): 23–24.

Carlson, Verne. "Realities vs. Differences." *Behind the Lens Annual Newsmagazine* (1992): 11–12.

Chaney-LeBlanc, Michele. "Polishing the Lens: 'Professionalism'—A Major Portion of the Battle." *Behind the Lens Annual Newsmagazine* (winter 1989–90): 9.

————. "Women's Limitations on the Set: Fact or Myth?" *Behind the Lens Annual Newsmagazine* (January 1988): 20.

Comer, Brooke. "*Visions of Light: The Art of Cinematography*: ASC Takes Part in an AFI-NHK Documentary Film That Turns the Cameras on Some of Motion-Picture Photographers' Leading Lights." *American Cinematographer* 74, no. 2 (February 1993): 59–64.

Coulson, Catherine. "Making Peace with Video: One Woman's Journey." *International Photographer* 55, no.10 (October 1983): 20–21.

Deren, Maya. "Cinematography: The Creative Use of Reality." In *Women in Focus*, edited by Joanne Betancourt, 169. Dayton Ohio: Pflaum, 1974.

Eller, Claudia. "A Tribute or a Demeaning Reflection? Movies: Hollywood Is Abuzz over *Vanity Fair*'s Focus on the Industry, Some Calling It Sexist and Insulting." *Los Angeles Times*, Calendar Section (16 March 1995): F1, 8.

Fisher, Bob. "Artfully Rendering *An Ambush of Ghosts*: Cinematographer Judy Irola lends award-winning approach to familial drama." *American Cinematographer*, 75, no. 4 April 1994): 44–46, 48, 50–52.

Ford, Charles. "The First Female Producer." *Films in Review* 15, no. 3 (March 1964): 141–145.

Gimbel, Peter. "Blue Water, White Death." *American Cinematographer* 52, no. 9, (September 1971): 872.

Goldman, Debra. "Woman with a Movie Camera." *The Independent* (July/August 1985): 4.

Greenbaum, Elisabeth. "Marina Goldovskaya." *UCLA Film and Television Archive Newsletter* (January/February 1994): 5.

Irola, Judy. "The Cinematography of 'Northern Lights.' " *Filmmakers' Monthly* 12, no. 12 (October 1979): 16–18.

"Judy Irola Wins Sundance Film Festival Honors." *Eastman Images* 5 no. 2 (spring 1993): 1.

Jungmeyer, J. "Team of Wildlife Naturalist-Photographers." *Audio-Visual Guide*, no. 22 (November 1955): 30.

Krasilovsky, Alexis. "Kelly Elder McGowen." *Angles: Women Working in Film & Video* 2, no. 4 (1995): 11–13.

————. "A Sharper Image." *Angles: Women Working in Film & Video 2, no. 4 (1995): 10–11.*

————. "An International Perspective." *Behind the Lens Newsletter* 3, no. 4 (June 1985): 18.

————. "In Praise of the Men Who Defend Us." *Behind the Lens Newsletter* 2, no. 3 (April 1985): 1–2.

————. "The Art of Being a Camerawoman: Part II." *Behind the Lens Newsletter* 2, no. 2 (January 1985): 6–8.

Kudaka, Geraldine. "Technical Women: A Personal View." *Behind the Lens Annual Newsmagazine* (January 1988): 24–26.

Laccasin, Francis. "Out of Oblivion: Alice Guy Blaché." *Sight and Sound* 40, no. 3 (summer 1971): 151–154.

"Lisa Rinzler Brings Lighting Sensitivity to Tough Subjects." *Eastman Images* 7, no. 2 (spring 1995): 7.

Maslin, Janet. "Just What Did Leni Riefenstahl's Lens See?" *The New York Times* (13 March 1994): H15, 23.

Miner, Jan. "The World Comes Full Circle: Documentary DP Judy Irola Shoots Spots." *Backstage* (9 October 1987).

Most, Madelyn. "From the Heart." *Eyepiece: The Magazine of Moving Images* 11, no. 3 (May–June 1990): 20.

————. "The Most Report: Real Stories, Real People, Real World." *Eyepiece: The Magazine of Moving Images* 17, no. 4 (Aug./Sept. 1996): 36–37.

O'Reilly, Kathleen. "Framing the Shot." *Behind the Lens Newsletter*, Special Annual Issue 4, no. 1 (December 1986): 19–20.

Orr, Eileen. "Who's That Woman Behind the Lens?" *L.A. Reader* 6, no. 47 (14 September 1984): 2.

Pedersen, Marie. "Documenting *The Great Peace March*." *Behind the Lens Newsletter*, Special Annual Issue 4, no. 1 (December 1986): 8–9.

"The Photography of 'Exorcist II: The Heretic.' " *American Cinematographer* 58 (August 1977): 806–13 passim.

"P.O.V.: Our Brothers and Sisters." *Behind the Lens Newsletter*, Special Annual Issue, 4, no. 1 (December 1986): 6–7,45–47.

"Prolifics: The Women Behind the Lens." *Film Crew*, no. 8 (May–June 1995): 24–25.

Robley, Les Paul. "Pumping Iron II." *American Cinematographer* 65, no. 7 (July 1984): 76.

Rosen, Marjorie. "Shirley Clarke; Videospace Xplorer." *Ms.* 63, no. 16 (April 1975): 107–10.

Schiller, Marc. "F-Stop Troop: A Look at Today's Independent Cinematographers." *Filmmaker* 1, no. 2 (winter 1992–93): 46–47, 60.

Seidenberg, Lisa. "Haiti 'Invasion' Seen through the Eyepiece: Newsgathering in the Hot Spots of the World Can Be Unnerving." *American Cinematographer* 76, no. 6 (June 1995) 96–98, 100–102.

————. "IDC/2 Takes Stock of Documentaries." *American Cinematographer* 77, no. 1 (January 1996): 18–26.

Struzzi, Diana. "Close-Ups: Lisa Seidenberg." *Millimeter* 18, no. 7 (July 1990): 148.

Tucker, Karen. "Dyanna Taylor." *Spotlight* (2 February 1990): 14, 28, 34.

Wiley, Lorna. "Women in Film Festival." *Behind the Lens Newsletter*, Special Annual Issue 4, no. 1 (December 1986): 20–22.

Wynne, Robert. "Lady of the Lens." *University of Southern California Chronicle* 15, no. 13 (27 November 1995): 16.

Zheutlin, Cathy. "Nicaragua Documentary." *Behind the Lens Newsletter* 3, no. 4 (June 1985): 6–7.

Zwilling, Susan. "Zen and the Art of Camera Operation." *Behind the Lens Newsletter* (June 1988): 3.

BOOKS

Changing Focus: The Future for Women in the Canadian Film and Television Industry. Toronto: Toronto Women in Film and Television, 1991.

Kuhn, Annette, ed. *Women in Film: An International Guide.* New York: Fawcett Columbine, 1990.

Seger, Linda. *When Women Call the Shots: The Developing Influence of Women in Television and Film.* New York: Henry Holt, 1996.

Stockly, Ed, ed. *Cinematographers, Production Designers, Costume Designers and Film Editors Guide.* 5th ed. Los Angeles: Lone Eagle, 1996.

Index

Aerial cinematography, 50–51, 202
Aguilera-Hellweg, Max, 65
Alcott, John, 104
Allred, Gloria, xxiv
Alonzo, John, 41, 50, 196
American Society of Cinematographers (ASC), xvii, 3, 13, 32, 159
Anderson, Erica, xxi
Arnold, Chuck, 45, 82
Ashton, Marie, 128
Association of Independent Video and Filmmakers, 76
Aviv, Nurith, xix

Bailey, John, 41, 50–52, 78, 82, 127
Bailey, Liz, 91–97
Barbee, Chuck, 84–85
Barbee, Elizabeth, 88
Bean, Karen Edmundson, xviii
Beato, Alfonso, 128

Beatty, Warren, 49
Behind the Lens, xxiv–xxv, 76, 92, 120, 139, 141, 155, 201–2; formation of, 10–11, 54, 78, 83–84, 102, 192; leadership of, 78, 91, 114, 165, 196
Bianchi, Ed, 134
Biren, Joan, 116
Bivens, Loren, 197
Blaché, Alice Guy. *See* Guy Blaché, Alice
Blaylock, Rob, 98, 99
Bleecker, Katherine Russell, xxi
Boelens, Larry, 57
Bongers, Sally, xix
Breastfeeding, 96
Brenner, Jane, 95
Brooke, Ralph, 3, 8–9
Bryant, Baird, 156
Burrill, Chris, 135

Burum, Stephen, 59
Butler, George, 128
Butler, Sandy, 189–95

Camaraderie, 52, 56, 87, 159, 170,
    176, 179, 181, 185, 187, 195
Camera Assistant Training Program,
    18, 19, 41, 81–83, 165, 167; en-
    trance exam, 42–43, 81, 173, 174,
    178–9
Cameras, 22, 28, 72; Aaton, 158; Ar-
    riflex, 22, 45, 57, 89, 180, 196;
    Auricon, 9, 22; Beaulieu, 72, 152;
    Betacam, 22, 69, 74, 113, 120–21;
    BNC, 16, 48, 181; CP-16, 113,
    117; Eclair, 160; hidden cameras,
    137; Ikegami, 191; Image 300,
    183, 187; Mitchell, 7, 22, 168–69;
    Panaflex, 49, 50, 78, 93, 180;
    Panavision, 22; Sony, 191; Vis-
    tavision, 169
Carson, Jo, 54, 164–70
Chamberlain, Pia, 43, 82
Chandler, Sandra, xviii
Chen, Carolyn, xviii
Childbirth, 91, 95–96, 114. See also
    Pregnancy
Children, 64, 70, 91, 96–97, 122–23,
    129, 189, 191, 194–95, 203. See
    also Breastfeeding; Childbirth;
    Pregnancy
Chopra, Joyce, 160
Christie, Julie, 49
Churchill, Joan, xviii, 61, 135
Cine Manifest, 31, 33
Cinewomen, xxiv
Clairmont, Denny, xxiii
Clarke, Shirley, xxvi, 154, 157 n.2,
    191–92
Collective for Living Cinema, 148,
    150, 151
Commercials, 57, 60, 66–67, 91, 132,
    134, 167, 183

Connors, Kathy, 43
Contract Services, 81, 82–83, 174
Coppola, Francis Ford, 91
Corliff, Risa, 133
Coulson, Catherine, xviii, 43, 54, 87
Crabe, James, 7, 41
Craft, Alicia. See Sehring, Alicia
    Craft
Crenshaw, Michelle, xviii, 182 n.1

D'Agostino, Lou, 35
Daviau, Allen, 59
Demme, Jonathan, xxiii, 124, 128
Deschanel, Caleb, 59
Diano, David, 82
Directors Guild of America, xxv, 42,
    54–55, 192
Di Santo, Roxanne, xviii
Discrimination: Anti-Semitism, 20,
    22, 23; Racial, 14, 16–17, 20, 23,
    24, 27–28, 83, 140, 142, 144, 156,
    173, 177, 179; See also Behind the
    Lens; Sexual Discrimination;
    Strength; Stress; Women in Film
Documentaries, xvii, xxi; Bailey, Liz,
    91, 95; Carson, Jo, 164; Glover,
    Kristin, 60, 66; Hill, Leslie, 42, 52,
    54; Irola, Judy, 31–36; Kudaka,
    Geraldine, 141, 146; Most, Made-
    lyn, 109–10; Omori, Emiko, 25,
    29; Schreiber, Nancy, 158–63;
    Seidenberg, Lisa, 69–77; Sissel,
    Sandi, 131–38; Taylor, Dyanna,
    124–30; Walsh, Susan, 79, 88;
    Zheutlin, Cathy, 113–23

Edwards, Blake, 109
Equal Employment Opportunities
    Commission (EEOC), 120
Evans, Mary Anne, 169
Experimental filmmaking, xix, 159;
    Independent Film Oasis, 150. See
    also Collective for Living Cinema;
    Halpern, Amy; Jacobs, Ken

Farmer, Mary, 116
Film schools: American Film Institute, 56, 196, 198–99; California State University, Northridge, 113, 148; Columbia College, 4; London Film School, 103; New York Institute of Photography, 159; New York University, 153; North Carolina School of the Arts, 42; Northwest Film Center, 114, 123; San Francisco Art Institute, 118; San Francisco City College, 191–92, San Francisco State University, 25–26, 191; Southern Methodist University, 132; State University of New York, Binghamton, 148, 150–51; U.C.L.A., 42, 53, 140, 141–42, 148, 153–54, 164, 166, 191; U.C. Santa Cruz, 124, 126; University of Austin, Texas, 196–98; University of Miami, 186; University of Southern California, 25, 32, 148, 173, 174; University of Wisconsin, 132
Findlay, Roberta, xix
Forsyte, Joey, xviii
Foster, Candy, 82–83, 178–79, 182 n.1
Fraker, William, xxiii, 41, 45, 49
Franklin, Warren, 124, 126
Friedberg, Beth-Jana, 199, 200, 202
Friedkin, William, 199–200
Fujimoto, Tak, 128

Gaffers. *See* Gainey, Celeste; Halpern, Amy; Schreiber, Nancy
Gainey, Celeste, 158
Gilbert, Craig, 60
Glover, Kristin, 43, 51, 54, 59–68, 82, 84, 87
Goldblatt, Stephen, 59
Goldovskaya, Marina, xix
Gordon, Melinda Sue, xix

Gornick, Aimee, 88
Gornick, Alan, 78
Gottlieb-Walker, Kim, xix
Griffiths, Mark, 53
Gunn, Mairi, xix
Guy Blaché, Alice, xx-xxi, xxv, xxvii n.14

Halpern, Amy, 148–57
Herron, J. Barry, 82
Hill, Leslie, 25, 41–58, 82, 83, 166
Hill, Patricia, xviii, 83

IA (International Alliance of Theatrical and Stage Employees) Local 16, 189
IA Local 600, xvii, xxv, 91, 181, 182 n.1, 190. *See also* IA Local 644; IA Local 659
IA Local 644, xxv, 14, 115, 17, 19, 31–32, 35–36, 102, 107, 124, 133, 158, 184; entrance to, 107, 127, 131, 133, 183
IA Local 659, xvii, xx, xxv, 4, 7, 9, 41, 43, 59, 78, 98, 99, 101, 102, 107, 136; entrance procedures, 62, 99, 101, 119–20, 173, 183, 186–87, 201; Executive Board, 78, 84, 85
Industrial Light & Magic, 98, 164, 168–69
Iris Films, 116
Irola, Judy, 25, 27, 28, 31–37, 115, 135

Jacobs, Ken, 150–51

Kane, Karen Williams, 183–88
Kirsh, Estelle, 18–24, 43, 82, 167, 192
Klick, Laurel, 98–101
Kovacs, Laszlo, 3, 7, 41, 43
Kozachik, Peter, 170
Kudaka, Geraldine, xxiv-xxv, 139–47
Kuras, Ellen, xviii

Kurland, Cindy, 52

Lange, Dorothea, 37, 124, 125–26
Littlefield, Nancy, 52, 53
Littlejohn, Dorothy, 27
London Women's Film Group, 106
Longinova, Tatiana, xix

McGowen, Kelly Elder, xviii, 95
MacKenzie, Heather, xviii
MacLaine, Shirley, 159–60
Maibaum, Paul, 179
Mangolte, Babette, xix
Maple, Jesse, xix, 182 n.1
Marriage and relationships, 8–9, 29,
    53, 55, 87, 88–89, 96, 99–100,
    122, 161, 203. *See also* Children
Mayers, Jo, xviii
Medina, Teresa, xviii
Miller, Margo, 43
Mitchell, Rod, 47
Moore, Bill, 181
Morgan, Patrick, 183, 185, 188
Most, Madelyn, 102–10
Müller, Robbie, 134, 199
Murphy, Brianne, 3–13, 43, 47, 54,
    87, 115, 136

Narita, Hiro, 59
National Association of Broadcast
    Employees and Technicians (NA-
    BET), 3, 7, 14, 15, 25, 28, 31, 33,
    34–45, 61, 69, 102, 107, 114, 162,
    189; entrance tests, 117, 124, 126–
    27; Third World and Women's
    Training Program, 139, 142
Nemenz, Otto, xxiii, 196, 198–99,
    203
Norton, David, 183, 185, 188
Nykvist, Sven, 108

Obenhaus, Mark, xxiii, 161
Omens, Woody, xxiii
Omori, Emiko, 25–30, 32, 118

Ophüls, Marcel, 109
Optical effects. *See* Special effects
    cinematography
O'Reilly, Kathleen, xviii

Parker, Bonnie, 63
Pedersen, Marie, xviii, 95
Pollard, Tama Takahashi, xviii
Poster, Steven, xxiii,
Pregnancy, 91, 94, 122–23, 193–94.
    See also Childbirth
Primes, Robert, xxiii

Reid, Frances, 116
Rinzler, Lisa, xviii
Rivetti, Tony, 176, 179
Robertson, Cathryn, xix
Rose, Sid, 7

Safety, 18–19, 45–47, 50, 74, 84, 137
Santa Cruz Women's Film Collec-
    tive, 114
Sato, Ted, 6
Schneeman, Carolee, xix
Schreiber, Nancy, 158–63
Scott, Ridley, 186
Sehring, Alicia Craft, 196–204
Seidenberg, Lisa, 69–77
Semler, Dean, 179
Sexual discrimination, xxiii–xxvii, 7,
    18–20, 28, 100–101, 104–5, 190;
    anxiety and, 21–22, 28–29, 162;
    crews and, 22, 33–34, 48, 86–87,
    90, 143–45, 161–62, 175, 199–
    200; film schools and, 92, 140,
    154, 191; films about women's is-
    sues and, 77; "glass ceiling," 61,
    62; mechanical training and, 105,
    119; sexual harassment, 20–21,
    44, 88, 93, 155; unions and, 7, 23,
    64, 119–20, 184; wages, 99, 163
Simmons, Sabrina, 173–82
Sissel, Sandi, 131–38

Society of Operating Cameramen, xxiv, 91

Special effects cinematography, 98–101, 164–70

Stephens, Elizabeth, 116

Steuben, Joe, 61

Storaro, Vittorio, 108

Strength: asking for help, 13; carrying cameras (Arri 35 BL, BNCR, Panavision), 48, 89, 181; carrying lighting equipment, 162; job interviews and issue of, 200–201; positive attitudes regarding, 94, 137; weight lifting, 193

Stress: alcohol and drugs and, 58, 192; hiding, 12, 169, 193; quitting jobs and, 72, 178; responsibilities of camerawork and, 46, 106–7; yoga and meditation and, 86; *See also* Sexual discrimination, anxiety and

Summers, Tara, xviii

Taylor, Dyanna, 25, 115, 124–30, 135

Television: ABC, 42, 69, 71, 74, 132, 134; BBC, 103; CBS, 14, 15, 17, 42, 69, 125, 139, 174, 196, 198; HBO, 132; KCET, 79; KQED, 25, 26–28, 331–33; NBC, 4, 9–10, 16, 25, 42, 52, 133; PBS, 25, 42, 75, 159; Showtime, 159; TBS, 122; WBRZ, 91; WNET-13, 60, 69, 71; WPLX, 71

Towers, Laurie, 202

Turos, Mia, xix

Underwater cinematography, 78–79, 82, 84–85

Unions: A.C.T.T., 102, 107; IBEW, 69, 91, 136. *See also* Directors Guild of America; IA Local 16; IA Local 600; IA Local 644; IA Local 659; National Association of Broadcast Employees and Technicians; Writers Guild of America

Valert, Frank, 154

Vanover, Patty, xviii

Video, 70, 139–40, 192, 195. *See also* Butler, Sandy; Cameras, Betacam, Ikegami, Sony; Documentaries

Villalobos, Ray, 46–47

Vincent, Amy, xviii

von Schmidt, Peter, 16

Waite, Ric, 41, 44

Walden, Richard, xxiii, 82, 84, 89–90

Walsh, Susan, 43, 51, 52, 54, 78–90

Wang, Juliana, 14–17

Wayne, John, 63–64

Weber, Alicia, xviii, 16, 127, 133, 135

Weidman, Joan, xviii, 159

Weill, Claudia, xviii, 160

Wexler, Haskell, xxiii–xxiv, 59, 62–63, 79, 134

Wiley, Bess, 169

Wiley, Lorna, xviii

Williams, Lawrence, Jr., 184, 185

Williams, Lawrence, Sr., 184

Willis, Allen, xxiii

Women in Film, xix, xxiv, 4, 10, 15, 42, 53–54, 76, 106; in New York, 127

Women Make Movies, xxiv, 116

Writers Guild of America, xxv, 42, 54

Zheutlin, Cathy, 25, 76, 113–23

Ziegler, Elizabeth, xviii

Zsigmond, Vilmos, 3, 7

Zwerin, Charlotte, 60

About the Author

ALEXIS KRASILOVSKY is a Professor at California State University, Northridge, where she teaches screenwriting and film production. Her films, videos, and holograms include *End of the Art World*, starring Andy Warhol and Robert Rauschenber, and *Epicenter U.*, a film about surviving the Northridge Earthquake. Krasilovsky is also the author of several poetry collections, including *Some Women Writers Kill Themselves*.